DICKSON ON PRINCIPLES OF BUSINESS LAW

Text, Cases, and Materials

With foreword by Carl S. Sloane
Professor Emeritus, Harvard Business School (HBS)

OSEI BONSU DICKSON

LLM, LLB, BA (UG), ECNIS (HARV), PhD Fellow (SMCU), Barrister
Faculty of Law, Wisconsin University

Lex Mundus & Cencla
Rule of Law Project

OTHER BOOKS BY THE AUTHOR

Dickson on Principles of Security Law
Dickson on Principles of Medical Law and Ethics
Dickson on Civil Procedure Precedents

DICKSON ON
PRINCIPLES OF
BUSINESS LAW

TEXT, CASES AND MATERIALS

For students and corporate managers

OSEI BONSU DICKSON

Icon Publishing Limited
P. O. Box OD 972
Odorkor, Accra, Ghana
enquiries.icongh@gmail.com

Books published by Icon Publishing Limited are available at special discounts for bulk purchases in Ghana by corporations, institutions, and other organisations. For more information, please call the Special Markets Department on +233268505055 or send an e-mail to enquiries.icongh@gmail.com.

Cover and Layout Design by DKO, +233244890432

ISBN: 978-9988-8567-6-2

In treasured honor of my mum
ESTHER APPIAH

ACKNOWLEDGEMENTS

I am exceptionally grateful to Carl S. Sloane, Ernest L. Arbuckle Professor Emeritus of Business Administration, Harvard Business School, for accepting to write the foreword to this work. I thank you deeply.

I owe a debt of gratitude to the commercial law firm Lex Mundus & Cencla (West Africa) for the painstaking research provided in pursuance of this publication. A similar debt is due my former lecturers at the Faculty of Law, University of Ghana, Ghana School of Law and Harvard University.

I thank my wife, Sandra for reading through the early manuscripts and reverting with perceptive comments. I thank our son, Kwesi Poku for providing healthy distraction and causing me to stumble upon fresh ideas.

I also thank a number of institutions for permission to cite or reprint materials - the Assembly Press for permission to cite the Constitution of Ghana, 1992 and various legislations; The Council for Law Reporting for permission to cite reported cases from the Ghana Law Reports; and Cavendish Publishing Limited for permission to cite briefs of various English cases. Efforts have been made to trace and contact copyright holders of cited works, but this has not been possible in every case, if notified, the author undertakes to rectify any errors or omissions at the earliest opportunity.

I thank the students and staff of the Law Faculty and the Graduate School, Wisconsin University, for their insightful comments. His Lordship the Judge, Mr. Justice S.S. Appiah, Dr. Ebenezer Appiah-Denkyirah and Mrs. Dinah Hayford, my uncles and aunt respectively, are deserving of thanks. I thank Dr. Kwaku Darkwa and Kingsley Sarkodie of Sanford World Clinics (Ghana) for advice and assistance readily given. I thank my sister Akosua for her invaluable comments, and my brother Ernesto for his support. I am grateful to Irene Awuah, Odette Buckner, Isaac Kuditchar, Elorm Fugar, Fredrick Johnson, Joyce Ababio and the publishers, Icon Publishing for secretarial, editorial and publishing assistance. Finally, I thank all my former classmates at the Faculty of Law, University of Ghana (LL.B '03), for the opportunity to contribute ideas and generate remedies to common problems.

I am solely responsibility for all the shortcomings, defects or errors that have remained uncorrected in this work.

FOREWORD BY PROF. EMERITUS CARL S. SLOANE

This book brings together exciting new work focusing on one of the foremost areas of law — business law. It presents fresh insights to further advance our understanding of the constantly shifting legal environment of business.

The text is comprehensive, authoritative, and reader-friendly. Its focus is on general principles which have remained the subject of practice and policy, and it is authored in a manner that makes it accessible to students who are approaching this area of legal scholarship for the first time.

Writing, however, across a broad province — the legal system, the law of obligations, company law, agency law, the sale of goods law, employment law, the law of mortgages, and land law, is by no means an easy undertaking. Yet, it is this extensive coverage of the text, that makes it worthy of recommendation to the teeming students of business law, lecturers new to the discipline, attorneys, judges, corporate managers, and indeed the reading public — who I suspect, badly require such a book, for transactional guidance.

Whatever its defects or omissions, the author can be confident that there will be many grateful readers who will have gained a broader perspective of business law as a result of his effort.

Carl S. Sloane
Ernest L. Arbuckle Professor of Business Administration Emeritus
Harvard University
Cambridge, Massachusetts
6 March, 2014

PREFACE

The study of business law (i.e. commercial law) provides huge insights into the law and its application to business. As any learner would at once realize, a litany of laws affect business entities. The case law in this area is thus profound. The focus of the present work is on the following segments of the curricular:

- **The elements of the legal system** – this topic covers the meaning of law, types of law, sources of law, structure and jurisdiction of the courts in the Ghanaian legal system.
- **The law of obligations** – this topic covers two vital obligations that all businesses are subject to, namely contract and tort. When a business enters into an agreement, a legally enforceable contract comes into formation. If or when the contract is breached, it could lead to payment of damages or some equitable remedies. Similarly, business entities, like individuals, have a duty not to harm others. If or when this duty is breached, it might occasion the payment of damages.
- **Agency law** – this topic covers the rules that come into force when one person, called an agent, acts for or on behalf of another person, called a principal.
- **Company law** – this topic covers the forms of business entities under the *Companies Act,* 1962 (Act 179), the role of promoters, directors, the company secretary, legal personality, among others.
- **Sale of goods law** – this topic covers the Legal rights of sellers and buyers under the *Sale of Goods Act,* 1962 (Act 137), the rules on transfer of property or risk in goods sold, are among other issues of unique interest here.
- **Employment law** – this topic overs the legal rights and obligations of employers, employees and related issues under the *Labour Act,* 2003 (Act 651).

Also covered are the law of mortgages, intellectual property law and land law. An attempt has made to cover in one single volume as wide an area of the law as possible. The merit of that approach inheres in a need to make the text relevant to a wide array of learners – those reading ICA, GAT, DBS, RSA III, HND, and business law at undergraduate and post-graduate levels.

How to pass business law - To pass a paper in law you first of all need technical knowledge. The current curricular has a vast amount of technical content by way of case law and legislation which you need to know. You need to master this and be able to identify which aspect of the knowledge is essential to a particular question. Secondly, you need to be able to apply knowledge to specific problems and scenarios and solve specific problems.

For students needing help you can enroll in our annual exam clinic by dialing 0241 022 964 or by emailing obdickson@gmail.com.

Osei Bonsu Dickson
Wisconsin University, 9 October, 2014

Table of Cases

Adams v. Lindsell (1818) 1 B &Ald 681; 106 ER 250

Ampofo v. Fiorini [1981] G.L.R. 829

Anning v. Kingful [1980] G.L.R. 404

Asare v. Antwi [1975] 1 GLR 16, C.A

Baidoo v. Sam [1987-88] 2 G.L.R 666 CA

Balfour v. Balfour [1919] 2 K.B. 571

Bank of West Africa Ltd v. Appenteng [1972] 1GLR 153

Barclays Bank v. Sakari[1996-97] S.C.G.L.R. 639

Bell v. Lever Bros. [1932] AC 161

Bettini v. Gye (1876) 1 QBD 183, [1874-80] All ER Rep 242

Boakyem and Others v. Ansah [1963] 2 G.L.R. 223

Board of Directors Orthodox Secondary School v. TawlmaAbels [1974] 1 G.L.R. 419

Brogden v. Metropolitan Railway Co. (1877) 2 App Cas 666, H L

Byrne & Co. v. Leon Van Tienhoven (1880) 5 CPD 344

C.A.S.T. v. Nketia [1971] 1 GLR 363

Carlill v. Carbolic Smokeball Co. [1892] 2 Q.B. 484; affd. [1893] 1QB 256

Central London Property Trust Ltd v. High Trees House Ltd [1947] K.B. 130; [1956] 1 All ER 256

CFC Construction Company (WA) ltd & Read v. Attitsogbe [2005-2006] SCGLR 858, SC

City & Country Waste Ltd v. Accra Metropolitan Assembly [2007-2008] SCGLR

D & C Builders Ltd v. Rees [1965] 3 All ER 837; [1966] 2 Q.B. 617

De Francesco v. Barum (1890) 45 Ch. D 430

Deegbe v. Nsiah & Antonnelli [1984-86] 1 G.L.R. 545

Delle & Delle v. Owusu-Afriyie [2005-2006] S.C.G.L.R. 60

Delmas Agency Ghana Ltd v. Food Distributors International Ltd [2007-2008] 2 S.C.G.L.R. 748

Derry v. Peek (1889) LR 14 App. Cas. (1889) 5 TLR 625; [1886-90] all ER 1, HL

Domins Fisheries Ltd v. Bremen-Vegesacker-Fisheries [1973] 2 G.L.R. H.C

Dormenyor v. Johnson Motors Ltd [1989-90] 2 G.L.R. 110

Dunlop Pneumatic Tyre Co. Ltd v. New Garage & Motor Co [1975] A.C. 79

Erlanger v. New Sombrero Phosphaste Co (1878) 3 App Cas 1218; [1874-80] All ER Rep 271, HL

Errington v. Errington [1952] 1K.B. 290; [1952] 1 All E.R. 149

Esso Petroleum v. Mardon [1976] Q.B. 801

Felthouse v. Bindley (1862) 11 C.D. (N.S.) 869; 142 ER 1037

Fish & Meat Co Ltd v. Ichnusa Ltd [1963] 1 G.L.R. 314

Fisher v. Bell [1960] 3 All ER 731; [1961] 1 Q.B. 394

Fofie v. Zanyo [1992] 2 G.L.R. 475 S.C

Frafra v. Boakye [1976] 2 G.L.R. 332 C.A

Frederick E. Rose Ltd v. William Pim [1953]2 All ER 739, CA

Gibbons v. Proctor (1891) 64 L.T. 594

Gibbon v. Manchester City Council [1978] 2 All ER 583, CA

Grainger & Son v. Gough [1896] A.C. 325

Great Northern Railway v. Witham (1873) L.R. 9 C.P. 16

Hammond v. Ainooson [1974] 1 GLR 176

Harris v. Nickerson (1873) L.R. 8 QB 286

Hornal v. Neuberger Products Ltd [1957] 1 Q.B. 247

Joseph v. Boakye [1977] 2 GLR 392

Kessie v. Charmant [1973] 2 G.L.R. 194

Koah v. Royal Exchange Assurance [1976] 1 G.L.R. 158

Kwaddey v. Okantey [1972] 2 GLR 84

Kwarteng v. Donkor [1962] 1 GLR 20

Lartey v. Bannerman [1976] 2 G.L.R. 461

Leaf v. International Galleries [1950] 1 All ER 693

Lewis v. Averary [1971] 3 All ER 907; [1972] 1 Q.B. 198

Mabsout v. Alderson (1883) 8 App. Cas 467

Motor Parts Trading Co v. Nunoo [1962] 2 G.L.R 195

Nash v. Inman [1908] 2 K.B. 1, CA

Nkrumah v. Serwah& Others [1984-86] 1 GLR 190

NTHC Ltd v. Antwi [2009] SCGLR 117

Nutakor and Another v. Adzrah [1965] GLR 445

Olatiboye v. Captan [1968] GLR 146

Partridge v. Crittendon [1968] 2 All E.R. 421

Payne v. Cave (1789) 3 Term Rep. 148

Pinnel's Case (1902) 5 Co. Rep. 117a

Pokua v. State Insurance Corporation [1973] 1 G.L.R. 335

Pousard v. Spiers (1876) 1 QBD 410, 45 LJQB 621, 34 LT 572

Prah& Others v. Anane [1964] GLR 458

Quao v. Squire [1978] 1 G.L.R. 270

Quartey v. Norgah [1967] G.L.R. 319 CA

R. v. Clarke (1927) 40 C.L.R. 227

R.T. Briscoe (Ghana) ltd v. Essien [1961] 2 G.L.R. 265

Raffles v. Wichelhaus (1864) 2 Hurl & C 906; 159 ER 375

Redco Ltd. v. Sarpong [1991] 2 GLR 457,CA

Rockson v. Armah [1975] 2 G.L.R. 116

Roscorla v. Thomas (1842) 3 Q.B 234

Rose & Frank Co v. Crompton Bros [1923] 2 K.B. 261

Routledge v. Grant (1828) 4 Bing 653

Royal Dutch Airlines (KLM) and Anor. V. Farmex Ltd [1989-90] 2 G.L.R. 623

S.A Turqui & Brothers v. Lamptey [1961] 1 GLR 190

Schandorf v. Zeini [1976] 2 GLR 418

Shanska Jensen International v. Klimatechnik Engineering Ltd [2003-2004] SCGLR 698

Smith v. Hughes [1960] 2 All ER 859

Stilk v. Myrick (1809) 2 Camp 317

Thornton v. Shoe Lane Parking Ltd [1971] 1 All ER 686; [1971] 2 Q.B. 163

Tinn v. Hoffman & Co. Limited v. Tungsten Electric Company [1955] 1 W.L.R. 761

White & Carter (Councils Ltd v. McGregor [1961] 3 All ER 1178, HL

Wilson v. Brobbey [1974] 1 GLR 250

Yeboah & Anor. V. Krah (1969) C.C. 42. Civil Appeal No. 27/64. (Judgment delivered on 23rd December, 1968 by Amissah J.A. on behalf of the Court of Appeal)

Zagloud Real Estates Co Ltd (No 2) v. British Airways Ltd [1998-99] SCGLR 378

TABLE OF STATUTES

Banking Act, 1989 (PNDCL 225)

Bill of Exchange Act, 1961 (Act 55)

Children's Act, 1998 (Act 560)

Companies Act, 1963 (Act 179)

Contract Act, 1960 (Act 25)

Conveyancing Act, 1973 (NRCD 175)

Electronic Transaction Act, 2008 (Act 772)

Environmental Protection Act (Act 490)

Factories, Offices and Shops Act, 1970 (Act 328)

Financial Institution (Non-Banking) Act, 1993 (PNDCL 328)

Finance Lease Law, 1993 (PNDCL 331)

Incorporated Partnership Act, 1962 (Act 52)

Income Tax Act, 2015 (Act 896)

Insolvency Act, 2003 (Act 657)

Insurance Act, 1989 (PNDCL 227)

Labour Act, 2003 (Act 651)

Limitation Act, 1972 (NRCD 55)

Minerals and Mining Act, 1986 (PNDCL 153)

Mortgages Decree, 1972 (NRCD 292)

Motor Insurance (Third Party Insurance) Act No. 42 of 1958

National Pensions Act, 2008 (Act 766)

Patent Act, 2003 (Act 657)

Registration of Business Names Act, 1962 (Act 151)

Sale of Goods Act, 1962 (Act 137)

Securities Industry Act, 1993 (PNDCL 333)

Stock Exchange Act, 1971 (Act 384)

Stamp Duty Act, 2005 (Act 689)

Trade Marks Act, 2004 (Act 664)

Workmen's Compensation Act, 1987 (PNDCL 187)

Constitution of the Republic of Ghana, 1992

CONTENTS

1. Introduction to Law and Legal Reasoning

LEARNING OUTCOMES

This opening topic examines the nature of law from the perspective of different schools of thought. After studying this topic, you would become familiar with the various legal philosophies that underpin law generally, as well as the nature, types, and role of law within the business environment.

INTRODUCTION

Why should people who conduct their private businesses be concerned with law? Two answers are at once probable. First, a person's ignorance of the law is no excuse for crimes or wrongs committed by that person (expressed in the well-known latin maxim – *ignorantia legis neminem excusat*[1]). Secondly, law affects all business decisions, and in that regard, business decisions ought generally to take law into account. With this in mind this, we can proceed to discuss the obvious question, "what is law"?

THE DEFINITION OF LAW

Law may be defined as a system of rules, promulgated or imposed by the state on its members, and enforced through threats of sanctions by institutions of social regulation and law enforcement. Alternatively, law may be defined as a system of rules governing relationships, between individuals (civil law) and between individuals and their society (criminal law). The famous English jurist, William

---

1   A legal principle which holds that a person who is unaware of a law may not escape liability for violating that law merely because he or she was unaware of its content.

Blackstone, contended that law was "a rule for civil conduct prescribed by the supreme power in a state, commanding what is right, and prohibiting what is wrong." In his book, *'The Path of the Law'* (1897), Oliver Wendell Holmes, the great United States Supreme Court Judge, whoever, described law as nothing but the *"prophesies of what the courts will do in fact, and nothing more pretentious."* In short, for Holmes the law is what the courts do – we may thus not know the law until a matter has been submitted to the courts. The American authors, Roger Miller and Gaylord Jentz, arguedin their book *'Business Law'* (2007) that "law consists of enforceable rules governing relationships among individuals and between individuals and society". For others like George Paton, law is a body of principles recognized and applied by the State in the administration of justice. In other words, law consists of rules recognized and acted upon by courts of justice. For most Ghanaians, law is a body of written and unwritten rules recognized and enforced by state institutions. This regulatory nature of law was well described by the Ghanaian academic and Supreme Court Judge Tawiah Modibo Ocran in his work, *'Law in Aid of Development'* (1978) as follows "... every society, save one that is anarchic, finds it necessary to regulate the behavior of its members; to make them refrain from certain acts, which, for some reasons, are considered detrimental to society; and to perform other acts, which for other reasons are considered useful to that society."

JURISPRUDENCE – THE PHILOSOPHY OF LAW

The word 'jurisprudence' is derived from the Latin phrase *juris prudential*, which means 'knowledge of the law.' Jurisprudence is thus the study of law or broadly put, the study of theories and philosophies of law. The argument is that if we understand the theories and philosophies behind law, we may better understand our laws.

To start with, the question "what is law" has generated diverse answers. Very divergent views or schools of thought have been expressed over the last two million years in careful explanation. Among these the leading schools of thought, have been the Natural law school, the Legal positivist school, the Marxist school, the Realist school, the Historical and Sociological schools, and more recently the Feminist school. Collectively these schools of thought have affected how states have made laws and how judges have similarly interpreted laws.

THE NATURAL LAW SCHOOL

Natural law theory was very keenly articulated by St. Thomas Aquinas. The leading proponents of natural law philosophy generally assume that law, rights and ethics are based on universal moral principles which are inherent in nature which can be discovered through human reason. This sort of reasoning dates back to the ancient Greek philosopher Aristotle. That said, natural law philosophy is, however, alive and present with us even today. The 1992 Constitution of Ghana, like the Constitution of the United States and the United Nations Universal Declaration of Human Rights subscribe to natural law thinking.

Advocates of natural law philosophy maintain that natural law is superior to positive law (the state's laws). They also argue that justice derives from God, and therefore only a just rule can be law. Correspondingly, an unjust rule is no law at all.

They argue that human beings are born with inalienable rights, certain notions of good and evil or right and wrong. In his book, "Summa Theological", Aquinas argued that a rule took on the character of "a law" only where it had an appropriate moral dimension. Thus, "that which is not just is no law at all" and such a law ought not to be obeyed, he argued. Aquinas argued for obedience to natural law, a perfect code, which was immutable or unchangeable and which was made known to man through reason.

THE LEGAL POSITIVIST SCHOOL[2] - LAW AS COMMANDS OF A SOVEREIGN

Legal positivism is a philosophy of law that emphasizes that law is socially constructed. To positivists, law is what has been posited by the State (ordered, given, decided, practiced, or law as it is, etc.). Law is the supreme will of the State and it applies only to the citizens of that nation at that time.

Positivists assume that laws, and thus rights and ethics, are not universal. Morality of a law (i.e. whether a piece of law is "bad or good,") is irrelevant; until repealed, laws ought to be obeyed even if they are unjust.

---

2   The term legal positivism is used here to signify a doctrine which rejects any metaphysical speculation concerning law. It involves a total rejection of statements that are not based on tested or verified experiences of the senses.

The greatest apostles of legal positivism — John Austin, Jeremy Bentham, Lon Fuller, Herbert Hart and Hans Kelsen, saw law as the command of a sovereign. Writing in the 19th century, the English Philosopher John Austin contended that law was a rule laid down *"..for the guidance of an intelligent being, by an intelligent being, having power over him."* To Austin, a "Sovereign is a determinate human superior, whom the bulk of the population in a given nation habitually obey, but who does not himself habitually obey any higher power of authority." To positivists, citizens have a duty to obey all valid laws (i.e. laws made in accordance with the appropriate procedures).

THE SOCIOLOGICAL SCHOOL

The sociological school in contrast, viewed law as a reflection of society's beliefs. Law was seen as a product of social organization. Three prominent sociologists and jurists could be singled out for attention: Jhering (1818–92), Weber (1864–1920) and Pound (1870–1964). Jhering in his highly influential treatise, *'Law as a Means to an End'* (1877), contended that "Law is the sum of the conditions of social life, in the widest sense of that term, as secured by the power of the State through the means of external compulsion." To its proponents, law was a mixture of rules for regulating social behavior.

THE MARXIST SCHOOL

Marxist jurisprudence stemmed primarily from the writings of Karl Marx (1818-83), Fredrick Engels (1820–95) and Vladimir Lenin (1870 – 1924), and involved the application of Karl Marx's philosophy of dialectical materialism. In his book, the *'Communist Manifesto'*, Marx viewed law as an ideological weapon of the ruling class (the bourgeoisie) which was employed by the State to maintain class rule and the subjugation of the working class. Marx rejected the view of an orderly human movement towards any spiritual destiny or perfection. To Marx, history was a record of class struggle, with law being used to perpetuate class domination. Thus slave-owning societies had laws recognizing and protecting the ownership of slaves. Similarly, capitalist society had laws recognizing the exploitation of labor and the preservation of dominance of the owners of capital.

THE REALIST SCHOOL

The realist school came into prominence in the 1930s. Its chief proponents were Holmes (1841–1935), Frank (1889–1957) and Gray (1839–1915), among others.

To its proponents, law was the activity of judges or officials involved in adjudication. Oliver Wendell Holmes, a notable American jurist, who exerted great influence as a jurist and US Supreme Court Judge, summed up this theory of law in his famous epigrammatic quote in the ***Harvard Law Review*** as follows: "The prophesies of what the court will do in fact, and nothing more pretentious, are what I mean by the law." [3]

Realists rejected abstract legal concepts in preference for law in action. Holmes' views have, however, been criticized by Goodhart and Cohen. Both have suggested that Holmes' formulation that, "Law is what the courts do", can be no more satisfactory to the jurist than the statement, "Medicine is what the doctor gives you."

THE HISTORICAL SCHOOL

Proponents of the historical school have argued that laws evolve. They point to historical doctrines of ages gone by as having rather guided and shaped our present laws. **The historical school emphasizes that laws evolve through a peoples' history. Adherents of this school concentrate on the origins of the legal system. They assume that law derives its legitimacy and authority from standards that have withstood the test of time. They also advocate the view that judges must follow settled decisions in earlier cases.**

In contrast, however, the sociological school argues that laws must be viewed within their social context, and judges should take economic and social realities into account, and not feel bound by past decisions. Sociological jurisprudence tends to be activist, many civil or human rights decisions exemplify this view.

Savigny (1799-1861) and Maine (1822-88) argued that today's legal systems, rules and concepts all developed over long periods of time and reflect the historical experiences of a people. To Savigny, there is a connection between a society's law and its history.

In the celebrated case of ***Tuffuor v. Attorney General,*** Chief Justice Sowah JSC speaking of the Ghanaian Constitution, echoed the views of the historical school as follows:

"A written Constitution such as ours is not an ordinary Act of Parliament. It embodies the will of a people. It also mirrors their history. Account therefore needs to,

---

3   Harvard Law Review Vol.10

be taken of it as a landmark in a people's search for progress. It contains within it, their aspirations and their hopes for a better and fuller life".[4]

FEMININE JURISPRUDENCE

Proponents of feminist legal theory project two major concerns. First, it explains ways in which the law played a role in women's former subordinate status. Second, it is dedicated to changing women's status through reworking the law and its approach to gender.

THE NATURE AND FUNCTIONS OF LAW

By nature or by character, law is normative, obligatory, institutionalized, and coercive. Law regulates human conduct, social behavior and has a certain degree of stability, fixity and uniformity. It is backed by stately authority or power, so violation of law could occasion punishment. Law is an expression of the will of the political class and is generally written down to give it definiteness and relative rigidity.

Among its assorted functions, law brings order into the business environment. It provides a platform for business co-operation, acts as a medium for commercial dispute resolution and functions as a tool for commercial relations. It is also a mechanism for social re-engineering, a bulwark against unethical practices and a means to protect commercial rights and attain economic justice.

CLASSIFICATION OF LAWS

Laws may be classified into public and private; substantive and procedural; criminal and civil, domestic and international. A single legal issue could, however, be classified under all three. For example, murder can be classified under criminal law, public law and also substantive law. Contract law can be classified under civil, substantive and private law.

Public Law versus Private Law

Public law is law that regulates relationships between individuals (or organizations) and the State. Criminal law, immigration law, human rights and constitutional law are examples of public law. Private law, on the other hand, regulates

---

4   See Tuffuor v. Attorney General [1980] GLR 637 at 647

the relationships between private individuals, organizations and companies. Examples include contract, tort, land, and company and employment law.

Substantive Law versus Procedural Law

Substantive law consists of all laws that define, describe, regulate and create rights and obligations. Procedural law, on the other hand, consists of all laws that state procedures and processes for enforcing legal rights.

Criminal Law versus Civil Law

Criminal law is a form of public law that regulates certain forms of conduct prohibited or proscribed by the state. In criminal cases, the State (i.e. the Republic) is the prosecutor because it is the State as a whole which is deemed to have suffered as a result of the criminal violation.

Civil law, in comparison, regulates disputes between private individuals, and their legal rights and obligations when dealing with each other or when they seek for compensation for wrongs done by one party.

Equally, the terminologies used in civil and criminal cases differ. In civil cases, the claimant or the plaintiff sues the defendant. In criminal cases, the State or Republic prosecutes the accused. While criminal law imposes fines and imprisonment, civil law imposes damages and equitable remedies.

Domestic Law versus International Law

Domestic law refers to the internal or municipal law of a given State. International law, on the other hand, refers to law that governs the relations between States and other entities with international legal status, such as the World Trade Organization and the United Nations.

THE IMPORTANCE OF LEGAL KNOWLEDGE IN REGULATED ENVIRONMENTS

The business environment in Ghana is a highly regulated field. Ghanaian businesses are accordingly impacted by a variety of laws – key among them, the constitution; various parliamentary enactments; orders, rules and regulations, common law (court decisions, doctrines of equity, and customary law) and in some cases by the rules of private international law.

The *World Investment Directory 2008: Africa by United Nations Conference on Trade and Development (UNCTAD)* recites a litany of laws that affect for instance businesses operating in Ghana[5]. Key among them, are the *Exchange Control Act; the Registration of Business Names Act; the Incorporated Private Partnerships Act; the Insolvency Act; the Trade Marks Act; the Stamp Duty Act; the Labour Act: the Factories, Offices and Shops Act; the Ghana Standards; the Workmen's Compensation Act; the Stock Exchange Act; the Social Security and National Insurance Act; the Patent Acts Law; the Securities Industry Act; the Stamp Duty Act and the Income Tax Act.*

As stated from the very outset, ignorance of the law is no excuse; which is why persons who manage business organizations must be familiar with the principles of business law.

Understanding contract law for example is very important. This is because contracts create enforceable legal rights and obligations where none existed. But then, the law of contract permits the parties to freely manage their risks, uncertainties and the extent of their own obligations. When a party fails to meet its obligations under a contract, it may become liable for breach of contract and thus for payment of damages.

Chapter 1 – Quick Review

Law is a system of rules, promulgated or imposed by the state on its members, and enforced through sanctions by institutions of social control. The study of law is probably appropriate because it affects business decision-making, and ignorance of law is no excuse. There are, however, several different schools of thought – positivism, natural law, realism, marxism, historical and sociological schools and each school espouses a different view of law.

Positivists for example see law as a set of rules enacted and enforced by the state, hence until repealed, enacted rules must be obeyed. Proponents of natural law, however, believe in divine law, accordingly they hold that man-made laws must take divine law into account and must be based on morality and ethics. Conversely, realists say law is only what the courts interpret or state them to be, but proponents of the historical and sociological schools argue that law as merely a product of a community's history and social evolution - their historical,

---

5   http://www.afribiz.info/content/2010/ghana-laws-affecting-transnational-corporations. A number of these legislations have been amended or otherwise repealed.

societal traditions, accepted norms, beliefs and shared customs. For Marxists law, however, law is a tool of class rule – a means by which all dominant classes keep the less dominant and oppressed classes in check.

Law serves several useful functions and may be classified into criminal or civil; substantive or procedural; domestic or international law.

2. Sources of Law in Ghana

The multiple rules that affect business

LEARNING OUTCOMES

Ghana operates a legal system that is premised on English common law. The laws of Ghana comprise the 1992 Constitution; enactments made by Parliament; orders, rules and regulations made by persons or authorities with power conferred under the Constitution; the existing law; and Common Law, which is defined as the rules of law generally known as the doctrines of equity and the rules of customary law, which are rules of law that by custom are applicable to particular communities in Ghana, including those determined by the Superior Court of Judicature. On completion of this chapter, you should be able to outline, discuss and distinguish between the various sources of Ghanaian law.

SOURCES OF GHANAIAN LAW

Article 11 (1) of the 1992 Constitution of Ghana provides an overview of the main sources of Ghanaian law as follows:

a)   The Constitution;
b)   Enactments made by or under the authority of the Parliament;
c)   Orders, Rules and Regulations made by persons or authorities acting under powers conferred by the Constitution;
d)   The Existing law; and
e)   The Common law.

THE CONSTITUTION

The 1992 Constitution is the supreme law of Ghana. Article 1(2) declares the Constitution to be the supreme law to which all other laws must be compatible with.

Provisions of the Constitution are arranged in articles and clauses. Knowledge of these provisions is vital since many of the provisions impose compliance duties on business entities (remember that businesses are deemed to be artificial legal persons, as well as the State).[6]

The human right provisions in Chapter 5 of the Constitution apply to businesses of all strips. Every business entity is under an obligation to respect and uphold human rights at the workplace. For example, the Constitution prohibits the use of slave or forced labor (Article 16) at any place of work (office, farm, camp etc). It prohibits companies from polluting the environment (Article 46), and similarly prohibits companies from denying or depriving their employees of their constitutional right to unionize for the protection of their interest (Article 21).[7] Recent media reports have revealed growing interest in corporate violation of human and constitutional rights. For example, Newmont Ghana Gold Limited has since 2011, been accused of several human rights violations at its Kenyasi, Ntotroso, and Atronie Ahafo mines in Ghana. Livelihood and Environment Ghana (LEG), a human rights and advocacy group, alleged that Newmont had provided unsafe living and working conditions; inadequate compensation and relocation packages; created noise and water pollution and was non-compliant with recommendations by local institutions including CHRAJ.

PARLIAMENTARY ENACTMENTS

The term enactment refers either to the whole or part of a piece of legislation. The word "enactment" does not therefore mean the same thing as "Act." An "Act" means the whole Act, whereas a section or part of a section in an Act may be an enactment.[8]

---

6   In *Bimpong-Buta v. General Legal Council and Others* [2003-2005] 1 GLR 738 at P783 Justice Kludze thus rightly observed that "...every justiciable issue can be spun in such a way as to embrace some tangential constitutional implications. Even a simple land dispute can be denominated a constitutional issue because of the implication that taking the property of another person is a constitutional violation. Similarly, the deprivation of liberty by unlawful detention or unlawful imprisonment is arguably inconsistent with the guarantee of personal liberties in the Constitution, 1992."

7   Article 21 (e) All persons shall have the right to freedom of association, which shall include freedom to form or join trade unions or other associations, national and international, for the protection of their interest;

8   In *Wakefield Light Railways Company v. Wakefield Corporation,* [1906] 2 KB 140 at 144 Ridley J. correctly stated the law thus "The word "enactment" does not mean the same thing as "Act." "Act" means the whole Act, whereas a section or part of a section in an Act

Examples of enactments include the *Minerals and Mining Law,* 1986 (PNDCL 153); the *Contract Act,* 1960 (Act 25), 1960; the *Insurance Law,* 1989 (PND-CL 227); the *Banking Law,* 1989 (PNDCL 225); the *Finance Lease Law,* 1993 (PNDCL 331); and the *Financial Institution (Non-Banking) Law,* 1993 (PND-CL 328).

ORDERS, RULES AND REGULATIONS
Orders, Rules or Regulations are delegated or subsidiary legislation enacted by persons or authorities acting under powers conferred by Parliament. Delegated legislation is therefore law made on behalf of Parliament. It consists of statutory instruments made by Government ministers using powers delegated by Parliament and the bye-laws enacted by the various Assemblies in Ghana.

THE EXISTING LAW
The existing law refers to all the laws of Ghana (written and unwritten) which existed immediately before the promulgation of the 1992 Constitution. This includes enactments dating from the colonial era which have not been repealed, and which therefore are legally binding. Examples of the existing law include (i) Laws of the Gold Coast (1951 Rev); (ii) the 1952-57 Ordinances of the Gold Coast; (iii) 1957-60 Acts of Ghana; (iv) 1960-66 Acts of the First Republic; (v) 1966-69 Decrees of National Liberation Council; (vi) 1969-72 Acts of the Second Republic; (vii) the 1972-79 Decrees of the National Redemption Council and the Supreme Military Council; (viii) 1979 Decrees of the AFRC; (ix) the 1979-81 Acts of the Third Republic; and (x) the Laws made by the PNDC since 31 December 1981, which have not been repealed are which are not inherently inconsistent with the Constitution.

GHANAIAN COMMON LAW
Article 11 (2) points to Ghanaian common law as another source of law in Ghana. Ghanaian common law– comprises three species of law, the English common law (a body of law that developed through "case law" or cases decided by judges); the Doctrines of Equity (a body of rules that were developed by the Court of Chancery in the 15th century to administer justice to parties aggrieved with common law remedies), and the rules of customary law including those determined by the Superior Court of Judicature. Ghanaian customary law refers to the rules of law, which by custom are applicable to particular communities in Ghana.

---

may be an enactment".

By its nature customary law is largely unwritten and thus not easily ascertainable. Customary laws may be discovered from reported decisions of the courts, and from a handful of textbooks.

THE COMMON LAW – A CONCISE HISTORY

The origins of English Common Law could be traced from **AD 1066** when William the Conqueror was crowned English King. Unlike previous monarchs, William decreed that he alone would resolve disputes in the Kingdom. He vested lands in the Crown, and parceled out lands in exchange for services to his kingdom, thereby establishing a system of governance that became known as feudalism.

After becoming inundated with cases, he reluctantly delegated his powers to representatives—judges—to decide disputes in his name, subject to his review.

The judges gradually realized, however, that their decisions in similar cases had to become consistent across England. They met regularly, reported and studied each other's cases. If a case presented similar facts or issues, they followed the reasoning and the rule of law laid down by the judge in a preceding or similar case. Following a rule established in a similar case (precedent) became known as the doctrine of **stare decisis** (Latin for "stand by that decided"). Judges, overtime, made their judicial decisions common to all England. This became known as the common law.

JUDICIAL PRECEDENT– DOCTRINE OF STARE DECISIS

The doctrine of **stare decisis** or judicial precedent required that, decisions of higher courts bind courts that were lower in the hierarchy. The doctrine binds judges to apply established principles laid down by superior courts in previous cases to current cases possessing similar facts. Where appropriate, the courts may apply settled legal principles established in superior courts in other common law jurisdictions such as England, the United States, Canada, Nigeria, etc. except that (as indicated by Justice Cardozo):

> "The judge, even when he is free, is still not wholly free. He is not to innovate at pleasure. He is not a knight-errant, roaming at will in pursuit of his own ideals of beauty or of goodness. He is to draw his inspiration from consecrated principles. He is not to yield to spasmodic sentiments, to vague and unregulated benevolence. He is to exercise a discretion in-

formed by tradition, methodized by analogy, disciplined by system, and subordinated to 'the premodial necessity of order in social life.'"

Ratio Decidendi

Generally, not every decision of a court sets a binding precedent. A rule of law which is laid down or abstracted from the facts of a case is known as the ratio decidendi of the case, which in effect becomes the binding precedent.

Obiter dictum

As a rule, not every statement of the law is an essential part of the ratio decidendi. They are non-binding and only of persuasive authority.

THE LAW OF EQUITY – A CONCISE HISTORY

During the course of the 13th and 14th centuries, judges of the English courts developed the common law - a system of accepting and deciding cases based on principles of law developed and shaped by preceding cases. Aggrieved parties, who felt that they were being denied justice due to the absence of an enabling statute or precedent, began sending their petitions directly to the King, who referred such requests to another royal court, called Court of Chancery. The Chancery was headed by a Chancellor who possessed power to settle disputes and order **equitable remedies** according to his conscience. The decisions of the Chancellor were made without regard for the common law, and they gradually became the basis of the law of equity.

EQUITABLE REMEDIES

The Courts of Equity provided special **reliefs** known as equitable remedies. This came in several forms. For example through **specific performance,** a judge could order one party to perform a specific act. For example, a seller who had breached a contract for the sale of a house could be ordered to complete the sale, instead of repaying the money to the buyer or a **restraining order or an Injunction,** by which a court could order a party to do or refrain from doing something, or **rescission,** by which a court could discharge the parties from their obligations under a contract.

THE DOCTRINES OF EQUITY

The Equitable Doctrine of Notice

Notice refers to knowledge of existing facts – therefore the buyer of a legal estate with notice of a prior equitable interest affecting the property takes the property subject to the prior equitable interests. **There are three types of notices – actual, constructive and imputed.**

Actual notice

Actual notice would exist, for example, where a buyer had actual or express notice of a prior interest at the time of purchase, or before a purchase was completed. Thus, in **Sempa Mbabali v. W K Kidza,** Odoki J held that a plea by the defendants, of being bona fide purchasers could not stand as they knew, and were aware all along, that a part of land they had purchased was actually for burial grounds, further that the seller had sold them that land well before his own share of the entire land had been ascertained, which therefore meant that their hands were not clean.

Constructive notice

Constructive notice was defined by Salden J in **Williamson v. Brown** to exist where a purchaser had prior knowledge of any fact sufficient to put him on inquiry as to the existence of a right or title in conflict with that which he was about to purchase. Such a purchaser was presumed to have made the inquiry and to have ascertained the extent of such prior right or to have been guilty of a degree of negligence equally fatal to his claim. The rule that a prior interest in land should always be put into consideration was illustrated in **U.P.T.C v. Lutaaya** where Karokora JSC held thus, "A proprietor takes land subject to the interests of any tenant in the land in possession even if he or she had no actual notice of the tenant".

Imputed notice

Imputed notice – where notice is neither actual nor constructive it may be imputed to the buyer through actual notice to the agent. It is well established in agency law that notice to an agent is taken as having knowledge of whatever the agent gets to know.

The Equitable Doctrine of Election

The doctrine of election means that a person cannot claim benefits and reject burdens under the same instrument. Thus in **Codrington v. Codrington,** per

Lord Cairns, a person cannot accept a benefit under a deed or will without the same time conforming to all its provisions.

The Equitable Doctrine of Satisfaction

The doctrine of satisfaction is based on the maxim, "equity imputes an intention to fulfill an obligation" and may be best explained with an illustration. Suppose W is under an obligation to give X something of value, but does not but later purports to gift X something of value, it will be presumed that W's gift was made with the intention of satisfying his obligation to X.

The Equitable Doctrine of Performance

The doctrine of performance is based on the maxim that "equity imputes an intention to fulfill an obligation" – where a person covenants to perform a particular act and later performs an act "which may be converted to a completion of this covenant", it will be supposed that he meant to complete his covenant per Kenyon MR, in *Sowden v. Sowden.*

Equitable Conversion – Under the doctrine of equitable conversion, a Court of Equity can order the completion of a sale when the death of a seller occurs between the signing of the sale agreement and the date of the actual sale. In such a case, a judge will convert the title to the purchaser. This is in fulfillment of the time-honored Maxim that "Equity looks upon that as done which ought to have been done."

Equitable Distribution – Under the doctrine of equitable distribution, a Court of Equity could order the fair allotment or division of, for instance, property between a husband and wife upon divorce. Under this doctrine, the needs and contributions of each spouse are considered when property is divided between them.

Equitable Estoppel – Under the doctrine of equitable estoppel, a Court of Equity could prevent, or stop a person from claiming a legal right, out of fairness to the opposing party.

Equitable Lien – A lien is an interest in property given to a creditor to secure the satisfaction of a debt. An equitable lien may arise from a written contract if the contract shows an intention to charge a party's property with a debt or obligation. An equitable lien may also be declared by a judge in order to fairly secure the rights of a party to a contract.

Equitable Recoupment – The doctrine of equitable recoupment prevents a party from collecting the full amount of a debt if she or he is holding something that belongs to the debtor. It is usually invoked only as a defense to mitigate the amount a defendant owes to a plaintiff.

Equity of Redemption – Equity of redemption is the right of a homeowner with a mortgage (a mortgagor) to reclaim the property after it has been forfeited. Redemption can be accomplished by paying the entire amount of the debt, interest, and court costs of the foreclosing lender. With equity of redemption, a mortgagor has a specified period of time after default and before fore-closure, in which to reclaim the property.

Maxims of Equity

Over the course of many years, equity developed its own hackneyed principles, among the following:

- *Where equity and the law conflict, equity prevails* — This maxim means that where rules of law and equity are at variance on some particular point, the rules of equity ought to prevail.[9]

- *He who seeks equity must do equity* — Anyone who wishes to be treated fairly must be ready to treat others fairly.

- *Where the equities are the same, the law must prevail*— The law should be used to determine the outcome of a controversy in which the merits of both sides are equal.

- *He who seeks equity must come with clean hands* — This maxim means that a party who comes seeking fairness from a Court of Equity should himself/herself equally not have acted unfairly or dishonestly against the other party.

- *Equity will not suffer a wrong to be without a remedy* — Equitable relief will be awarded when there is a right to a relief, and there is no relief available at law.

- *Equity regards substance rather than form* — This maxim implies that a Court of Equity is more concerned with fairness and justice rather than with mere legal technicalities.

---

9   Cheshire's Modern Real Property [9th ed], p 350

- ***Equity aids the vigilant, not the indolent*** — This maxim implies that a Court of Equity will not assist a party who neglects/sleeps on their rights for an unreasonable period of time.

- ***Equity follows the law*** — This rule of equity means that, a Court of Equity will neither depart from statutory law nor refuse to follow common law rules except in exceptional cases. For example, in a land dispute, a Court of Equity will respect and not override the legal interest if shown evidence of valid land registration documents.

- ***Equity imputes an intention to fulfill an obligation*** — Where a party is obliged to perform an act and that party did some other act which could be regarded as a performance of it, then it will be so regarded by a Court of Equity. The text writers give an example of a debtor leaving a legacy to his creditor equal or greater to his obligation. A Court of Equity will regard such a gift as performance of the obligation to the creditor. Thus the creditor will not be permitted to claim both the legacy and payment of the debt.

- ***Equity regards as done which ought to be done*** — This maxim means that where a contract is specifically enforceable, a Court of Equity will regard the promisor as having done what he has promised to do.

- ***Equity acts in personam*** — This rule of equity implies that, a Court of Equity has jurisdiction over a party personally. The personal nature of this jurisdiction is illustrated by the fact that failure to comply with the order such as specific performance or an injunction is a contempt of court punishable by imprisonment.

- ***Delay defeats equity*** — This rule of equity means that, a Court of Equity will assist a vigilant and not an indolent party. This is the primary foundation for the doctrine of larches and acquiescence where a party who slept on his rights cannot obtain equitable relief. Anytime a party suffers some wrong or injury, that party must act immediately or timeously. When you relax on your rights a court of fairness cannot assist you right a wrong that you could have prevented if you had been vigilant.

- ***Equity does not require an idle gesture*** — This rule of equity means that, a party cannot compel a Court of Equity to undertake a vain thing or issue empty orders. For example, it would be an idle gesture for a Court of Equity to grant rectification of a contract and then to deny to a prevailing party the opportunity to perform it as modified.

- *Equity delights to do justice and not by halves* — This maxim means that, where a Court of Equity is presented with a good claim to equitable relief, and in the same breath it is clear that a party has also sustained monetary costs, a Court of Equity has jurisdiction to, as well, give the injured party legal reliefs like monetary damages. A Court of Equity will therefore not stop at granting only an equitable relief, but will proceed to give a complete raft of remedies.

- *Equity will not allow a statute to be used as a cloak for fraud* — This maxim means that, a Court of Equity will prevent a party from relying upon an absence of a statutory formality, if to do so would be unconscionable and unfair. This can occur in secret trusts and also constructive trusts and so on.

STATUTORY INTERPRETATION

The task of interpreting statutes is a major duty of our courts. To apply any legislation, a judge has to determine what the legislation means. Sometimes they have to determine the legality or constitutionality of an enactment; to do that however, judges apply one of three rules — the literal rule, the golden rule, or the mischief rule.

The literal rule
Under the literal rule, a judge considers what the statute actually says rather than what it might mean. In doing this, the judge must give the words in the statute their literal, plain, ordinary, or everyday meaning, even if doing this would lead to an otherwise unjust or undesirable outcome.

The golden rule
The golden rule is applied in situations where applying the literal rule would probably lead to an absurd result, except that the court is not free to replace or ignore a statutory provision merely on the basis that it considers them absurd.

The mischief rule
When there is **ambiguity** in a statute, a court of law may go beyond the actual wording of a statute to consider the problem or mischief that the statute was enacted to remedy. In applying the mischief rule, the court must, however, consider the following four elements as indicated in *Heydon's case* (1584): what was the common law before the passing of the statute? What was the mischief in the law which the common law did not adequately deal with? What mischief did

Parliament intended to cure? Or what reason did Parliament have in mind for adopting this or that remedy?

CHAPTER 2 – QUICK REVIEW

The main sources of Ghanaian law are the Constitution, Parliamentary Enactments, Orders, Rules and Regulations, the Existing law, and Ghanaian common law. Our legal system is therefore pluralistic. Common law built up over centuries, through the application of judicial precedent. Equity developed rules of fairness at the courts of chancery to deal with rigidities of the common law.

The judiciary is required to interpret statutes made by the legislature. To do this, judges may resort to the literal, golden or mischief rule. The following rules apply: words should be given their literal meaning; words should be interpreted within context; words should be interpreted according to the purpose of the statute, and the meaning to be assigned general words should be limited to the type or class of things mentioned by specific words.

3. The Structure and Jurisdiction of the Courts

Understanding Dispute Resolution

LEARNING OUTCOMES

The 1992 Constitution and the *Courts Act,* 1993 (Act 459) as amended by L.I. 2211 provides for the composition and jurisdiction of the Supreme Court, the Court of Appeal, the High Court, the Circuit and District Court. This chapter provides an overview of the court system in Ghana. It covers also litigation and alternative dispute resolution (ADR) mechanisms for settling business disputes. Upon completion of this topic, you should master the various types of courts, their composition and jurisdiction and ADR mechanisms for dispute resolution.

INTRODUCTION

The Ghanaian court system comprises the following courts in a descending order of importance:

- The Supreme Court
- The Appeal Court
- The High Court (Fast Track Division; Commercial Division; Land Division; Human Right, Labour Division and the Financial Crimes Division).
- The Circuit Court, and
- The District Court

There are, however, a number of administrative and quasi-judicial institutions such as the National Labour Commission ("NLC"), the National Media Commission ("NMC"), and Commission of Human Rights and Administrative justice ("CHRAJ").

THE JUDICIARY

The Constitution and the Courts Act provide for a Judiciary that is headed administratively by a Chief Justice, and a court system that is structured into two broad divisions, namely, the "Superior Courts of Judicature" on the one hand and the "inferior" or "Lower Courts and Tribunals" on the other hand.[10]

The Superior Courts, consisting of the Supreme Court, the Court of Appeal, the High Court and Regional Tribunals, are creatures of the Constitution,[11] while the Lower Courts namely the Circuit Courts, District Magistrate Courts, Judicial Committee of the National House of Chiefs; the Judicial Committee of the Regional House of Chiefs and the Judicial Committees of the various Traditional Councils, are creatures of the Courts Act.[12]

In the exercise of their judicial functions, in both civil and criminal matters,[13] all Courts are empowered to issue any orders and directions that are necessary to enforce their judgments, decrees or orders. Indeed to cement their judicial independence, Article 127(1) of the Constitution provides expressly that, in the exercise of their judicial function, the Judiciary cannot be subject to the control or direction of any person or authority in Ghana.

---

10   The Chief Justice functions as the Administrative head of the Judiciary, with relatively wide supervisory powers. Thus Section 104 of the **Courts Act,** 1993 (Act 459) for example, reserves exclusively in the Chief Justice the power to transfer and thereby take away the jurisdiction of any judge, magistrate or tribunal to hear and determine any pending cause or matter to another competent judge, magistrate or tribunal be it a part-heard or a fresh matter, although, under section 104 (1) of Act 459 the transfer order should be under the hand and seal of the Chief Justice. And although under section 104 (2) of Act 459 the Chief Justice in a case of urgency could order a transfer by means of a telegraphic, telephonic or electronic communication, but section 104 (3) of Act 459 required that unless such an order was confirmed immediately by a written order signed and sealed by the Chief Justice, it would have no effect. When a judge's jurisdiction over any matter was taken away by the Chief Justice, the only manner by which the jurisdiction might be restored was by another formal transfer or retransfer under the hand and seal of the Chief Justice under section 104 of Act 459.

11   Article 126

12   Section 29 of Act 459

13   Civil matters relate to disputes between private individuals arising from a contract or tort etc. Criminal matters, on the other hand, are those matters that relate to crime or activities which are punishable either by a fine or imprisonment or both a fine and imprisonment.

THE SUPREME COURT

The Supreme Court is a superior court of record and the highest court of the land.[14] The Constitution empowers the Court to exercise jurisdiction in five main areas: General, Supervisory, Appellate, Review and Original jurisdiction. Historically, the first Supreme Court was created in the Gold Coast under the Supreme Court Ordinance of 1876. That court inherited the jurisdiction that the fused English High Court had under the Supreme Court of Judicature Act, 1873. Thus, our Supreme Court acquired jurisdiction in both common law and equity.[15] The Supreme Court was presided over by a Chief Justice who sat with puisne judges appointed by the Governor.

COMPOSITION OF THE SUPREME COURT

The Supreme Court consists of the Chief Justice and not less than nine other Justices of the Supreme Court, but is duly constituted for its work by not less than five Supreme Court Justices. The Chief Justice presides at sittings of the Supreme Court and in his absence, the most senior of the Justices of the Supreme Court presides. No person qualifies for appointment as a Justice of the Supreme Court unless he/she is of high moral character and proven integrity and is of not less than fifteen years' standing as a lawyer.

JURISDICTION OF THE SUPREME COURT

General Jurisdiction

Under Article 129 of the Constitution, 1992:

(1) The Supreme Court is the final court of appeal

(2) The Supreme Court is not bound to follow the decisions of any other court, and

(3) The Supreme Court may treat its own previous decisions as binding, but could depart from it when it appears appropriate; and all other courts would be bound to follow the Supreme Court on questions of law.

---

14   The Supreme Court is also Ghana's Constitutional court.

15   But not the review jurisdiction of the old Court of Chancery which had been transferred to the Court of Appeal established under the *Judicature Act,* (1873). And since the common law court had no review jurisdiction, the earlier Supreme Court could not be said to have inherited one under section 11 of the Ordinance.

Original Jurisdiction

Under Article 130 of the Constitution,

(1) The Supreme Court has exclusive original jurisdiction in:
(a) all matters relating to enforcement or interpretation of the Constitution; and
(b) all matters as to whether an enactment was made in excess of the powers conferred on Parliament or any other authority or person by law or under the Constitution.
(2) Where an issue that relates to a matter or question referred to in clause (1) arises in any proceedings in a court other than the Supreme Court, that court must stay the proceedings and refer the question of law involved to the Supreme Court for determination; and the Court in which the question arose must dispose of the case in accordance with the Supreme Court.

Appellate Jurisdiction

Under Article 130 of the Constitution:

(1) An appeal from a judgment of the Court of Appeal goes to the Supreme Court,
(a) as of right in a civil or criminal case where the appeal has been brought to the Court of Appeal from a judgment of the High Court or a Regional Tribunal in the exercise of its original jurisdiction; or
(b) with leave of the Court of Appeal, in any other cause or matter, where the case was commenced in a Court lower than the High Court or a Regional Tribunal and where the Court of Appeal is satisfied that the case involves a substantial question of law or is in the public interest.
(2) Notwithstanding clause (1) the Supreme Court may entertain an application for special leave to appeal to the Supreme Court in any cause or matter, civil or criminal, and may grant leave accordingly.
(3) The Supreme Court has however appellate jurisdiction, to the exclusion of the Court of Appeal, to determine matters relating to the conviction or otherwise of a person for high treason or treason by the High Court.
(4) An appeal from a decision of the Judicial Committee of the National House of Chiefs goes to the Supreme Court with the leave of that Judicial Committee or the Supreme Court.

Supervisory Jurisdiction

Article 132 of the Constitution, 1992 confers jurisdiction on the Supreme Court to supervise pending adjudication in any courts and by all adjudicating authorities. In the exercise of that jurisdiction, it may issue orders and directions in the nature of **habeas corpus, certiorari, mandamus, prohibition and quo warranto** for the purpose of enforcing or securing the enforcement of its supervisory power.

Review Jurisdiction
Article 133 of the Constitution, 1992 confers jurisdiction on the Supreme Court to review its own decisions. This jurisdiction is not frequently used. It is, however, exercised by the court only in exceptional circumstances, for instance, in situations where the Supreme Court has inadvertently committed a fundamental error of law, and if left uncorrected will occasion a gross miscarriage of justice.

THE COURT OF APPEAL

The Court of Appeal is immediately below the Supreme Court but above the High Court. It hears only cases on appeal, for example, from the High Court, Regional Tribunal and Circuit Courts. It has no supervisory jurisdiction and no original jurisdiction.

COMPOSITION OF THE COURT OF APPEAL
Article 136 of the Constitution, 1992 provides that:

(1) the Court of Appeal consists of
    (a) the Chief Justice;
    (b) subject to clause (2) and (3) of this article, not less than ten Justices of the Court of Appeal; and
    (c) such other Justices of the Superior Court of Judicature as the Chief Justice may, for the determination of a particular cause or matter by writing signed by him, request to sit in the Court of Appeal for any specified period.

CONSTITUTION OF THE COURT OF APPEAL
The Court of Appeal is duly constituted by any three of its Justices and when so constituted, the most senior of the Justices presides.

No person qualifies for appointment as a Justice of the Court of Appeal unless he is of high moral character and proven integrity and is of not less than twelve years standing as a lawyer. The Court of Appeal is not bound by its own precedents, and all courts below it are bound to follow its decisions on questions of law.

JURISDICTION OF THE COURT OF APPEAL

Under Article 137 of the Constitution:

(1) The Court of Appeal has jurisdiction throughout Ghana to hear and determine appeals from among others, judgments, decrees or orders of the High Court and Regional Tribunals. In general, an appeal lies, as of right, from a judgment, decree or Order of the High Court and Regional Tribunal to the Court of Appeal; and for the purposes of hearing the appeal, the Court of Appeal assumes all powers, authority and jurisdiction vested in the Court from which the appeal emanates.

THE HIGH COURT

In a descending order of importance, the High Court is next court after the Court of Appeal. Within the High Court, there are, however, specialized divisions, namely the Fast Track, Commercial, Finance, Land, Industrial/Labor, and Human Rights Divisions.

COMPOSITION OF THE HIGH COURT

Article 139 of the Constitution provides that:

The High Court consists of –

> (a) the Chief Justice;
> (b) not less than twenty Justices of the High Court; and
> (c) such other Justices of the Superior Court of Judicature as the Chief Justice by writing signed by him, request to sit as High Court Justices for any period.

CONSTITUTION OF THE HIGH COURT

The High Court is constituted by

> (a) a single Justice of the Court;
> (b) a single Justice of the Court and jury;
> (c) a single Justice of the Court with assessors; or
> (d) three Justices of the Court for the trial of the offense of high treason or treason as required by article 19 of this Constitution.

No person qualifies to be appointed as a High Court Judge, unless he is a person of high moral character and proven integrity and is of at least ten years' standing as a lawyer.

JURISDICTION OF THE HIGH COURT

1. The High Court exercises original jurisdiction in all civil and criminal matters, and other appellate jurisdiction conferred on it by law.

2. It has appellate jurisdiction in any judgment of the Circuit Court in criminal matters, and appellate jurisdiction in any judgment of the District Court or Juvenile Court;

3. The High Court also has exclusive jurisdiction to try acts of piracy;[16] and enforce the Fundamental Human Rights and Freedoms guaranteed by the Constitution. In a high treason or treason trial, the High Court has only power to convict a person for high treason or treason, and

4. The High Court exercises supervisory jurisdiction over all lower courts and adjudicating authorities, and in its exercise of that jurisdiction, it can issue orders and directions for enforcing its supervisory powers. And for hearing and determining appeals assume all the powers, authority and jurisdiction vested in the Court from which the appeal emanates.

5. In relation to its jurisdiction in relation to infants or persons of unsound mind,

(1) The High Court may

(a) on an application by a person, and after hearing the objections to the application, appoint a person as a guardian or as joint-guardian for an infant, make an order concerning the custody of an infant, the right of access to an infant, and weekly or other periodic payments towards the maintenance of an infant, or may, remove a guardian or joint-guardian and appoint a new guardian or joint-guardian; or may, in respect of an infant or person of unsound mind, make the orders and give the directions for the control and administration of the estate of that infant, including the investment of money, that the Court considers desirable having regard to the welfare of the infant; make the orders and give the directions permitting the use of moneys for the education of the infant, or for setting the infant up in an occupation or a career, that the Court considers desirable having regard to the welfare of the infant.

6 In relation to its jurisdiction in maritime matters,

(1) The High Court may, hear and determine:

---

16   See Section 21 of Act 459

(a) questions as to the title to, or ownership of, a ship, or the proceeds of the sale of a ship, arising in an action relating to possession, salvage, damage, necessaries, or wages; and

(b) questions arising between the co-owners of ships registered in Ghana as to ownership, possession, employment or earnings of that ship, or a share of it, with power to settle an account outstanding and unsettled between the parties in relation to it, and may direct the ship, or a share of it, to be sold, or make an appropriate order.

The Commercial Court

In fact, in order to make it easier for local and foreign investors to enforce their rights in Ghana, the judiciary in 2005 set up Commercial Courts (a division of the High Court) whose function is essentially to adjudicate on commercial matters only. Special rules govern proceedings at the commercial courts, notable among which is the 30 day compulsory mediation.

The Fast Track High Court

The Fast Track High Court is a highly automated court. It is not a new or separate court, but a division of a pre-existing court—the High Court.

THE REGIONAL TRIBUNAL

The Regional Tribunal was first created by the 1992 Constitution and is the court immediately after the Court of Appeal. Within the court structure, the Regional Tribunal has co-ordinate jurisdiction with the High Court.

COMPOSITION OF THE REGIONAL TRIBUNAL

In terms of Article 142 of the 1992 Constitution, the Regional Tribunal consists of:

(a) the Chief Justice,
(b) one Chairman, and
(c) members who may or may not be lawyers designated by the Chief Justice to sit as panel members.

CONSTITUTION OF THE REGIONAL TRIBUNAL

A Regional Tribunal, in the exercise of its original jurisdiction, is duly constituted by a panel consisting of the Chairman and not less than two and not more than four other panel members. No person qualifies to be appointed as a Chairman unless that person is qualified to be appointed a Justice of the High Court;

and no person qualifies to be appointed a panel member unless that person is a person of high moral character and proven integrity. The Chief Justice or a Justice of the High Court or of the Court of Appeal nominated by the Chief Justice can sit as Chairman.

JURISDICTION OF THE REGIONAL TRIBUNAL

Articles 142-143 of the Constitution and Section 24 of Act 459 relate to the Regional Tribunal. The Tribunal has concurrent original jurisdiction (i.e. powers) with the High Court in criminal matters, but has no civil or supervisory jurisdiction. The jurisdiction of the Tribunal is spelt out in detail in Articles 142-143 of the Constitution. For example, the Tribunal has jurisdiction to try offenses specified under the following statutes — Chapter 4 of the *Criminal Code, 1960* (Act 29); the *Customs, Excise and Preventive Services Management Law,* 1993 (P.N.D.C.L. 330); the *Income Tax Decree,* 1975 (S.M.C.D. 5); the *Narcotic Drugs (Control, Enforcement and Sanctions) Law,* 1990 (P.N.D.C.L. 236) and any other offense involving serious economic fraud, loss of State funds or property. A Regional Tribunal however is permitted by law to try criminal offenses requiring the participation of a jury or assessors. The decisions of a Regional Tribunals rest upon the majority opinion of the members hearing the case. Appeals against the decisions of the Tribunal go directly to the Court of Appeal.

THE CIRCUIT COURT

This court is located immediately below the High Court and Regional Tribunal but above the District Magistrate Court. The Circuit forms part of the inferior or lower courts.

JURISDICTION OF THE CIRCUIT COURT

Section 42 of Act 459

The Courts Act provides that the jurisdiction of the Circuit Court consists of:

(a) Original jurisdiction in civil matters;
(i) in personal actions arising under a contract or a tort, or for the recovery of a liquidated sum of money, where the amount claimed is not more than 100 million cedis;
(ii) in actions between a landlord and a tenant for the possession of land claimed under a lease and refused to be delivered up;
(iii) in [causes and matters] involving the ownership, possession, occupation of or title to land;

(iv) to appoint guardians of infants and to make orders for the custody of infants;

(v) to grant in an action instituted in the Court, injunctions or orders to stay
waste, or alienation or for the detention and preservation of property which
is the subject matter of that action, or to restrain breaches of contract, or
the commission of a tort;

(vi) in claims of relief by way of interpleader in respect of land or any other
property attached in execution of an order made by a Circuit Court;

(vii) in applications for the grant of probate or letters of administration in respect of the estate of a deceased person, and in [causes and matters] relating to succession to property of a deceased person, who had, at the time of
death, a fixed place of abode within the area of jurisdiction of the Circuit
Court, and the value of the estate or property in question does not exceed
100 cedis.

Criminal Jurisdiction of the Circuit Court

Section 43 of Act 459

A Circuit Court has original jurisdiction in criminal matters other than treason,
offenses triable on indictment and offenses punishable by death.

Appeals from the Circuit Courts

Section 44 of Act 459

(1) A person aggrieved by a judgment of a Circuit Court in a civil action may,
subject to this Act and the Rules of Court, appeal to the Court of Appeal.

(2) A person aggrieved by a judgment of a Circuit Court in a criminal trial may,
subject to this Act and the Rules of Court, may appeal to the High Court.

THE DISTRICT COURT

Section 45 of Act 459

These are Courts that are set up by the Chief Justice in respective districts of
the country. District Court is presided over by Magistrates who are appointed,
subject to the approval of the President, by the Chief Justice on the advice of the
Judicial Council. However, a person does not qualify to be appointed a Magistrate of a District Court unless that person is of high moral character and proven
integrity and is a lawyer of not less than three years' standing.

CIVIL JURISDICTION OF THE DISTRICT COURT
Section 47 of Act 459

A District Court has civil jurisdiction in the following matters:

(a) Personal actions arising under a contract or a tort for the recovery of a liquidated sum of money where the amount claimed does not exceed ten million cedis.

(b) Granting of injunctions or orders to stay waste or alienation, or for the detention and preservation of property which is the subject matter of that action, or restrain a breach of contract or the commission of a tort.

(c) Claims for relief by way of interpleader in respect of land or any other property attached in execution of [a decree] [an order] made by the District Court.

(d) Civil actions relating to the landlord and tenant of premises, or a person interested in the premises as required or authorized by a law relating to landlord and tenant.

(e) Actions relating to ownership, possession or occupation of land, where the value of the land does not exceed ten million cedis.

(f) Divorce and other matrimonial cases [causes or matters] and actions for paternity and custody of children.

(g) Applications for grant of probate or letters of administration in respect of the estate of a deceased person, and in [causes and matters] relating to succession to property of a deceased person, who had at the time of death a fixed place of abode within the area of jurisdiction of the District Court and the value of the estate or property in question does not exceed ten million cedis; and

(h) hear and determine charges and dispose of any other matters affecting juveniles, that is, persons under the age of eighteen.

CRIMINAL JURISDICTION OF THE DISTRICT COURT
Section 48 of Act 459

(1) In criminal matters, a District Court has jurisdiction to try summarily:

(a) an offense punishable by a fine not exceeding five hundred penalty units or a term of imprisonment not exceeding two years or both the fine and the imprisonment;

(b) any other offense, except an offense punishable by death or by imprisonment for life or an offense declared by an enactment to be a first degree felony, if the Attorney-General thinks that the case is suitable to be tried summarily, considering

(i) the nature of the offense,

(ii) the absence of circumstances which would render the offense of a grave or serious character, and

(iii) any other circumstances of the case;

(c) an attempt to commit an offense to which paragraph (a) or (b) applies;

(d) abetment of or conspiracy in respect of that offense.

STATUTORY UPDATE – LI 2211

The civil jurisdiction of the Circuit Court under Section 42(1)(a)(i) of Act 459 was limited to personal actions arising under contract or tort or for recovery of liquidated sums with value not exceeding GHC10,000.00. L.I. 2211 has, however, expanded the Court's jurisdiction to GHC50, 000.00. Similarly, under Section 47 of the Act the jurisdiction of the District Court has been expanded from GHC5, 000.00 to GHC20, 000.00. The District Court's jurisdiction to admit land related disputes with values not exceeding GHC5, 000.00 has also been expanded to GHC20, 000.00.

In matters relating to grant of Probate and Letters of Administration, L.I. 2211 has expanded the Jurisdiction of the Circuit Courts to admit applications in respect of estates whose values do not exceed GHC50, 000.00 and that of the District Court from GHC5,000.00 to GHC20,000.00.

THE JUVENILE COURT

The Juvenile Court is a specialized District Court that hears and determines actions under the **Children's Act,** 1998 (Act 560). It has jurisdiction in matters concerning parentage, custody of children, access to and maintenance of children. It hears cases concerning children in need of special care and protection. It can make care and supervision orders. The Tribunal sits with a panel consisting of a chairman and not less than two members, one being a Social Welfare Officer.

THE FAMILY TRIBUNAL

The Family Tribunal hears criminal or civil cases involving persons under the age of eighteen (18) years. The court is constituted by a District Magistrate and two other persons, one of whom must be a Social Welfare Officer. The Chief Justice designates a District Court Judge to preside over the court.

THE MOTOR COURT

The Motor Court is a specialised District Court created and mandated to handle motor traffic cases. It is therefore a special court for motor offenses and traffic violations.

THE CHIEFTAINCY TRIBUNAL

Under the 1992 Constitution chieftaincy disputes are to be heard by the Judicial Committees of the Traditional Authorities. Matters heard by Traditional Councils can be appealed to the Regional House of Chiefs and a further appeal to the National House of chiefs. The Supreme Court serves, however, as the final court of appeal for all Chieftaincy Tribunal cases.

BUSINESS DISPUTE RESOLUTION IN THE GHANAIAN LEGAL SYSTEM

Civil Litigation

Civil litigation is the conduct of a lawsuit in a court of law. Litigation is an important procedure as it offers disputing parties an opportunity to resolve legal disputes in accordance with law. Litigation is an intensely procedural process. It is governed by rules and generally starts when one or more parties (called the plaintiff or plaintiffs) or their lawyers filing a claim against one or more parties (called the defendant or defendants) for specified reliefs.

The 1992 Constitution and the Courts Act[17] provide for the composition and jurisdiction of the courts. By virtue of Article 125 (3) of the Constitution, final judicial power, that is the ultimate power to adjudicate, or resolve disputes vests in the Judiciary.[18] Under Article 125(3), neither the President, nor Parliament nor any other organ or agency created by the President or Parliament, has the power to exercise the final say in judicial matters. Ultimately, in criminal matters, a person's guilt can only be determined by a court of competent jurisdiction.

---

17   Act 469 of 1993 as amended by the *Courts (Amendment) Act* of 1993 (Act 464)
18   In *Akainyah v. The Republic* (1968) GLR 548, it was decided that an essential attribute of judicial power was the power to decide on claims by disputing parties in accordance with established legal principles, as well as, the power to enforce those claims.

ALTERNATIVE DISPUTE RESOLUTION (ADR)

The Code of Ethics of the Ghana Bar Association obliges lawyers to advise their clients to avoid or terminate litigation whenever a dispute admits of fair settlement.[19] Given that litigation can be costly, harmful to reputation and also time-consuming, many disputing parties are increasingly opting for alternative dispute resolution.

Alternative Dispute Resolution (ADR) refers to a range of procedures that serve as a substitute to traditional litigation for the resolution of disputes and generally involves the assistance of a neutral or impartial third party.

With the passage of the *Alternative Dispute Resolution Act,* (Act 798) of 2010, ADR practice received a major boost. Disputing parties in many cases undergo some pre-trial mediation, before a case goes for trial. The rising popularity of ADR is explained by the increasing caseload of traditional courts, as well as awareness that ADR imposes lesser costs than litigation. There is also confidentiality, and parties could have greater control over the selection of the third party who can decide their disputes.[20]

TYPES OF ADR MECHANISMS

There are various methods of resolving disputes using ADR. These methods include; arbitration, negotiation, conciliation, mediation, customary-arbitration, mediation-arbitration and neutral case evaluation.

Arbitration

Arbitration is an out of court settlement of a dispute by an independent person chosen by the disputing parties themselves. Where a contract has a clause requiring the parties to submit a dispute first to arbitration, the court will enforce that clause and will not permit a party to proceed to litigate, unless an arbitral process has first been exhausted.

The parties themselves are involved in choosing the person who is going to settle their dispute. This means that they can request the services of an expert in the particular commercial area they operate in.

Arbitration is also less formal, fully private, quicker and less expensive in comparison with litigation. Where a particular dispute covers, for example, a com-

---

19   Section 43 (1) and (2)

20   *http://en.wikipedia.org/wiki/Alternative_dispute_resolution*

mercially sensitive matter, this may actually be more helpful to avoid negative publicity. Courtroom proceedings, on the other hand, are usually placed on record and are accessible by the public.

Negotiation

Negotiation is a process by which parties to a dispute or their representatives discuss the issue(s) in dispute with the intention of settling the dispute without the intervention of one or more third parties. For negotiation to succeed, the parties must be willing and ready to compromise. And they must act in good faith and be responsive to the legitimate interests, concerns and fears of each other.

Mediation

Mediation is a process by which a neutral or impartial third party, known as a mediator, acts to assist the disputants to find ways to resolve their dispute. The duty of the mediator is to facilitate dialogue between parties to assist them to arrive at a mutually acceptable settlement. The mediator works with the parties to find the situation that best fits them all and not to decide who is right or wrong (Kelsey, 2013). There are three types of mediation approaches that the mediator can opt for. The amount of control the disputing parties have is the main difference between these types:

- **Evaluation Mediation:** This type focuses on the legal rights of the parties disputing. The mediator hears the different sides of the issue and evaluates it based on the legal rights and fairness to bring out a solution that fits all. The mediator used in this type needs to have a legal background.
- **Facilitative Mediation:** The parties here have more control over the process. The mediator does not give an opinion about the solution but ensures that the parties come to an agreement of their own.
- **Transformative Mediation:** Like the facilitative mediation, the power of settling disputes lies with the disputing parties. The parties determine and layout the process and the mediator only helps them understand each other's values and points of view. This type is mostly used to resolve interpersonal disputes (Legal Service Article, 2011).

Mediation offers the various parties the confidentiality needed to settle their case. The confidentiality involved is such that mediators cannot be forced to testify in court about the case. Parties can have the privacy to settle their differences without spewing it out in public. During mediation there is a mutual attempt to arrive at a solution that suits all parties involved. This goes a long way to maintain and repair the relationship between the disputants. The main characteristics of mediation are, however, as follows:

- It is confidential. This means the parties cannot be compelled to disclose information that they prefer to keep confidential. That information cannot be provided to anyone including even a court outside the context of the mediation.

- It is a non-binding process controlled by the parties. This means that a party to mediation cannot be forced to accept an outcome that it does not like. Unlike an arbitrator or a judge, the mediator is not a decision-maker. The mediator's role is, rather, to assist the parties in reaching a settlement of the dispute. Indeed, even when the parties have agreed to submit a dispute to mediation, they are free to abandon the process at any time after the first meeting if they find that its continuation does not meet their interests. However, parties usually participate actively in mediations once they begin. If they decide to proceed with the mediation, the parties decide on how it should be conducted with the mediator.

Customary Arbitration

Customary Arbitration involves a voluntary submission of a dispute to one or more arbitrators acting under customary law or according to customary traditional norms.

It is the process of voluntary submission of a dispute to one or more neutral persons for a final and binding determination or settlement. Arbitration can start only if there exists a valid Arbitration Agreement between the parties prior to or after the emergence of the dispute. Usually it is advisable if such an agreement is in writing.

Conciliation

Conciliation is similar to mediation. In this type of dispute resolution, a third party (Conciliator) helps the parties to reach a resolution and the third party plays a more active role in bringing the parties together and suggesting solutions. Conciliation is a less formal form of arbitration. Conciliation does not require the existence of any previous agreement. Any party may request the other party to appoint a conciliator. A single conciliator can be appointed but two or three are also acceptable. Where there are multiple conciliators, all must act jointly. Where a party rejects the offer to conciliate, no conciliation can be held.

Parties may submit statements to the conciliator describing the general nature of the dispute and the facts in issue, and to each other. The conciliator may request further details, and the parties may even submit suggestions for the settlement of the dispute to the conciliator. Where the conciliator finds that settlement exists, he can draw up the terms of settlement and serve it to the parties for their acceptance. If the parties accept to sign the terms of settlement it becomes final and binding on them. The effects of conciliation include the fact that the parties involved maintain their autonomy and control over the process. Conciliation is also a good way of saving time and cost due to the fact that the parties have the advantage of doing things to suit their time and financial situations. Parties involved also enjoy the confidentiality that comes with having to settle the dispute with only the other parties and the conciliator.

THE ADVANTAGES OF ADR

ADR is increasingly being used, locally and internationally. In many countries it has been integrated into the legal system. Among its merits are the following:

a)   ADR is suitable in multiparty disputes;
b)   Is flexible in procedure as the process is determined and controlled by the parties to the dispute
c)   Costs tend generally to be lower
d)   Has processes which are less complicated
e)   Enables parties to choose their own third party "judge" to direct negotiations/adjudicate
f)   Has greater likelihood of generating speedier settlements
g)   Provides solutions that can be tailored to suit the parties' interests
h)   Has a better likelihood of obtaining a durable agreement
i)   Generally, confidentiality is assured with ADR
j)   Enhances the preservation of relationships and reputations

INTERNATIONAL INSTITUTIONS AND ADR MECHANISMS

International Chamber of Commerce (ICC)

Expansion in international trade led to the creation in 1919 of the International Chamber of Commerce (ICC). The ICC's international secretariat was established in Paris and its International Court of Arbitration was created in 1923. The ICC promotes international trade and investment, open markets for goods and services, and the free flow of capital.

The ICC produces and promotes trade standards relating to carriage and passage of risk called International Commercial Term (Incoterms). Incoterms are used principally in international sales contracts. They were developed to address issues on which buyers and sellers have to agree if a contract was to be performed satisfactorily. These issues included how far insurance costs are included in the contract price; what time risk and property in goods passed; how far carriage costs are included in the contract price; who would bear the risk of damage or loss at any particular point in time; who had responsibility for customs documentation, and how far customs are included in a contract price.

International Court of Arbitration (ICA)

The ICA promotes the use of arbitration in commercial disputes, as an alternative to litigation. The ICA engages in arbitral proceedings, maintains a list of arbitrators, decides challenges involving arbitrators, approves arbitral awards and fixes arbitrator fees. States which have ratified the ICC's New York Convention of 1958 agree to recognize arbitration agreements, and also agree not to submit such disputes to national courts.

World Trade Organization (WTO)

The WTO emerged out of the General Agreement on Tariffs and Trade (GATT) of 1995 and deals with rules of international trade between nations. WTO has more than 150 members and is devoted to the promotion of international free trade, in goods, intellectual property and services. The WTO settles international trade disputes through its Dispute Settlement Body (DSB). The DSB comprises of a panel of experts. Although rulings of the panel are generally binding, they can be appealed.

United Nations Commission on International Trade Law (UNCITRAL)

UNCITRAL is a body within the UN which focuses on international trade law. UNCITRAL was created in 1966, when the General Assembly recognized that differences in national laws governing international trade were hampering trade.

The International Institute for the Unification of Private Law (UNIDROIT)

UNIDROIT was set up in 1926 as an independent intergovernmental organization based in Rome. It is concerned with modernizing, harmonizing and coordinating commercial law between States and groups of States as well as formulating uniform law instruments, principles and rules to achieve those objectives. Since UNIDROIT is an intergovernmental structure, its rules take the form of international conventions.

Chapter 3 – Quick Review

The Ghanaian court system comprises the Supreme Court, the Appeal Court, the High Court, the Circuit Court, the District Court, Family Tribunals and the Juvenile Courts. Generally litigation and Alternative Dispute Resolution (ADR) offers the two (2) dominant forms of dispute settlement. ADR is a way of settling disputes out of court. Generally ADR assures greater privacy, informality, speed, cost effectiveness, expertise, finality and neutrality. Unfortunately, there are a few demerits too, among them, lack of legal expertise, no right of appeal, and less predictability than a court decision.

In the conduct of international trade, ADR is the subject of the UN Model law on international commercial Arbitration. UNIDRIOT, UNCITRAL, the ICC and ICJ all offer various forms for business dispute resolution at the international level.

4. Offer and Acceptance

Formation of contract

LEARNING OUTCOMES

A contract is a voluntary, deliberate, legally binding agreement between two or more competent parties. Contracts are usually written, but may also be oral or implied. A contractual relationship is characterized by a valid offer, acceptance, consideration and an intention to be legally bound. When these elements are in place, each party acquires rights and duties which can be enforced in a court of law.

At the end of the lesson, you should be able to define a contract, and identify the elements of a valid offer and a valid acceptance; the distinction between bilateral and unilateral agreements; identification of a valid offer; termination of an offer; identification of a valid acceptance; communication of acceptance, certainty of terms and incomplete agreements.

THE DOCTRINES OF CONTRACT LAW

Doctrine of Freedom of Contract

The doctrine of freedom of contract is based on the notion that parties to a contract are the best judges of their own interests. Accordingly, where two parties have voluntarily entered into a genuine contract, the courts would enforce the terms of the contract as they stood and not interfere with the agreement if it was freely entered into.

Doctrine of Sanctity of Contract

The doctrine of sanctity of contract is another dogma of contract law. It is to the effect that parties to a contract are free to determine the terms of their contract, and obligations voluntarily undertaken under a contract are "sacred" and should be performed by all means. This doctrine held that parties ought to be made to keep their promises. The rule developed that a party should not be excused from performing his contractual obligations even if they become onerous or impossible to perform due to events outside his control, unless he could rely on the stipulations of the contract to do so.

DEFINITION – WHAT IS A CONTRACT?

A contract was defined as "an agreement constituted by an offer and an acceptance with the mutual intention that it should be binding and enforceable at law". (See the Court of Appeal case of **Kobaku Associates v. Owusu**[21]).

FORMS OF CONTRACT

Under Ghanaian law, contracts may be oral, written or by conduct. Section 11 of the **Contracts Act,** 1960 (Act 25) provides that a contract is not void simply because it is not in writing.[22] An oral contract will be binding long as there is clear evidence as to its essential terms and also the actual intention of the parties. The existence of a binding agreement, is generally a matter of evidence and that can be established by the actual conduct of the parties[23] (see **Brogden v. Metropolitan Railway** (1877)). The general rule is that where a contract is not required to be in writing, the existence and contents of such a contract must be proved. A court would in that case look at all material facts upon which the contract is based in order to ascertain what was really decided by the parties.

The law of contract is based on the Latin maxim, *"pacta sunt servanda"*, which means agreements are binding and must be kept. This notwithstanding, not all agreements are binding or contractual. This is because some promises may not

---

21   [2003-2005] 1 GLR 611

22   Section 11 of Act 25: Subject to this Act, and to any other enactment, a contract whether made before or after the commencement of this Act, is not void or unenforceable by reason only that it is not in writing or that there is no memorandum or note of the contract in writing.

23   In so far as conduct, which creates a binding contract is concerned, the principle summed up in **Freeman v. Coke** and adopted by Lord Blackburn's famous articulation in **Smith v. Hughes** (1871) LR 6QB 597, at 607 that, *"If, whatever a man's real intention may be, he so conducts himself that a reasonable man would believe that he was assenting to the terms proposed by the other party, and that other party upon that belief enters into a contract with him, the man thus conducting himself would be equally bound as if he had agreed to the others terms"* remains good law.

have an intention to create legal relations, such as social or domestic agreements (see ***Balfour v. Balfour***).

TYPES OF CONTRACTS

Contracts may be classified in a number of ways. Ghanaian law recognizes three (3) species of contracts or transactions. These are namely:

a) **Unilateral contracts,** that is, contracts in which a promise is met, not by a reciprocal promise, but with the performance of a requested act.

b) **Bilateral contracts,** that is, contracts in which a promise is met with a re-ciprocal promise; and finally

c) **Formal contracts,** that is, contracts made by deed. Contracts for the sale of land and hire-purchase agreements are, for example, generally required to be in writing.[24]

FORMATION OF CONTRACT

In order to constitute a binding contract, certain ingredients should be present. These are namely:

a)   Offer and Acceptance
b)   Intention to create legal relation
c)   Consideration, and
d)   Capacity and Legality

---

24   Section 2 of the ***Conveyancing Act,*** (NRCD 179) states that "*A contract for the transfer of an interest in land is not enforceable unless it is evidenced in a writing signed by the person against whom the contract is to be proved or by a person who was authorized to sign on behalf of that person*". (b) it is relieved against the need for a writing by Section 3.

However, Section 3 provides that Sections 1 and 2 do not apply to a transfer or contract for the transfer of an interest in land which takes effect (a) by operation of law; (b) by operation of the rules of equity relating to the creation or operation of resulting, im-plied or constructive trusts; (c) by order of the Court; (d) by will or on intestacy; (e) by prescription; (f) by a lease taking effect in possession for a term not exceeding three years, whether or not the lessee is given power to extend the term; (g) by a licence or profit other than a concession required to be in writing by section 3 of the ***Concessions Act,*** 1939; 2 or (h) by oral grant under customary law. (2) Sections 1 and 2 are subject to the rules of equi-ty including the rules relating to unconscionability, fraud, duress and part-performance.

OFFER AND ACCEPTANCE (AGREEMENT)

Agreement is a key element. Agreement implies that there must be a valid offer by one party and a valid acceptance by the other party. Agreement, is the act of the parties assenting to the same terms which results from a valid promise (an offer) made by the offeror and valid acceptance by the offeree. Not all agreements, however, are contractual in the sense that since certain promises, for instance, social or mere domestic agreements are normally made without any intention of creating binding legal relations.

An offer may be oral, written or by conduct. For oral agreements and agreements based on conduct, however, there can be unique problems, as to whether there has been a valid offer made by one party, and a valid acceptance by the other party. Again for oral offers, one party can easily lie.

THE DEFINITION OF AN OFFER

An offer is an expression of willingness to contract on certain terms, made with the intention that it shall be binding as soon as it is accepted by the other party to whom it is addressed.

In *NTHC v. Antwi,* an offer was defined as an indication in words or by conduct by an offeror that he or she is prepared to be bound by a contract in terms expressed in the offer, if the offeree communicates to the offeror his or her acceptance of those terms.[25] A person who makes an offer or promise is known as an offeror or promisor. The person to whom an offer or promise is made to is the offeree or promisee.

FORMS OF OFFER

Under Ghanaian law, an offer can be made orally, or in writing or by conduct. It must, however, be clear and precise, unconditional, unqualified and communicated to the offeree, since the offeree cannot accept the offer unless he knows of the existence of that offer.

a.   Offers by Words

An offer may be made in any form. Therefore, it may be made orally. This rule is, however, subject to some exceptions, in that certain contracts are required to be reduced into writing. Examples include contracts for the sale of land. Under the Conveyancing Act a conveyance of an interest in land must be made in writing,

---

25   [2009] SCGLR 117

signed by the person making the transfer or by his or her duly authorized agent in writing (i.e. by deed).[26]

An offer must, however, be clear and precise, unconditional, unqualified and communicated to the offeree, since the offeree cannot accept the offer unless he knows of the existence of the offer.

b. Offer in Writing

An offer may be made in writing. The general rule is that, once the other party accepts the offer and communicates back his or her acceptance, a binding contract can arise.

By law certain contracts are required to be written done and signed. For example, Section 2(a) of the *Conveyancing Act,* 1975 (N.R.C.D. 175) requires a transfer of an interest in land to be in writing, signed by the transferor.[27]

c. Offer Inferred from Conduct of the Parties

A contract by conduct usually arises where a person conducts himself in such a manner that, any reasonable person in the position of the other party would think that he intended to contract on certain terms. If the other party in reliance upon the party's conduct responds affirmatively to the terms of his offer, a contract could legally be implied from the conduct. (*Kobaku Associates v. Owusu*)

---

26   The online law dictionary, the law.com defines a deed as a writing or instrument, under seal, containing some contract or agreement, which has been delivered by one person to the other. The word "deed" is normally used to describe the document which transfers the ownership of land or real estate. See Section 1 and 2 of the *Conveyancing Act,* 1973 (NRCD 175).

27   This requirement of writing notwithstanding, a court of law is entitled in certain cases to permit a contract to be proved by oral evidence, even though of a kind required to be proved in writing, when the party seeking to enforce the contract had done acts in performance of his obligations under it. The court would exercise its discretion where (a) the act of part performance was referable to only the contract alleged; (b) they were such as would render it a fraud in the defendant to take advantage of the contract not being in writing; (c) the contract by its own nature was enforceable by the court; and (d) there had to be proper parole evidence of the contract let in by the act of part performance. See *Fofie v. Zanyo* [1992] 2 GLR 475.

CHARACTERISTICS OF A VALID OFFER

A valid offer:

- Must be communicated so that the other party can accept or reject it. Thus in *Taylor v. Laird* (1856), the master of a ship gave up his command during a voyage, but helped to sail the ship home. It was held that the owners did not have to pay for his assistance, as an offer to assist had not been communicated to them, hence they had not had an opportunity to accept or reject any offer.
- May be communicated in any manner whatsoever that is in writing, in words, or by conduct. There is no general requirement in law that an offer must at all times be in writing.
- May be made to a particular person, to a group of persons, or to the whole world. Thus in *Carlill v. Carbolic Smoke Ball Company* (1893) one of the best known cases in contract law, the defendants, manufacturers of 'carbolic smoke balls', advertized offering to pay £100 to any person who used smoke ball and succumbed to influenza within a stated time. Mrs. Louisa Elizabeth Carlill, who saw the advert bought and used one of the smoke balls as required but went down with influenza on 17 January 1892. She sued for the £100. The defendants however argued that an offer to the 'whole world' was impossible under English Law. It was held however that the advert was not a unilateral offer to the entire world, but an offer restricted to persons who acted upon the stated terms of the advert. That using the smoke ball constituted acceptance of the offer, and purchasing the smoke ball constituted consideration, since it was a distinct detriment incurred at the behest of the company, and that, an offer could be made to the whole world.
- Must be definite in substance
- Must not be an 'invitation to treat' – An invitation to treat means an invitation to the other party to make an offer.

WHAT IS NOT A VALID OFFER

Counter-Offer

A counter offer is an offer that is made in response to a previous offer by the other party during negotiations for a final contract. Making a counter offer automatically rejects the prior offer, and requires an acceptance under the terms of the counter offer or there is no contract. For example: Serwaa (Seller) offers to sell her house for GHC150,000, to be paid in 60 days; Baffour (Buyer) receives the offer and gives Seller an offer of GHC140,000, payable in 45 days. The original offer is dead, despite the shorter time for payment since the price is lower. Seller then can choose to accept at GHC140,000, counter again at some compromise price, reject the counter offer, or let it expire. Thus in the 1873 case of *Tinn v. Hoffman,* it was held that a counter offer rejected or nullified the original offer and therefore it could not create a binding contract.

Invitation to Treat

An invitation to treat, as stated above, is simply put, an invitation to the other party to make an offer – it is an indication that the invitor is willing to enter into some negotiations but is not yet prepared to be bound. An invitation to treat cannot be accepted as a valid offer, so it cannot give rise to a valid contract. The classic case of **Gibson v. Manchester City Council** (1979) illustrates this point. In Gibson, the Council's letter stated expressly that 'we may be prepared to sell you'. Mr. Gibson read the letter, and treated the words of the letter as an offer. His claim was, however, rejected. It was held that there was never an offer available for acceptance. A response to an invitation to treat may itself be an offer. In **NTHC v. Antwi,** the Supreme Court of Ghana expatiated on the difference between an offer and an invitation to treat as follows:

> "…..the offer has to be definite and final and must not leave significant terms open for further negotiation.….if a communication during negotiation is not the final expression of the alleged offeror's willingness to be bound, it may be interpreted as an invitation to the other party to use it as a basis for formulating a proposal emanating from him or her that is definite enough to qualify as an offer…an invitation to treat is thus to be distinguished from an offer on the basis of the proposal's lack of an essential characteristic of an offer, namely, its finality."

Examples of Invitation to Treat

At common law, the courts have already held that there is no intention to be bound in any of the following cases.

Most Advertisements

The general rule is that an advertisement is an invitation to treat and not an offer.

Partridge v. Crittenden (1968) illustrates the position of the law on advertisements. In that case, the defendant placed an advert in a magazine which said 'Bramblefinch cocks and hens – 25s each'. It was held that the advertisement was an invitation to treat and not an offer. The advertisement stated that the birds were for sale, not that the seller would sell to all purchasers. Therefore, he could not have intended the advertisement to be an offer.

Exception to the general rule that an advert is not an offer

There is an exception to the general rule that an advertisement is not an offer in itself. Note that an advert would be an offer if no further negotiations were intended or expected. This is the position in *Carlill v. Carbolic Smoke Ball Co* (1893), where the advertisers made it clear that they would pay money to anyone complying with the terms of their advertisement.

Goods displayed on shelves at shopping malls

In *Pharmaceutical Society of GB v. Boots Cash Chemists Ltd* (1953), it was held that goods displayed on shelves were mere invitations to treat. That the sale contract actually takes place at the cash counter, when the assistant accepts the customer's offer to buy the goods.

Shop window displays

In *Fisher v. Bell* (1961), it was held that a 'flick knife' displayed in a shop window with a price attached was not an offer but only an invitation to treat.

Shop window displays

In *Grainger & Son v. Gough* (1896) it was held that price lists, catalogue and brochures were invitations to treat.

Auctions

An auctioneer's request for bids. In *Payne v. Cave* (1789) it was held that the auctioneer's request was an invitation to treat. The offer was made by the bidder.

A notice of an auction

In *Harris v. Nickerson* (1873), it was held that a notice that an action would be held on a certain date was not an offer which could be accepted by turning up at the stated time.

Tenders

A request for tenders is normally taken in law to be an invitation to treat. It was held in *Blackpool and Fylde Aero Club v. Blackpool BC* (1990), however, that if the request is addressed to specified parties, this amounts to a unilateral offer that serious consideration will be given to each tender.

'Subject to contract'

The words 'subject to contract' may be placed on top of a letter in order to indicate that certain statements are not to be legally binding in the case of *Walford v. Miles* (1992).

TERMINATION OF OFFERS

The general rule is that an offer, once accepted, cannot be terminated. A valid offer can, however, be terminated in a number of ways, as follows:

a.   Revocation

Revocation is the withdrawal of an offer by the offeror. The general rule is that an offeror may withdraw an offer at any time before it has been accepted. There are a number of rules which must however be noted.

The revocation of the offer must be communicated to the offeree, that is, it must be brought to his actual notice. For revocation to be effective, it must be communicated to the offeree. The offeror cannot revoke his offer arbitrarily or simply by a personal unilateral decision that he no longer wishes to proceed. This is the legal position even if the postal system is used as the main channel of communication. The case of *Byrne v. Van Tienhoven* (1880) illustrates this point.

Byrne v. Van Tienhoven (1880)

Facts: In this case, the Defendants posted a letter in Cardiff to the Plaintiffs in New York on 1st October, offering to sell them 1,000 boxes of tin plates. On 8th October, the Defendants posted a letter revoking their offer. On 11th October, the Plaintiffs received the Defendants offer letter and telegraphed their acceptance. On 20th October the Defendants letter of revocation finally reached the Plaintiffs.

Held: that the revocation took effect only on 20th October, but since the Plaintiffs had already accepted the offer on 11th October, the revocation had not been communicated in time.

Secondly, a revocation of an offer can be communicated by the offeror or by a reliable third party. The case of *Dickinson v. Dodds* illustrates this point

Dickenson v. Dodds (1876)

Facts: In this case, the Defendant (Dodds) actually agreed to keep an offer open for two days. However, the Defendant sold the property to a third party. The

Plaintiff (offeree) was told of the sale by a third party, but he nonetheless attempted to accept the original offer.

Held: That at the time of his 'acceptance' he the Plaintiff was clearly aware that the offer had been validly revoked. The offer was therefore properly revoked and could not be accepted.

While at Common Law, whereas a bare promise to keep an offer open for acceptance is not binding on the promisor in the absence of consideration,[28] in Ghana on the other hand, such a promise may be binding because of Section 8 (1) of the **Contract Act,** 1960 (Act 25).

Section 8 (1) states as follows:

"A promise to keep an offer open for acceptance for a specified time is not invalid as a contract by reason only of the absence of a consideration for that promise."

This means that a promise to keep an offer open for acceptance for a specified period of time is binding on the promisor, whether or not the promisee gives or does not give any consideration to the promisor for the promisee.

b.   Lapse of Time
The general rule is that if an offer is stated to be open until a particular time, any purported acceptance after that time is invalid. The offer lapses and thus cannot be accepted.

If no time is stated, an offer would lapse after a reasonable time. What constitutes "reasonable time" would actually depend on the facts of each case. Thus in **Ramsgate Victoria Hotel Co v. Montefiore** (1866), an attempt to accept an offer to buy shares in the Plaintiff's company after five months failed since the offer had clearly lapsed.

c.   Death

Death of the Offeror
As a general rule an offeree who has not yet accepted an offer made by an offeror to him (offeree), during the lifetime of the offeror, cannot purport to accept the offer after notice of the offeror's death. However, if the offeree does not know

---

28   See the case of **Routledge v. Grant** (1828) 4 Bing. 653, where the defendant stated that his offer would be open for a period of 6 weeks, but before the expiration of the stipulated time revoked his offer. The Plaintiff sued, and the court held that the defendant was entitled to revoke his offer at any time before the offer was accepted, since no consideration had been given to him for the promise to keep the offer open.

of the offeror's death and there are no personal elements involved, then he may accept the offer. The case of **Bradbury v. Morgan** (1862) illustrates this point.

Bradbury v Morgan (1862)

Facts: One L, guaranteed his brother's account with the Plaintiffs. L died but the Plaintiffs were not aware and continued to supply goods. The Defendants (L's Executors) refused to pay for goods supplied after L's death.

Held: That L's offer continued until the Plaintiffs knew about his death and they were therefore entitled to be paid.

Death of the Offeree

Where the offeree dies, someone else cannot purport to accept the offer on the offeree's behalf.

d.   Rejection

Counter–Offer

Traditionally, an acceptance must be a mirror image of the offer. If any alteration is made, or anything added, then this will be a counter-offer and will terminate the offer. The case of **Hyde v. Wrench** (1840) illustrates this position.

Hyde v Wrench (1840)

Facts: In this case, the Defendant offered to sell a farm for £1,000. The Plaintiff said he would give £950 for it.

Held: That this was a counter-offer which terminated the original offer which was, therefore, no longer open for acceptance.

Conditional or Qualified Acceptance

A conditional acceptance may be a counter-offer capable of acceptance, e.g. 'I will pay £500 for your car if you paint it red', or it may be qualified acceptance as in the phrase, 'subject to contract'.

e.   After Offeree has stated to carry out the acceptance

Where the agreement is a unilateral contract, a problem may arise with revocation if the offeror attempts to revoke the offer after the offeree has commenced performance or acceptance. This position of the law is classically illustrated in the case of **Errington v. Errington** (1952).

Errington v Errington (1952)

Facts: In this case, a father purchased a house on mortgage for his son and daughter in law and promised them that if they paid off the mortgage, they could have ownership of the house. The couple commenced paying off the mortgage, but before they could finish, the father died, and the executor purported to claim the house.

Held: That the father's offer could not be revoked while the couple were paying the mortgage. That once the offeree had started to perform the contract, the offeror cannot withdraw the offer without giving them a reasonable chance to complete.

THE DEFINITION OF ACCEPTANCE

An acceptance is an unqualified or unconditional assent by the offeree to all the terms of an offer.

Acceptance is vital to the formation of a valid contract, in that, once an offeree had accepted the terms of an offer, all other contractual ingredients being present, a binding contract comes into existence. Both parties are in that case bound to perform their side of the contract. The offeror can no longer withdraw his offer and neither can the offeree withdraw his acceptance.

Just like an offer, acceptance may be express or implied. An express acceptance may be oral or in writing. An implied acceptance is usually, however, inferred from conduct. Thus in **Carlill v. Carbolic** it was held that, general offers were acceptable by conduct, and that such an acceptance was valid even without prior notice to the offeror about the acceptance.

THE ELEMENTS OF A VALID ACCEPTANCE

An acceptance is a final and unqualified assent to all the terms of the offer. The main elements of a valid acceptance are as follows:

- It must be made while the offer is still in force.
- It must be made by the offeree.
- It must exactly match the terms of the offer, that is, it must be a 'mirror image' of the offer.
- It may be written, oral, or implied from conduct – **Carlill v Carbolic Smoke Ball** (1893).

- The offeror can require the acceptance to be made in a certain way. If the requirement is mandatory, it must be followed. If the requirement is directory, then another equally effective method will suffice. Thus in **Manchester Diocesan Council for Education v. Commercial and General Investments Ltd** (1969), an invitation to tender stated that the person whose bid was accepted would be informed by a letter to the address given in the tender. The acceptance was eventually sent not to this address, but to the defendant's surveyor. It was held that the statement in the tender was not mandatory; the tender had therefore been validly accepted.

RULES ON ACCEPTANCE

Acceptance must be communicated — As a general rule acceptance is not effective until it is communicated to the offeror. **Entores v. Miles Far Eastern** (1955) illustrates this rule.

Entores v Miles Far Eastern (1955)

Facts: The Plaintiffs, who were based in London, made an offer by telex to the Defendants in Amsterdam. The Defendants accepted by telex. The issue of dispute was where the acceptance had taken place. That is in Amsterdam at the time the Defendants sent the telex or in London when it was received. It can be vital which country the contract was concluded in as different countries may have different legal rules.

Held: Acceptance is not effective until it was communicated. Therefore the contract was made in London.

Also in **Fofie v. Zanyo,** the Supreme Court of Ghana held, inter alia, that before it could be said that there had been an acceptance of an offer by an offeree, there had to be (a) positive evidence by words, in writing or by conduct from which the court might infer acceptance; and (b) the acceptance had to have been communicated to the offeror.

A cross offer is not an acceptance — A cross-offer refers to two identical offers made in ignorance of each other. In law, cross offers do not constitute an agreement. **Tinn v. Hoffman & Co** (1873) illustrates this principle.

Tinn v. Hoffman & Co (1873)

Facts: H wrote to T offering to sell him a quantity of iron on stated terms. On that same day, T wrote to H offering to buy on the same terms.

Held: It was held that instantaneous cross offers made in ignorance of each other, could not bind the parties.

A counter offer is not an acceptance — An offeree whose response deviates from the terms of an offer will usually be regarded as having made a counter-offer. A counter offer terminates the original offer, so that the offeree can no longer accept the original offer after it has been rejected. The case of ***Hyde v. Wrench*** illustrates this rule.

Hyde v. Wrench

Facts: In this case an offer was made to sell a house at 1,000 pounds. The offeree rather proposed to buy it at 950 pounds.

Held: It was held that the offeree's proposal amounted to a counter offer.

A conditional acceptance is not an acceptance —An acceptance which contemplates that further conditions have to be satisfied or that some further steps need to be taken, as a more formal contract generally renders the agreement incomplete and non-binding

Silence is not acceptance — The offeror can expressly or impliedly dispense with the need for communication of acceptance as in the case of ***Carlill v. Carbolic Smoke Ball Co.*** However, an offeror may not stipulate that the silence of the offeree will amount to an acceptance. The case of ***Felthouse v. Bindley*** (1862) is authority for this proposition.

Felthouse v Bindley (1862)

Facts: In this case, the plaintiff wrote to his nephew offering to buy a horse, and adding, *'If I hear no more … I will take it that the horse is mine'*. The nephew did not reply to this letter, but told the defendant, an auctioneer who was to sell his stock, that this horse was to be kept out of the sale.

Held: It was held there was no contract. Acceptance had not been communicated to offeror.

EXCEPTIONS TO THE RULE ON COMMUNICATION

* Where failure of communication is the fault of the offeror. This was suggested by Lord Denning in ***Entores Ltd v. Miles Far East Corporation (1955)*** where he stated, 'if the listener on the telephone does not catch the words of acceptance, but nevertheless does not ask for them to be repeated, or if

the acceptance is sent by telex during business hours but is simply not read by anyone in the offeror's office when it is there transcribed on his machine'.

- Where the post is deemed to be the proper method of communication. The case of *Adams v Lindsell* (1818), illustrates this position of the law.

Adams v Lindsell (1818)

Facts: The defendants wrote to the plaintiffs offering to sell them a quantity of wool and requiring acceptance by post. The letter arrived late, having been incorrectly addressed by the defendants. The plaintiffs immediately posted an acceptance on 5 December.

Held: It was held that the contract was completed on 5 December.

THE POSTAL RULE

The postal rule states that where an acceptance is communicated by post, the acceptance is complete, and takes effect, when the acceptance letter, properly addressed, is posted, not when it is received (*Adams v. Lindsell* (1818)). The postal ruleis thus an exception to the rule that acceptance must be communicated.

The postal rule applies only when the use of the postal service is reasonable in the circumstances – as it will be, for example, where an offer has been made by post and the offeror has indicated the use of the post for the purpose of making the acceptance. The reason underlying the postal rule is that the key risks associated with use of the postal system lies with the offeror who would, in most cases, have indicated the post as the medium for communication. If that is the case then it is apt that the offeror bear the risks involved in its use.

Then again, acceptance is deemed effective upon posting, even when the letter is lost in the post. Thus in *Household Fire Insurance Co Ltd v. Grant* (1879), where the defendant offered to buy shares in the plaintiff's company, a letter of allotment was posted to the defendant. However, it never reached him. It was held that the contract was completed when the letter was posted.

Limitations of the postal rule

Limitations of the postal rule are such that:

- It only applies to letters and telegrams.
- It does not apply to methods of instantaneous communication.
- It must be reasonable to use the post as the means of communication (e.g. an offer by telephone or by fax might indicate that the rapid method of response was required).

- Letters of acceptance must be properly addressed and stamped.
- The rule is easily displaced. E.g. it may be excluded by the offeror either expressly or impliedly. Thus in Holwell Securities Ltd v Hughes (1974), it was excluded by the offeror who insisted upon being given 'notice in writing'. It was also suggested by the court that the postal rule would not be used where it would lead to manifest inconvenience.

ACCEPTANCE BY ELECTRONIC MAIL (E-MAIL)

An acceptance of an offer by email is binding. Section 23 of the *Electronic Transaction Act,* (Act 772) provides that 'an agreement is valid even if it was concluded partly or wholly through an electronic medium'.

According to Section 18 of the Act,an offer, acceptance or payment of consideration which is expressed by email is generally deemed to have been sent at the time the record enters the information processing system (online -unless otherwise agreed between the originator and the addressee, the dispatch of an electronic record occurs when it enters an information processing system outside the control of the originator or agent of the originator.

OFFER AND ACCEPTANCE OF REWARDS

As a general rule, advertisements promising rewards for the recovery of lost property are generally construed as offers. The Australian case of *Williams v. Cawardine* is illustrative of this rule.

Williams v. Cawardine (1833)

Facts: Upon Walter Cawardine's murder, the Plaintiff, Mrs Williams, gave evidence against two suspects, but both suspects were acquitted. The victim's brother and defendant, Mr. Cawardine, published a handbill, stating there would be a reward for information leading to the discovery of Cawardine's murderer. Mrs Williams then gave more information leading to the conviction of two men (including John Williams, her own husband). She later claimed the reward but Mr. Cawardine refused to pay. At the trial it was found that although she knew about the reward, she had not revealed the information specifically to get the reward.

Held: The Court held that the Plaintiff was entitled to recover the reward – motive was irrelevant.

A person cannot, however, accept an offer that he has no knowledge of. Thus in *R v. Clarke* (1927), information was given in connection with a reward. The informer's motivation was to obtain a royal pardon. The High Court of Australia held that motive was irrelevant.

Chapter 4 - Quick Review

An offer is a statement of willingness by the offeror to enter into a contract on stated terms, provided those terms are accepted by the offeree. An acceptance, on the other hand, is an unqualified expression of assent to the terms proposed by the offeror. Acceptance must generally be communicated to the offeror. Ads are invitations to treat; they are not offers. Except for unilateral contracts, ads and display of goods are invitations to treat.

As a general rule, acceptance cannot be implied from the silence of an offeree. Under the postal rule, acceptance letters take effect when posted, provided the offeree's use of the post was reasonable. This rule applies even if the letter fails to reach the offeror.

Offers could be terminated by revocation, rejection by the offeree, lapse of time, the occurrence of a stipulated event and the death of one of the parties. In cases of revocation, the rule is that the revocation must actually be brought to the attention of the offeree.

5. Consideration

LEARNING OUTCOMES

As a general rule, when a contract is unsupported by consideration it may be incapable of enforcement in a court of law. And while a gratuitous promise or bare offer is generally unenforceable in Ghanaian courts, there are exceptions. Section 8 (1) of the **Contract Act,** 1960 (Act 25) for example makes it possible to have a valid and binding contract even if it is unsupported by any consideration.

You should thus be familiar with the meaning of consideration, the types of consideration, the common law rules on consideration, statutory changes to common law rules on consideration and promissory estoppel.

THE DEFINITION OF CONSIDERATION

The classic definition of consideration was set down in **Currie v. Misa** (1875) as "A valuable consideration in the eyes of the law may consist either in some right, interest, profit or benefit to one party, or some forbearance, detriment, loss or responsibility given, suffered or undertaken by the other". Also in **Dunlop Pneumatic Types Co v. Selfridge & Co Ltd** (1915) consideration was defined as "an act of forbearance (or the promise of it) on the part of one party as the price of the promise made to him by the other party to the contract".

The English jurist Sir Frederick Pollock defined consideration as 'the price for which the promise of the other is bought', a statement that was approved by the House of Lords in **Dunlop Pneumatic Tyre Co Ltd v. Selfridge** stated above. Treitel was, however, critical of this definition on grounds that it was vague.

Consideration is concerned with the exchange of promises or the doing of an act in a unilateral contract, in return for the promise. Subject to statutory changes effected by the **Contracts Act,** 1960, a promise that is unsupported by consideration from the promisee is said to be a gratuitous promise incapable of enforcement in court.[29]

---

29   The position of the common law is stated by the learned authors, Cheshire and Fifoot in their book The Law of Contract (6th ed.) at p. 57 as follows: "To sustain an action

TYPES OF CONSIDERATION

a. Executory consideration – Executory consideration is given where there is an exchange of promises to do something in the future. An executory act is an act which is yet to be done or performed. In this respect, an executory consideration is a promise to do something at a future date. Let's take a simple example for clarification. If in a sales transaction Nana, a buyer, makes a promise to Sandy that he would pay an amount of money (GH¢10,000) to her, a seller, and Sandy agrees to deliver the goods requested by Nana on credit, we could say that both Sandy and Nana have provided executory consideration to each other. This type of consideration is valid and binding even though neither Sandy nor Nana has actually done anything. Neither party can withdraw, although actual performance cannot be claimed until the future due date.

b. Executed consideration – An executed consideration, on the other hand, refers to consideration in the form of an act performed immediately a contract is entered into. Again let us take a very simple example to illustrate the point being made. If Nana offers a vehicle for sale to Sandy, and Sandy accepts and pays Nana the sum of GH¢ 35,000.00, Sandy's consideration is considered executed, and if Nana delivers the car to Sandy in consideration for the sum of GH¢ 35,000.00 received, his consideration is also executed. Hence, if a party makes a promise in exchange for an act performed by the other party, then the other party's performance is complete.

c. Past consideration – Past consideration is defined as an act done before a contract is made. It is consideration that is already given or some act that is already performed and therefore cannot be induced by the other party's act, or promise in exchange.

Thus if Nana gives Sandy a lift from Haatso to Ho, and after their mutual arrival, Sandy were to promise Nana GH¢ 700.00 towards the fuel, Nana cannot enforce Sandy's promise as his right for giving Sandy the lift (his consideration) as his consideration is past. In Eastwood v Kenyon, the guardian of a young lady raised a loan to educate the young lady and to

---

on a promise made by the defendant the plaintiff must show either that it is contained in a document under seal or that it is supported by the presence of consideration." The ramifications and intricacies of this doctrine are well indicated in any book on the law of contract. That doctrine is part of Ghanaian common law of, subject to changes made by the *Contracts Act,* 1960.

improve her marriage prospects. After her marriage, her husband promised to pay off the loan. It was held that the guardian could not enforce the promise as taking out the loan to raise and educate the young lady was past consideration, because it was completed before the husband promised to repay it.

Then again, where a contract exists between two parties and one party, subsequent to formation of the contract, promises to confer an additional benefit on the other party to the contract, that promise is not binding because the promisee's consideration, which is his entry into the original contract, had already been completed (or "used") at the time the next promise is made.

In *Roscorla v. Thomas,* Roscorla and Thomas contracted to buy a horse for £30. After the sale, Thomas promised Roscorla that the horse was sound; the horse turned out to be vicious. It was held that Roscorla could not enforce the promise, as the consideration given for entering into the contract to buy the horse had been completed by the time the promise was made; in a sense, the consideration was "used up" completed, unenforceable.

EXCEPTIONS TO THE PAST CONSIDERATION RULE

Under Ghanaian law, there are a number of exceptions with respect to past consideration. This means that in those cases it is possible for past consideration to be considered as good consideration. These include the following:

(a) Firstly, under the **Bill Of Exchange Act, 1961** (Act 55), consideration provided for a cheque or bill of exchange can be constituted by an "antecedent debt or liability" that is, by a past consideration. This implies that past consideration is sufficient to create liability on a bill of exchange.

(b) Secondly, under the **Limitation Act, 1972** (NRCD 55), the right to sue for debt recovery becomes statute-barred after six (6) years. If after the 6 year period, the debtor, however, makes a written claim of the creditor's claim, the debt will still be enforceable at law, notwithstanding that the debt is past consideration.

(c) Thirdly, where a service was rendered at the request of the promisor on the understanding that a payment would be made, a subsequent promise to pay a certain sum will be enforced on the basis that it merely identified the amount (see **Lampleigh v. Braithwaite** (1615)).

THE COMMON LAW RULES ON CONSIDERATION

a) Consideration must be sufficient, but need not be adequate – Under both common law and statutory law, the rule that consideration must be sufficient but need not be adequate applies. This rule implies that the court will only look to see whether the purported consideration has any economic value, but will not question its adequacy, even if one party is apparently making a good bargain while the other is not. The case of **Mountford v. Scott** (1975) illustrates this position of the law. In that case, £1 was paid for an option to purchase a house, and this was found to be good consideration. Also in **Chappell & Co v. Nestle** (1960), three wrappers from the defendant's chocolate bars were held to be part of the consideration.

b) Consideration must move from the promisee – The rule at common law is that consideration must move from the promisee to the promisor. This rule means that only a person to whom the promise is made can enforce such promise provided he, and not a third party, has provided consideration for that promise.

Under this common law rule, a party cannot sue if a third party provided the consideration. Thus if X Financial Ltd promises Y Ltd GHC100,000 that if Z Engineering Ltd would perform engineering works at X Financial, and Z Engineering did so, Y Ltd cannot enforce X Financial Ltd's promise, unless Y Ltd procured or had engaged Z to do the required works.

c) At common law a promise to waive payment of debt (section 8 (2) of Act 25) is unenforceable in the absence of fresh consideration – The general rule at common law is that a promise to waive or forgo a debt or part payment of debt is not binding on the promisor unless there is some fresh consideration coming from the promisee. Thus in **Foakes v. Beer,**[30] Mrs. Beer agreed with Dr Foakes to forgo the interest on a judgment debt owed Mrs. Beer if Dr. Foakes could pay the principal money promptly on agreed terms. Even though Dr. Foakes eventually paid the judgment debt, Mrs. Beer brought an action to recover the interest. The House of Lords held that Mrs. Beer's claim should be upheld because Foakes only did what he was contractually bound to do and that part payment cannot constitute a discharged of the whole debt. Furthermore the agreement was unenforceable because it lacked consideration.

---

30   (1884) 9 App. Cas. 605

d) At common law, consideration must not consist of a pre-existing legal obligation – The general rule at common law is that, a promise to perform a pre-existing legal obligation does not constitute sufficient consideration for another promise. The position of the common law is that since the promisor is already legally bound to perform the act, he suffers no detriment in performing it and the promisee obtains no benefits from the performance since the promisor is already bound to perform the obligation. Thus in **Collins v. Godefroy** (1831) the defendant promised to pay the plaintiff if the plaintiff would attend court and give evidence for the defendant. The plaintiff had, meanwhile, been served with a subpoena already. It was held that as the plaintiff was legally obliged to attend court, promise to do this was not valid consideration.

e) At common law a promise to keep an offer open for a specified period is not binding in the absence of consideration – at common law, a promise by the promisor to keep an offer open for acceptance for a specified period of time is not binding on the promisor unless it is supported by consideration by the promisee. **Routledge v. Grant** (1832)[31], illustrates this position. In Routledge, the defendant offered to take a lease of the plaintiff's premises and stated that his offer would be opened for acceptance for a period of six weeks. Before the expiration of the six weeks, the defendant revoked his offer and the plaintiff sued. The court held that the defendant was entitled to revoke his offer at any time before the offer was accepted since no consideration had been given for the promise to keep the offer open.

STATUTORY CHANGES DONE TO THE COMMON LAW RULES ON CONSIDERATION BY THE CONTRACT ACT, 1960 (ACT 25)

The **Contract Act,** 1960 (Act 25) has amended significantly the common law rules on consideration, and provides a contrary position. The changes made by Act 25 can be found under Sections 8(1), 8(2), 9 and 10 of the Act.

SECTION 8 (1)

a) Section 8 (1) of the Contracts Act abolishes the common law rule on a promise to keep an offer open for acceptance for a specified period. In Ghana, Section 8 (1) of Act 25 has modified and abolished the common law rule in **Routledge v. Grant**. Section 8 (1) does not make consideration

---

31   (1928) 4 Bing 653

a prerequisite for the enforceability of a promise to keep an offer open for acceptance for a specified period of time. Section 8(1) of Act 25 provides that "a promise to keep an offer for acceptance for specified time shall not be invalid as a contract by reason only of the absence of any consideration thereof".

SECTION 8 (2)

b)   Section 8 (2) of the Contracts Act also abolishes the common law rule on promise to waive the part payment of a debt. Generally at common law, a promise to give up or waive a part payment of a debt is not binding on a promisor if the promisee having accepted this promise, failed to give consideration for it. This is known as a gratuitous promise to waive a debt and is thus unenforceable against the promisor. The classic case which illustrates this rule is the case of *D & C Builders Ltd v. Rees.* In that case, the defendant owed the plaintiff company 482 pounds but refused to pay. The plaintiffs eventually agreed to waive the remaining debt if the defendant would pay 300 pounds. However, the plaintiffs later sued for the 182 pounds outstanding. It was held that since the promise to waive the 182 pounds was unsupported by consideration from Rees, the plaintiffs were not bound by their promise and thus be precluded from suing Rees for the money.

The general rule at common law is that part payment of a debt is not good consideration for a creditor's promise to forgo the unpaid outstanding balance. In paying part of the debt, the promisee is doing no more than performing an existing contractual duty owed to the promisor.

This rule, that payment of a lesser sum on the day cannot be satisfaction for the whole, is known as the rule in Pinnel's case, which principle was finally established in *Foakes v. Beer.*

Section 8 (2) of the **Contracts Act,** 1960 (Act 25) has, however, abolished the common law rules on part payment of debts by providing that "A promise to waive the payment of a debt or part of a debt or the performance of some other contract and legal obligation shall not be invalid as a contract by reason only of the absence of any consideration thereof". This implies that under Ghanaian law, a promise to waive a debt or part of it is binding on the promisor even in the absence of any fresh consideration.

SECTION 9

c) **Section 9 of the Contracts Act, 1960, amends the common law rules on consideration given for pre-existing legal duties.**

Section 9 of the **Contracts Act,** 1960, has amended the common law rules on pre-existing legal obligation, by providing that "the performance of an act or the promise to perform an act may be sufficient consideration for another promise notwithstanding that the performance of that act may already be enjoined by some legal duty whether enforceable by the other party or not". This implies that, if Fred already has a legal duty to perform a given task, but has not yet performed it before Dickson promised giving a reward to Fred to perform that pre-existing duty, then after performing the said duty, Fred will be entitled to Dickson for the reward in issue. **Kessie v. Charmant** (1973)[32] illustrates this position of the law. In that case, the plaintiff, an ambassador, was promised a position and a stake in the defendant's company if he could use his office to help win the defendant a contract. The defendant later refused to comply, saying he was acting on his official duties. However, the court held that under Act 25, section 9, there was a binding contract but could not be enforced because it would encourage corrupt practices in future. Section 9, thus, abolish the common law rules on consideration illustrated in **Stilk v. Myrickand** and **Collins v. Godefroy.**

SECTION 10

d) **Section 10 of the Contracts Act, 1960 (Act 25) also abolishes the common law position that consideration must move from the promisee to the promisor.**

Section 10 provides that 'no promise shall be invalid as a contract by reason only that the consideration therefore is supplied by someone other than the promisee'.

The statutory position of the Ghanaian Law of contract, unlike English law, is that consideration need not move from the promisee himself to the promisor. Section 10 therefore departs from the English common law position illustrated by **Tweedle v. Atkinson** and **Dunlop Pneumatic Tyre Company Ltd v. Selfridge** (1915) which maintains that only a party who

---

32   2 GLR 194

has provided consideration for a promise can enforce that promise.[33] Section 10 must be read in tandem with section 5 of Act 25, which provides that a third party can enforce a contract if it purports to confer a benefit on that third party.

Therefore, where there is sufficient consideration to support a promise, then an authorized third party may acquire legal capacity to sue to enforce the contract. The case of *Ejura Farms v. Harley.*

PROMISSORY ESTOPPEL

In the law of contract, the doctrine of promissory estoppel provides that if a party changes his or her position substantially either by acting or forbearing to act in reliance upon a gratuitous promise, then that party can enforce the promise although the essential elements of a contract are not present.

There are, however, certain key elements that must be established to enable one invoke promissory estoppel. First, there must be a Promisor – that is, a party who has made a promise to another – in this case a gratitutious promise that he should reasonably have expected would induce an action or forbearance of a definite and substantial character on the part of the promisee, the person to whom a promise is made. The promisee must have justifiably relied on the promise, and suffered substantial detriment – that is severe economic loss should have ensued to the promisee from the action or forbearance such that injustice can only be avoided by enforcing the promise. A leading case which established this doctrine is *Central London Property Trust Ltd v. High Trees House Ltd* (1947).

Facts: In *Central London Property Trust Ltd v. High Trees House Ltd* (1947), the Plaintiffs let a block of flats to the defendants. In January 1940, they agreed to accept half-rent since many of the flats were un-let. In 1945 the flats were all let and the plaintiffs claimed full rent again.

Held: Lord Denning held that the arrangement was only intended to last during the war and gave judgment for the plaintiffs. He also stated that if the plaintiffs had sought to recover past rents, they would have failed. They would, he said, be

---

33   See the case of *Dunlop Pneumatic Tyre Company Ltd v. Selfridge* (1915). In this case, Dunlop sold tyres to Day who resold them to Selfridge. Day, on the request of Dunlop, inserted a term prohibiting Selfridge from re-selling the tyres below list price. Selfridge broke the term. Dunlop sued for breach of contract. It was held that even if Day had acted as agents for Dunlop, Dunlop could not enforce the contract as they had not provided any consideration for the promise by Selfridge.

estopped by their promise from asserting their legal right to demand payment. He based his judgment on **Hughes v. Metropolitan Rly Co** (1877) where Lord Cairns stated:

> Where one party leads the other to suppose that the strict rights arising under the contract will not be enforced … the person who otherwise might have enforced those rights will not be allowed to enforce them where it would be inequitable.

LIMITATIONS OF PROMISSORY ESTOPPEL

There are however numerous limitations to the doctrine of promissory estoppel. Some of the main limitations are as follows:

a) There must have been a promise that is clear, unequivocal, precise and unambiguous. This was illustrated by the case of **Woodhouse A.C Israel Cocoa Ltd SA v. Nigerian Produce Marketing Co. Ltd** [1972] AC 741 (HL).

b) The promise must have been given voluntarily.

c) The promise must have been made with the knowledge and intention that it would be acted upon by the promisee, who will thus be altering his or her position in reliance upon it.

d) **The promisee must have actually acted in reliance upon the promise.**

    That is, the promisee must have had no other reason for completing the alleged act of reliance. The case of **E.A. Ajayi v. R.T. Briscoe** (Nigeria) Ltd [1964] 3 All ER 556 (PC) provides a good example of a case where there had not been sufficient reliance. This reliance need not be detrimental to the promisee. This was established by Lord Denning in **W. J. Alan & Co. Ltd v. El Nasr Export and Import Co.** [1972] 2 QB 189 (CA)

e) **It must be inequitable for the promisor to go back on the promise.**

    This point was stressed by Lord Denning in **D & C Builders Ltd v. Rees** [1966] 2 QB 617 (CA).

f) **There must have been a prior existing legal relationship between the parties.**

    That is, promissory estoppel cannot occur in a vacuum. It can only arise when there is an existing relationship between the parties. Normally, this will be a contract.

g) **The doctrine cannot be used as a "sword"**

The doctrine cannot be used to found a cause of action. Instead, it can only be used as a defense. This is explained well in the case of **Combe v. Combe** [1951] 2 KB 215 (CA).

Chapter 5 – Quick Review

A contract is valid only if it is for mutual consideration. This means the contract must involve an exchange of things of value. Gratuitous promises or bare offers are rarely enforceable in Ghanaian courts, except that consideration need only be sufficient, but not adequate.

Several changes have been made by the **Contract Act,** 1960 (Act 25) to the common law rules on consideration. For example, (a) by virtue of Sections 5 (1) and 10, a promise can be enforced by third parties (e.g. creditor beneficiary, donee beneficiary or incidental beneficiary) who are not privy to the contract if the contract purports to confer a benefit on them (b) consideration need not move to the promisor. It is all right if the promisee suffers a detriment at the promisor's request but confers no corresponding benefit (c) also by virtue of Section 9, where a person is under a public duty or is legally bound to do an existing task, agreeing to perform that task may still be sufficient consideration **(Kessie v. Charmant)**. (d) Section 8(2) also abolished the principle in **Foakes v. Beers** on part-payment of a debt. Section 8(1) also abolished the principle in **Routlegde v. Grant,** by providing that a promise to keep an offer open for a specified time could be valid during that period, even if the promisee had not given the promisor any consideration.

6 Intention to create legal relations

LEARNING OUTCOMES

For a party to a contract to be capable of enforcing the promise of another, the promise must have been intended to be a contractual one. Absent such an intention and there is no contract. At the end of this chapter, you should be familiar not only with the presumption in favor of an intention to be bound in commercial agreements, but also with cases where no such presumption exists, as in domestic or general social agreements.

INTENTION TO CREATE LEGAL RELATIONS

In order to create a contract, both parties must clearly intend to enter into a legally binding relationship. Traditionally, contract law has required the parties to a contract to have the objective or intention of creating legal relations. If it is not clear or apparent from the contract that the parties intended legal consequences, then the law presumes the intention of the parties based on the type of agreement.

PRESUMPTION TO BE BOUND IN COMMERCIAL AGREEMENTS

In commercial or business agreements the law presumes that the parties intend to create legal relations, unless it can be proven otherwise. This means the presumption may be rebutted, but the onus of rebuttal with evidence is on the party seeking to exclude legal relations. Thus in *Esso Petroleum Ltd v. Commissioners of Custom and Excise* (1976), Esso promised to give one world cup coin with every four gallons of petrol sold. A majority in the House of Lords believed that the presumption in favor of legal relations had not been rebutted.

CASES IN WHICH THE EXISTENCE OF AN INTENTION TO BE LEGALLY BOUND IS DENIED BY COURT OR STATUTE

- 'Agreement may not be subject to the jurisdiction of any court' (**Rose & Frank v. Crompton Bros** (1925)).
- Agreements to be binding 'in honor only' (**Jones v. Vernon Pools** (1938)).
- Letters of comfort - that is statements to encourage lending to an associated company.

It was held in **Kleinwort Benson Ltd v. Malaysia Mining Corp** (1989) that a defendant's statement that 'it is our policy to ensure that the business is at all times in a position to meet its liabilities to you', was a statement of present fact and not a promise for the future. It was not intended to create legal relations.

PRESUMPTION AGAINST AN INTENTION TO BE BOUND IN SOCIAL OR DOMESTIC AGREEMENTS

Social agreements cover agreements between family members, friends and colleagues. In social and domestic agreements there is a presumption against legal relations. This can be rebutted by evidence to the contrary. As a rule, the law of contract does not want to become involved or implicated in social agreements for public policy reasons, since if all such agreements were to be deemed binding, the courts would be inundated with cases of families suing each other:

- **Agreements between husband and wife**

In **Balfour v. Balfour** (1919), the court refused to enforce a promise by the husband to give his wife £50 per month whilst he was working abroad. In that case it was held that there was no legally binding contract between the parties. The reasoning was that, as it was a domestic agreement, it was presumed that the parties did not intend to be legally bound.

The usual presumption that agreements between spouses who are living happily together are unenforceable does not apply if the couple are about to separate or are separated. In such circumstances, the situation on the ground can be used to show or be shown to rebut the presumption. In that case, a court will enforce a clear agreement between the separating or separated parties as was held in **Merritt v. Merritt** (1970).

Merritt v. Merritt (1970)

Facts: A husband separated from his wife, wrote and signed a document stating that in consideration of his wife paying off the outstanding mortgage debt of

£180 on their matrimonial home, he would transfer the house standing in their joint names to her sole ownership. The wife paid off the outstanding mortgage, but the husband refused to transfer the title in the house to her, claiming that his promise was just a domestic arrangement and did not give rise to a legally-binding obligation.

Held: The Husband's promise was legally enforceable, the agreement having been made when the couple were not living together amicably or peacefully. A legal relations is contemplated where a husband deserts his wife and an agreement is concluded on the ownership of the matrimonial home occupied by the wife and children. Thus, the circumstance of their separation was enough to rebut the presumption.

- **Agreements between members of a family**

In ***Jones v. Padavatton***(1969), Mrs Jones offered a monthly allowance to her daughter if she would come to England to read for the Bar. Her daughter agreed but was not very successful. Mrs Jones stopped paying the monthly allowance but allowed her daughter to live in her house and receive the rents from other tenants. Mrs Jones later sued for possession. The daughter counter-claimed for breach of the agreement to pay the monthly allowance and/or for accommodation. It was held that (a) the first agreement may have been made with the intention of creating legal relations, but was for a reasonable time and would, in any case, have lapsed; and (b) the second agreement was a family arrangement without an intention to create legal relations. It was very vague and uncertain.

Intention may, however, be inferred where one party has acted to his detriment on the agreement (***Parker v. Clarke*** (1960)) or where a business arrangement is involved (***Snelling v. Snelling*** (1973)) or where there is mutuality (***Simpkins v. Pays*** (1955)).

Simpkins v. Pays [1955]

Facts: A grandmother, granddaughter and a lodger entered into a weekly competition run by the Sunday Empire News. The coupon was sent in the grandmother's name each week and all three made forecasts and they took it in turns to pay. They had agreed that if any of them won they would share the winnings between them. The grandmother received £250 in prize money and refused to share it with the other two. The lodger brought the action to claim one third of the prize money.

Held: There was a binding contract despite the family connection as the lodger was also party to the contract. This rebutted the presumption of no intention to create legal relations.

CHAPTER 6 – A QUICK REVIEW

In domestic and social agreements, it is presumed that the parties do not intend to create enforceable legal obligations. This may, however, be rebutted by 'clear' evidence to the contrary, including the context within which the agreement was made and the reliance that was placed on it.

In commercial agreements, the presumption is that the parties do intend to create legal relations. This presumption is a 'heavy' one, and clear evidence is needed to rebut the presumption, which could be rebutted in cases of agreements to sell land 'subject to contract', collective agreement and 'honor clauses'.

7. Privity of contract

LEARNING OUTCOMES

Normally a person who is not a party to a contract cannot claim the benefits of the contract. At the end of this chapter you should be familiar with these areas: the meaning of the doctrine of privity, exceptions to the rule on privity and the statutory modifications to the law on privity in Ghana.

THE DOCTRINE OF PRIVITY

The doctrine of privity of contract consists of two distinct rules. Firstly, a contract cannot confer rights on a person who is not a party to a contract, and, secondly, a contract cannot impose obligations on a third party.

What this means is that, a person who is not a party to a contract cannot claim the benefits of that contract even if the contract was entered into with the object of benefitting that third party. Then also a third party cannot be subjected to a burden by a contract to which he is not a party. That is, he cannot sue or be sued on that contract. The case of *Tweddle v Atkinson* offers a classic example. In that case, the plaintiff married Mr Guy's daughter. The plaintiff's father and Mr Guy had agreed together that that they would each pay a sum of money to the plaintiff. Mr Guy died before the money was paid and the plaintiff sued his executors. The action was dismissed since the plaintiff was not a party to the contract which was made between the two fathers.

Also in *Dunlop Pneumatic Tyre Co Ltd v. Selfridge* (1915), Dunlop sold tyres to Dew & Co, a wholesaler, and included a term in the contract that Dew would obtain from any third party to whom they resold the tyres an undertaking that they would not retail the tyres under the list price. Selfridge gave Dew such an undertaking, but actually resold the tyres under the list price. Dunlop sued Selfridge for damages, but the suit failed on the grounds that Dunlop was not a party to the contract between Selfridge and Dew and only a party to the contract could enforce the contract. This case illustrates the second leg of the rule that, a third party or stranger who has not supplied consideration cannot be sued on the contract.

EXCEPTIONS TO THE RULE

a.   Assignment

An assignment is the transfer of the benefit of a contract by a contracting party to a third party. An assignment must be in writing. The effect of an assignment is that the third party becomes entitled to sue. Thus If Kofi enters into a contract with Ama's house Papa Kofi assigns his right to receive payment to Kweku, Kweku (the assignee) can sue Ama directly.

b.   Trust

The rules of equity developed the concept of a trust as an exception to the rule of privity. A trust is the right of property held by one party for the benefit of another, whereby the original owner of the property, called the settler, places the property in confidence or trust into the hands of a person, called the trustee, to hold the property for the benefit of another, called the beneficiary. The beneficiary under a trust needs not wait for a trustee to act where the trust is in danger, the beneficiary can sue directly.

b.   Agency

If an agent enters into an authorized contract with a third party on behalf of his principal, there is a contract between the principal and the third party. The third party for example can sue the principal.

c.   Leases[34]

The benefits and burdens of covenants in leases may be transferred to successors in title of the landlord and tenant if the covenants affect the land. Covenants inserted into a contract of sale of land may bind subsequent purchasers, and may thus enable landlords to sue successors in title although no direct contractual relations previously existed between them.

THE RELATIONSHIP BETWEEN PRIVITY AND CONSIDERATION

A person can be a party to the agreement, even though he or she has not provided any consideration. Thus if, at the request of A, B promises C that he (A) will pay C GH¢ 50.00 if C will dig his B's garden, A can be said to be party to the agreement, although A has not provide any consideration. See the case of ***Beswick v. Beswick*** (1968).

---

34   A lease is an interest in land that has a specified start and end date, subject to payment of annual ground rents and covenants.

THE GHANAIAN DOCTRINE OF PRIVITY - STATUTORY MODIFICATIONS MADE BY ACT 25

In 1960, the **Contracts Act,** (Act 25) amended the common law rules on third party contractual rights. According to Prof. Date-Baah third party rights consist of donee, creditor and incidental beneficiaries.

d.   DONEE BENEFICIARY

A donee beneficiary situation arises where, in a contract between two parties, Ms. Osei and Mr. Bonsu, Ms. Osei exacts a promise from Mr. Bonsu to confer a benefit on Mr. Dickson and Osei's intention in exacting the promise is to confer a gift on Mr. Dickson. In that case, Mr. Dickson becomes a donee beneficiary. Mr. Dickson is a donee in relation to Ms. Osei, not Mr. Bonsu, since Mr. Bonsu's performance is supported by consideration from Ms. Osei.

Failure to allow Mr. Dickson, the donee beneficiary, to sue means that Mr. Dickson is without a remedy, because he cannot sue Ms. Osei, since there is no pre-existing obligation between Ms. Osei and Mr. Dickson, the beneficiary. It is also impossible for Ms. Osei to sue Mr. Bonsu for failing to perform his promise, since Ms. Osei has not been injured by Mr. Bonsu's non-performance.

e.   CREDITOR BENEFICIARY

A creditor beneficiary situation arises where, in a contract between Ms. Osei and Mr. Bonsu for example, Ms. Osei owes Mr. Bonsu and agrees with Mr. Dickson that monies payable to him by Mr. Dickson should be paid to Mr. Bonsu. In that case, Mr. Bonsu becomes a donee beneficiary, but under Ghanaian law, Mr. Bonsu could sue. This is because Section 5(1) of the **Contracts Act, 1960** states that:

> "Any provision in a contract made after the commencement of this Act which purports to confer a benefit on a person who is not a party to the contract, whether as a designated person or as a member of a class of persons, may, subject to the provisions of this Part, be enforced or relied upon by that person as though he were a party to the contract."

Thus under Section 5(1) third parties can enforce the provisions of a contract where the parties to the contract contemplated conferring a benefit on that third party.

f.   INCIDENTAL BENEFICIARY

Incidental beneficiaries are generally unforeseen plaintiffs who come forward to sue from the wide category of people who would benefit in one way or another from the promisor's performance of his or her promise.

For instance, persons who have purchased tickets for a play might claim to have a right of action against an actress in the play for a breach of her contract of service with the theater company. Since her promised performance under such a contract would confer the benefit of entertainment on the ticket-holders, the latter would be beneficiaries of her contract of service. But such beneficiaries should obviously not be able to recover against the actress, since that would be imposing an onerous liability on her. The social policy interest in encouraging private economic enterprise requires that an overly burdensome and indefinite risk of liability is not imposed on promisors (Date-Baah: 1971).[35]

An incidental beneficiary is a third party on whom a contract neither confers a gift as beneficiary nor intends to discharge a legal duty owed to him. In *Yeboah & Sons v. Krah* (1969), it was held that the victim of a road accident is merely an incidental beneficiary of a contract of insurance between a motorist and his insurers. Thus, victims cannot sue on the contract. The parties must, however, contemplate or intend benefiting the third party and that intention must be shown in the contract either expressly or impliedly.

NAMED DRIVER POLICY OF INSURANCE

Third party motor insurance policies are also affected by Section 5(1). Third party policies provide insurance cover for the driver named in the policy. Koah v. Royal Exchange Assurance thus held that a driver, other than the named insured driver of the vehicle, at the time of the accident could not take advantage of the provisions of Section 5 of the *Contracts Act, 1960* because he was not a party to the policy and the terms did not confer a benefit upon him.

Under Section 6(1)(b), the policy must be such as would cover any liability which might be incurred by the person or classes of persons specified in the policy in respect of the death or bodily injury to third parties from the user of the vehicle agreed upon. The importance of section 6 lay in the guidance it gave to the person who proposed to take out a policy cover as to the extent of the cover

---

35   Enforcement Of Third Party Contractual Rights In Ghana [1971] Vol. Viii No. 2 UGLJ 76—97 Date-Baah S. K.*

he should take. Thus, even though the section did not prohibit the restriction of the user, liability arising from the user accepted by the insurer was limited to that "incurred by such persons or classes of persons as [might] be specified in the policy."

PREJUDICAL RELIANCE

Section 6 emphasizes the notion of prejudicial reliance by third parties. Prof. Date-Baah, in particular, contends that prejudicial reliance is any act promised or forbearance done in reliance on a purported contract which is not already due to the beneficiary. Section 6 (b) of the Contracts Act provides that a promisor and promisee can amend or rescind a contract to compromise a third party's right to enforce or rely on the contract, but only if the third party has not acted to his detriment, due to the rights conferred on him.

For example, if the third party is a donee creditor of GHS 600.00 from the promisee through a promise from the promisor, neither the promisee nor promisor can rescind or amend the amount to say GHS 200.00 if the third party can show that it will be to his detriment.

CHAPTER 7 – QUICK REVIEW!

Privity consists of two distinct rules. First, that a third party cannot be subjected to a burden by a contract to which he is not a party, and, second, that a third party cannot claim a benefit, even though the contract was entered into with the object of benefiting that third party (***Dunlop v. Selfridge***).

There are several exceptions to the doctrine of Privity, for example, assignment – the transfer of the benefit of a contract to a third party. An assignment must be in writing. Having received an assignment, an assignee has the right to sue. Then again, trusts - a right over property where the property owner (settler) places his property in confidence (trust) in the hands of another (trustee) for the benefit of some named person (beneficiary). The beneficiary gains proprietary rights in the trust property and can sue to directly enforce his rights. Other exceptions arise with agency and collateral contracts.

The rules on privity have, however, been substantially modified by the ***Contracts Act, 1960*** (Act 25). For instance, Section 5 (1) and 6 (a) allows third parties (like a donee beneficiary and creditor beneficiary) to benefit where the contract confers a benefit on them.

8. Capacity and Legality

LEARNING OUTCOMES

This focus is the legal rules on the capacity of a person to enter into valid and enforceable contracts. You will learn that some people do not have full capacity to enter into contractual relations. For public policy reasons such people are deemed to require legal protection when it comes to contracting. The main classes of people who lack full capacity include minors, mentally incompetent persons, and drunken or intoxicated persons.

CONTRACTUAL CAPACITY

Contractual capacity is the ability of a person to enter into a contract. Not all persons can contract. This is because certain categories of persons in the eyes of the law lack full capacity to enter into contractual relations. For public policy reasons these persons are deemed to require protection when it comes to both their creation of contractual relations and assumption of contractual liability.[36] These persons with limited contractual capacity include infants or minors, persons of unsound mind and drunken or intoxicated persons.

THE CONTRACTUAL CAPACITY OF MINORS

In Ghana, a minor or infant is a person below the age of 18 years. Article 28 of the 1992 Constitution states that "for the purpose of this article, 'child' means a person below the age of 18." Also, the *Children's Act,* 1998 (Act 560) defines a minor as a person below the age of 18 years.[37] Contracts with minors may be divided into three categories.

Valid contracts – which can be enforced against a minor.

---

36   Christine Dowuna-Hammond, p68
37   Section 1 of Act 560

Contracts for Necessaries

Necessary goods are defined in the *Sale of Goods Act,* 1979 as 'goods suitable to his condition in life, and to his actual requirements at the time of sale and delivery'.

In *Nash v. Inman* (1908), a student purchased 11 silk waistcoats while still a minor. The court held that silk waistcoats were suitable to the conditions of life of a Cambridge undergraduate at that time, but they were not suitable to his actual needs since he already had a sufficient supply of waistcoats.

It is important to distinguish between luxurious goods of utility and goods of pure luxury. The status of the minor can make the former into necessaries, but the latter can never be classified as necessaries. The burden of proving that the goods are necessaries is on the seller. Necessary services include education, medical and legal services and they must satisfy the same tests as necessary goods.

Nature of a minor's obligation under a contract for necessaries

The rule is that even though contracts for necessaries bind minors, a minor's obligation even under a contract for necessaries is statutorily limited.[38] The minor is required only to pay a reasonable price, not the actual contractual price.[39] It should be remembered that minors have a limited capacity to contract.

Beneficial contracts of service

A beneficial contract of service must be for the benefit of the minor. In *De Fransesco v. Barnum* (1890) the terms of the contract were burdensome and harsh on the minor. In that case, the court held that the contract was therefore void.

However, in *Doyle v White City Stadium* (1935), a minor had forfeited his payment for a fight because the contract provided that this should happen if a boxer was disqualified for fouling. It was held that the contract, which was provided by the Boxing Board of Control, was enforceable against the minor. Where a contract is, on the whole, for the benefit of a minor, it will not be invalidated because one term has operated in a way which is not to his advantage.

---

38   Section 2(2) of the *Sale of Goods Act* (Act 137)

39   Buckle L.J. stated the rule in *Nash v. Inman* that, an infant may contract, at a reasonable price for the supply of goods reasonably necessary to support his station in life, if he already has a sufficient supply.

Beneficial contracts must be contracts of service or similar to a contract of service. In *Chaplin v. Leslie Frewin (Publishers) Ltd* (1966), the court enforced a contract by a minor to publish his memoirs since this would train him in becoming an author, and enable him to earn a living. But trading contracts (involving the minor's capital) will not be enforced even if it helps the minor earn a living. Thus in *Mercantile Union Guarantee Co Ltd v. Ball* (1937), the court refused to enforce a hire purchase contract for a lorry which would enable a minor to trade as a haulage contractor.

Voidable contracts and minors' repudiation rights

Voidable contracts are agreements that are binding on all the parties to a contract, except that one of the parties will be entitled to rescind the contract.

A voidable contract binds a minor, except that the minor is entitled to repudiate (that is, to refuse to accept) the contract before he attains the age of 18 years or within a short time after attaining the age of 18 years. This is also called disaffirmation. To disaffirm, a minor must express his or her intent, through words or conduct, not to be bound by the contract. He or she must disaffirm the entire contract, not merely part or portions of it. For instance, the minor cannot decide to keep part of the goods purchased and return part. If the minor fails to disaffirm within a reasonable time after turning 18 years, a court will likely hold that the contract has been ratified. Examples of voidable contracts involving minors are contracts involving the lease of land, or purchase of land and subscription to shares in companies.

A minor can free himself from obligations under these contracts for the future, such as an obligation to pay rent under a lease, but will have to pay for benefits already received. He cannot recover money already paid under the contract unless there has been a total failure of consideration as held in the case of *Steinberg v. Scala (Leeds) Ltd* (1923).

An adult who enters into a contract with a minor cannot avoid his or her contractual obligations on the grounds that the minor can do so. Unless the minor actually exercises the option to disaffirm the contract, the adult party is normally legally bound by it.

RESTITUTION

The law is that where a contract is unenforceable against a minor or where he repudiates it, the courts have power to order the minor to turn over or give back any property he or she acquired under the contract, if it is just and equitable to do so. This power is actually expressly provided for under Section 3(1) of the *Contract Act, 1960.*

Section 2 also makes a guarantee of a minor's contractual obligations enforceable against a guarantor irrespective of the fact that the main contractual obligation itself is not unenforceable against the minor. This implies that the guarantee of an enforceable minor's contract is as effective as if the minor had been an adult. It is significant to note that this does not, however, affect contracts for necessaries, since the minor is contractually obliged to pay a reasonable price for them. Two other points are worth stating:

*   Equity will order restitution of property acquired by fraud, but there can be no restitution if the minor has resold the property (see *Leslie v. Sheill* (1914)).
*   An action may be brought in tort if it does not in any way rely on the contract. But although a minor is fully liable for all his torts, he may not be sued in tort if this is just an indirect way of enforcing a contract. Thus in *Leslie v. Sheill* (1914) a minor obtained a loan by fraudulently misrepresenting his age. It was held that he could not be sued in the tort of deceit since this would be an indirect way of enforcing a contract which was void.

PARENT'S LIABILITY

As a general rule, parents are not liable on contract made by their children. This is the reason why most businesses prudently require parents to co-sign any contract made with the minor. Where a parent co-signs with the minor, that parent becomes personally obligated under the contract, even if their child avoids future liability.[40]

THE CONTRACTUAL CAPACITY OF INSANE PERSONS

Mental health and legal competence

Mental health plays a significant role in contract formation. In order for a contract to be formed freely and voluntarily, both the offeror and offeree must be able to understand the nature and consequence of their agreement. If one party is mentally impaired through illness or intoxication by drugs or alcohol, the contract may be void, voidable or valid. The rule is that a person suffering from mental disorder or incapacity should not be liable on his contract if he is incapa-

---

40   Business Law, Clarkson, Miller, Jentz and Cross p. 269

ble of intelligent consent. Contracting with any person with a mental disability can, therefore, be highly risky.

When will the contract be void?

If a court has ruled that a person is mentally incompetent and has appointed a guardian to represent the patient, contracts made by the patient is void. This means no contract exist, as only the guardian can competently enter into binding legal obligations on behalf of the patient.

When will the contract be voidable?

Where the other contracting party is fully aware of the patient's disability, the resulting contract is voidable at the option of the patient. In that case, the patient just has the burden of proving or showing that his disability actually prevented him from understanding the transaction, and that the other party knew about this. The patient, however, becomes bound if he ratifies the contract after he is cured.

Generally, only mentally competent persons can contract. Mentally incompetent persons like minors must return any consideration and pay a reasonable price for any necessaries they received.

When the contract will be valid

Any contract made by a mentally incompetent person may be valid if the person had capacity at the time the contract was formed. A contract will be valid if the person does not lack contractual capacity. For example, an otherwise insane person or mental health patient may medically have a lucid-interval – this is a temporary restoration of sufficient intelligence, judgment and will, capable of enabling that individual to know and understand the nature and effect of the contract he or she is making.

CONTRACTUAL CAPACITY OF COMPANIES

In Ghana, all companies are formed by registration under the *Companies Act, 1963 (Act 179)*. By virtue of Section 24 of the Companies Act, every company has all the powers of a natural person of full capacity. What this means is that, companies registered in Ghana have contractual capacity to enter into legally binding agreements with third parties, they can sue and be sued in their own name, and they can also acquire, own or dispose of property.

Limitations on Corporate Contractual Capacity

By virtue of Section 125, however, a company does not have contractual capacity to enter into contracts that do not relate to its registered and authorized business. Where a company, however, enters into such a contract, the courts will recognize and enforce the agreement to protect those who enter into contracts with companies in respect of transactions that do not relate to the company's authorized business, and who do not know that the company lacks capacity to enter into the contract in issue.

Where the company is about to rather enter into such a contract, a member or a creditor of the company (whose credit is secured by a floating charge) is entitled to apply to the High Court for an injunction to restrain the company from entering into the contract.

Where the company suffers any losses after entering into the contract, the officers, normally the directors, will be held personally liable to compensate the company for any losses suffered.

LEGALITY

For a contract to be valid, legally binding and enforceable, its object and purposes must be lawful. This means the aim, subject matter and performance of that contract must be legal. A contract to do a prohibited act, such as operate a pornographic site, commit crime or a tort is illegal, and therefore void right from the outset *(ab initio)*.

Under legality we shall concern ourselves with three broad categories of illegal contracts. Firstly, contracts contrary to a statute. Secondly, contracts contrary to public policy and, lastly, unconscionable contracts or clauses.

Contracts Contrary to Statute (Statutory illegality)

Any contract in violation of a statute amounts to commission of a crime. The purported contract is unenforceable. Thus a contract to supply marijuana that has been paid for is unenforceable.

Contracts Contrary to Public Policy

Some contracts are unenforceable because of the negative effects they could have on social mores or the economy. The case of ***Kessie v. Charmant*** (1973) provides an illustrative authority.

Kessie v. Charmant (1973)

Facts: The Plaintiff, an Ambassador, was promised a position and a stake in the Defendant's company if he could use his office to win the defendant a contract. The Defendant later refused to comply with the promise, saying the Ambassador was merely performing his official duties.

Held: It was held that under Section 9 of the ***Contract Act,*** 1960 (Act 25), there was a binding contract; however, it was unenforceable because to do so would be to encourage corrupt practices in future.

Unconscionable Contracts or Clauses

Usually, a court will not look at the fairness or equity of a contract (for instance, the adequacy of consideration or length of time or terms granted to one party by the other). Every contracting party is presumed to be intelligent, wise and acting in their own best interest even if that is not obvious. Nonetheless, where the terms are oppressive, the courts may relieve the innocent party of part or all their duties. An agreement is deemed unconscionable if it is grossly unfair or devoid of conscience.

CHAPTER 8 – QUICK REVIEW

The general rule is that, a minor is not bound by a contract which he enters into during his minority, unless it is a contract of 'necessaries' or where the contract as a whole is for the benefit of the minor. He is also bound by a beneficial contract of employment. Excluding these exceptions contracts involving minors may be repudiated at the option of the minor in which case the minor must repudiate the contract during his minority or before attaining the age of majority. He may, however, incur liability if he ratifies the contract after attaining majority.

Persons suffering mental incapacity may make valid contracts during their lucid moments. At common law, mental incapacity itself is not a ground for setting aside a contract, unless the mental incapacity was clearly known to the other party.

9 Terms

LEARNING OUTCOMES

The terms of a contract define the nature and extent of obligation of each party to the contract. Terms may be either oral or written, or partly oral and partly written (see *Couchman v. Hill* (1947)). If a statement forms part of the contract, then it is a term. If it is made in the negotiations leading up to the formation of the contract and made to induce the other party to contact, then it is mere representation. Now in contract law, the terms agreed upon must not be in violation of a statute, which is why it may be important to involve an experienced lawyer. If any of the contractual terms violates a statute, the contract may be rendered unenforceable and any injured party that sues cannot recover –in some cases the outcome can be serious.

At the end of this chapter, you should be familiar with the legal distinction between terms and mere representations, interpretation of the express terms of a contract, identification of the implied terms, the different weights given to different terms and the parole evidence rule.

TERMS AND REPRESENTATIONS

A term is a statement which forms part of the express terms of contract, a representation, on the other hand, is a statement which does not form part of the contract, but merely help to induce it.

This distinction between terms and representations is an important one in contract law. If a representation is untrue, it is called a 'misrepresentation' and the untruth constitutes a breach of contract. Whether a statement becomes a term of contract, however, depends on the intention of the parties. In trying to ascertain the intention, the court may take into account the following factors:

a.   Importance of the statement to the parties
In *Bannerman v. White* (1861), the buyer stated 'if sulphur has been used, I do not want to know the price'. The presence of the sulphur was clearly important to the buyer and so was held to be a term of the contract.

b.   **Respective knowledge of the parties**

In *Oscar Chess Ltd v. Williams* (1957) it was held that a statement by a member of the public, a non-expert, to a garage, an expert, with regard to the age of a car was a mere representation not a term. On the other hand, a statement made by a garage owner, an expert, to a member of the public, a non-expert, concerning the mileage of a car was held to be a term (see *Dick Bentley Productions Ltd v Harold Smith* (Motors) Ltd (1965)).

c.   **The manner of the statement**

For example, if it suggests verification (*Ecay v. Godfrey* (1947)), it is unlikely to be a term. If it discourages verification 'If there was anything wrong with the horse, I would tell you' (see *Schawel v. Reade* (1913)), it is likely to be a term.

d.   **Where a contract has been reduced to writing**

The terms will normally be the statements incorporated into the written agreement of the parties(see *Routledge v. McKay* (1954)).

A contract maybe partly oral and partly written. In *Evans & Sons Ltd v. Andrea Merzario Ltd* (1976), an oral assurance that a piece of machinery would be stowed under, and not on the deck, was held to be a term of a contact, although it was not incorporated into the written terms. The court held that the contract was partly oral, and partly written and in such hybrid circumstances the court was entitled to look at all the surrounding circumstances.

TERMS OF CONTRACT

The nature, scope and extent of the obligations of the parties to a contract, as indicated above, is known as the terms of contract. The terms may be oral, written or implied from the conduct of the parties.

a.   **The Terms of Oral Contracts**

The terms of an oral contract are generally as enforceable as that of a written one. The problem with oral contracts, however, is proving their existence or terms. An oral contract may be proved by witness testimony – that is, if third parties were present. All actions taken by one or both parties in obvious reliance on the existence of a contract also offer another way to prove the existence and agreed terms[41] (see ***Brogden v. Metropolitan Railway*** (1877) 2 App Cas 666 at 669, HL).

b.   The Terms of Written Contracts

The terms of a written contract are generally stated in the contractual document agreed to by the parties. If there is any dispute, the parties must resort to the stated terms.

c.   The Terms of a Contract implied from conduct

The terms of a contract that is implied from conduct can be ambiguous or inexact. It is often difficult to prove precise terms when a dispute erupts. Note that this kind of contract is based on a meeting of minds, such that although precise terms have not been stated expressly, the terms are inferred, as a fact, from the conduct of the parties which in the light of the surrounding circumstances, reveals their tacit understanding.

d.   The Parole Evidence Rule

The parole evidence rule states that where a contract is reduced to writing, oral or other extrinsic evidence (i.e. evidence outside the document) is normally inadmissible to 'add to, vary or contradict', the terms of that written agreement. There are, however, important exceptions to the parole evidence rule.

Exceptions to the Parole Evidence Rule

- **To show a contract is illegal** – Parole evidence is admissible to show that the contract is not legally binding e.g. because of a mistake or misrepresentation.
- **To show that the contract is subject to a 'condition precedent'.** Thus in ***Pym v. Cambell*** (1856), oral evidence was admitted to show that a contract was not to come into operation unless a patent was approved by a third party.
- **Customs** — to establish a custom or trade usage (see ***Hutton v. Warren*** (1836).

---

41   In so far as conduct, which creates a binding contract is concerned, the principle summed up in ***Freeman v. Coke*** and adopted by Lord Blackburn's famous articulation in ***Smith v. Hughes*** (1871) LR 6QB 597, at 607 that, "If, whatever a man's real intention may be, he so conducts himself that a reasonable man would believe that he was assenting to the terms proposed by the other party, and that other party upon that belief enters into a contract with him, the man thus conducting himself would be equally bound as if he had agreed to the other's terms" remains good law.

- **To show that the contract is not the entire contract** – Parole evidence is admissible to establish that the written contract is not the whole contract. It is presumed that 'a document which looks like a contract is the whole contract', but this is rebuttable (see the case of **Couchman v. Hill** (1947) and **Evans v. Andrea Merzario**). A contract may be contained in more than one document (**Jacobs v. Batavia Plantation Trust Ltd** (1924).
- **To show existence of collateral contract** – Parole evidence is admissible to establish a collateral contract (**City & Westminster Properties Ltd v. Mudd** (1959); **Evans & Son Ltd v. Andrea Merzario Ltd** (1976)).

CLASSIFICATION OF TERMS OF CONTRACT

The law of contract makes a distinction between the terms of a contract which entitle an innocent party to terminate or rescind or treat as discharged a contract in the event of a breach, and terms which only enable a party to claim damages. Terms may, however, be classified into two main classes:

a. Express and Implied Terms, and
b. Conditions, Warranties and Innominate Terms

Express and Implied Terms

The terms of a given contract may be either express or implied. A term is express if the parties have stated, agreed and indicated an intention to be bound legally by it. An express term may be either written or oral, or partly written and oral.

A term is implied, however, if although the parties have not expressly stated it, it can be deduced or inferred from the express terms, or the conduct of the parties, or the circumstances and the nature of the transaction. A term may, however, be implied from one of three sources.

Terms implied by Custom

A contract may be deemed to incorporate any relevant custom of the market, trade or locality in which the contract is made. In **Hutton v. Warren** (1836) a tenant established a right to fair allowance for improvements to the land through a local custom.

Terms implied by Statute

When a contract made by two or more parties is governed by a statute, the statute may, in certain cases, imply some terms into the party's agreement. For example, in a sale of goods contract, the *Sale of Goods Act*, (1979) implies the following terms into contracts for the sale of goods:

- That the seller has the right to sell the goods
- That goods sold by description correspond with the description.

The *Conveyancing Act*, (1974) regulates contracts for property sale and lease (an agreement between two parties regarding of property) and other immovable properties in Ghana. In a conveyance of land, Section 22 of the *Conveyancing Act*, (1973) implies a right to convey. This means that the seller in a conveyance warrants (or assures) the buyer impliedly that he or she is the owner of the property to be conveyed, and therefore legally has the power to sell or lease it. If it turns out that he or she does not have the said right, he or she would be in breach of that term, and the buyer will be entitled to sue the seller for a refund of any monies paid, damages for any losses or injuries suffered.

In a sale of goods, there is also an implied term that the goods (the subject-matter of the sale) are of satisfactory quality. Goods are of a satisfactory quality if they meet the standard that a reasonable person would regard as satisfactory, taking account any description of the goods, the price, if relevant, and all other relevant circumstances; in particular that:

(a) Their fitness for all purposes for which goods of that kind are commonly supplied
(b) Appearance and finish
(c) Freedom from minor defects
(d) Safety; and
(e) Durability.

It does not cover matters specifically drawn to the buyer's attention before the contract is made; or, where the buyer examines the good, defects which that examination should have revealed:

- That the goods are fit for any special purpose made known to be seller
- That goods sold by sample correspond with the sample

Where an implied term is broken, then the buyer may reject the goods, provided he has not accepted them. However, where the buyer is not a consumer, and the breach is so slight that it would be unreasonable to reject them, then the right to reject is removed.

Terms implied by Court

The court may imply a term in the party's contract to give business efficacy to the contract. *The Moorcock* (1889) case illustrates this point.

The Moorcock (1889)

Facts: There was an agreement by a wharf owner to permit a ship owner to unload his ship at the wharf (a place where ships dock to load and off-load cargo or passengers). The ship was damaged when, at low tide, it was grounded on the bottom of the river on a hard ridge.

Held: The court would imply a term that the river bottom would be reasonably safe for ships to dry out on.

Also, in *Wong Mee Wan v. Hong Kong Travel Service* (1995), it was held that a travel company had undertaken that activities carried out by others, such as ferrying a party across a lake in China, would be carried out with reasonable care and skill.

TYPES OF TERMS

There are three types of terms known in Ghanaian contract law – conditions, warranties and innominate terms. The difference between the various types is important because it eventually determines the remedies available in the event of a breach of contract.

Conditions

A condition is a vital term going to the root of the contract itself. A breach of condition can result in the payment of damages (i.e. compensation) or in discharge of the contract or both. A discharge entitles the innocent party to repudiate the contract and claim damages. *Poussard v. Spiers & Pond* (1876) illustrates this position of the law.

Poussard v. Spiers & Pond (1876)

Facts: An opera singer failed to appear on the opening night.

Held: It was held that this was a breach of condition which entitled the management to treat the contract as discharged (i.e. as ended or terminated).

Warranties

A warranty is a relatively less important term which is secondary to the main purpose of the contract. If a warranty is therefore broken, it does not entitle the innocent party to terminate the contract (i.e. treat it as discharged); it just entitles him or her to damages. In this regard, the right to quiet enjoyment in a tenancy agreement is a warranty. If it is breached by the landlord, it may not allow the buyer to treat the entire tenancy as discharged, but to damages only. The English case of ***Bettini v. Gye*** (1876) is illustrative of this principle.

Bettini v. Gye (1876)

Facts: An opera singer was engaged to sing for a whole season. He undertook to arrive six days in advance to take part in rehearsals, but failed to turn up for rehearsals. The management therefore engaged another singer to replace him for the entire season.

Held: It was held that the rehearsal clause was subsidiary to the main clause – it was only a warranty. The management was therefore not entitled to treat the contract as discharged and employ a replacement singer. They should have kept to the original contract and merely sought damages for the three days' delay.

Innominate terms

An innominate or indeterminate term is one which is neither a condition nor a warranty. As such, the remedy for breach depends on the actual effect of the breach on the innocent party. If the effect or the gravity of the breach is minor or trivial, it will be treated as a warranty and the innocent party would be entitled to damages only. However, if it is major or serious, the innocent party would be entitled to damages, discharge or both. *The Hansa Nord* (1976) case illustrates this point.

The Hansa Nord (1976)

Facts: In this case, the seller had sold a cargo of citrus pellets with a term in the contract that the shipment be made in good condition. The buyer rejected the cargo on the basis that his term had been broken. The defect, however, was not serious and the court held that although the ***Sale of Goods Act*** 1979 had classified some terms as conditions and warranties, it did not follow that all the terms had to be so classified.

Held: That the court could consider the effect of the breach, and since this was not serious, the buyer had not been entitled to reject.

EXCLUSION CLAUSES

An exclusion clause is a term that seeks to exclude or limit a party's liability for a breach of contract. Through an exclusion clause, a party to a contract (e.g. a company or individual) can identify events or circumstances causing loss for which there will be no liability whatsoever for breach.

At common law, in order for an exclusion clause to be valid, it must satisfy two conditions. First, it must be incorporated into the contract and second, its wording must cover the loss.

Incorporation of Exclusion Clauses

Under Ghanaian contract law, there are three ways in which such term may be incorporated (i.e. inserted) into a contractual agreement – this is by signature, notice and previous dealing.

Signature

The rule is that if a person signs a contractual document, then they are bound by its terms, even if they did not read it. The illustrative case in point is *L'Estrange v. Graucob* (1934). The case of *L'Estrange v. Graucob* established the rule that a clause is incorporated by signature even if the signatory never read or understood the document.

The rule in *L'Estrange v. Graucob* will, however, not apply if there was misrepresentation. Thus in *Curtis v. Chemical Cleaning & Dyeing Co* (1951), it was held that a signature does not incorporate an exclusion clause if the effect of the term was misrepresented.

Notice

An exclusion clause will not be incorporated into a contract unless the party affected actually knew of it, or was given sufficient notice of it. In order for notice to be adequate, the document bearing the exclusion clause must be an integral part of the contract and given at the time the contract is made. The case of *Olley v. Marlborough Court Ltd* (1949) is a locus classicus for this rule. Whether the degree of notice given has been sufficient is a matter of fact, but in *Thorton v. Shoe Lane Parking Ltd* (1971), it was stated that the greater the exemption, the greater the degree of notice required.

Olley v. Marlborough Court Ltd (1949)

Facts: A couple checked into a hotel and later sued the hotel that it was responsible for their missing fur coat. The hotel sought to rely on a notice pasted in the room of the couple requesting them to declare all valuables at the reception desk, failure of which the hotel would not be responsible for any loss.

Held: It was held that a notice in a hotel room did not exclude liability as the contract was made at the reception desk.

Previous dealings

Where the parties have had previous dealings on the basis of an exclusion clause, that clause may be included in later contracts (***Spurling v. Bradshow*** (1956)). But it has to be shown that the party affected had actual knowledge of the exclusion clause (***Hollier v. Rambler Motors*** (1972)).

The wording must cover the loss

Under the ***contra proferentem rule*** (Latin for the rule that a contract is to be interpreted against the drafter), the courts interpret words narrowly against the person seeking to rely on the clause. ***Photo Production v. Securicor*** (1980) illustrates this principle.

Photo Production v. Securicor (1980)

Facts: A Security Guard burnt down a factory he was guarding. The contract between his employers, the security firm, and the factory limited his employers' liability for injurious acts and defaults of the guards.

Held: The clause was clear and unambiguous and effectively limited the security firm's liability even for this fundamental breach.

CERTAINTY OF TERMS AND INCOMPLETE AGREEMENTS

If the terms captured in a contract are too vague, the court will not enforce the vague terms. ***Scammell & Nephew v. Ousten*** (1941), illustrates this position of the law.

In Scammell, the court refused to enforce a sale which was stated to be made 'on hire-purchase terms', but in which neither the rate of interest, nor repayment period, nor the number of installments were stated.

CHAPTER 9 – QUICK REVIEW

A term is a statement that forms part of the agreed obligations under a contract, a representation, on the other hand, does not form part of the contract, but merely helps to induce it.

There are three types of terms, nominate clauses, warranties and conditions. As a general rule, a person is bound by a document which he signs, whether he reads it or not, except where his signature has been procured by fraud or misrepresentation or where the defense of non est factum is made out.

Exclusion clauses are terms that limit the obligations of the parties and provide a defense to alleged breaches of obligation. To be effective, however, exclusion clauses must be incorporated into the contract, by signature, by giving reasonable notice of the exclusion clause or by a course of dealing.

10. Vitiating Factors

LEARNING OBJECTIVES

When does a mistake by either party or fraud by a business partner invalidate a business contract? When can a party successfully claim that an agreement was reached under duress? The main purpose of this chapter is to examine these vital questions. The factors discussed below show that there are exceptions to the general rule that a contract, once formed, is enforceable. At the end of the chapter you should be able to:

- State the exceptional factors which negate consent and which render contracts unenforceable
- Recognize the different types of mistake and misrepresentations
- Differentiate between misrepresentation of fact and misrepresentation of law and
- Appreciate the effects of undue influence and duress.

VITIATING FACTORS

Vitiating factors are simply factors which negate the manifest consent of one or all the parties, and as a result render a contract unenforceable or voidable, and thus liable to be set aside on equitable grounds.

This means that a contract may be executed by parties with full legal capacity and for a perfectly lawful purpose. It may be supported by consideration and may reflect a clear intention to create legal relations, yet with all these ingredients, the contract may still be unenforceable. Factors which can make a contract unenforceable, such as mistake, misrepresentation, fraud, duress, undue influence, illegality might imply that no genuine consent or agreement was given by one or more of the parties. As intimated earlier, any consent which is induced by fraud, misrepresentation or duress cannot be genuine; on the contrary, the presence of these factors vitiates the contract, and a contract found to be vitiated will be set aside by a court of law (Bondzi-Simpson, 2010:71).

VOID AND VOIDABLE CONTRACTS

A void contract is a contract which is devoid of any legal effect and thus unenforceable. The parties cannot be held to its terms, and therefore every property transferred and every payment made under it is recoverable, because in actuality the contract was of no effect from its very beginning. Hence, it gave rise to no obligation to perform anything. A void contract is basically unenforceable. This can happen for various reasons, such as:

- The subject matter of contract involves illegal matters, such as drug dealing, prostitution, pornography, or some form of crime as spelt out in the *Criminal Offenses Act,* 1960 (Act 29)
- The contract is against public policy, and
- The contract required one party to perform acts that are impossible, or depends on impossible events.

A voidable contract, on the other hand, is a contract which remains valid until set aside by the party who has the right to set it aside, through a process known as rescission. Factors that may make a contract voidable include:

- Agreements in which one party is still a minor
- Contracts involving fraud, deceit, or other forms of trickery
- Mistake
- Duress
- Undue Influence, and
- Contracts that were made when one party was drunk or mentally incapacitated or not of sound mind at the time of the contract.

The distinction between void and voidable was drawn famously by Lord Denning in the case of *MacFoy v. United Africa Co. Ltd*[42], as follows:

> "If an act is void, then it is in law a nullity. It is not only bad, but incurably bad. There is no need for an order of the court to set it aside. It is automatically null and void without more ado, though it is sometimes convenient to have the court declare it to be so. And every proceeding which is founded on it is also bad and incurably bad. You cannot put something on nothing and expect it to stay there. It will collapse. So will this judgment collapse if the statement of claim was a nullity. But if an act is only voidable, then it is not automatically void. It is only an irregularity which may be waived. It is not to be avoided unless something is done to avoid it. There must be an order of the court setting it aside: and the

---

42   (1962) AC 152

account has a discretion whether to set it aside or not. It will do so if justice demands it but not otherwise. Meanwhile, it remains good and a support for all that has been done under it. So will this statement of claim be a support for the judgment, if it was only voidable and not void."

Importance of Enforcing Contracts

Once a contract is formed, the law then focuses on enforcing it in order to preserve the integrity and reliability of contractual relationships. If the aggrieved party's claim falls within any of the vitiating factors stated above, he has two alternatives: he may choose whether to keep the contract or have it brought to an end.

CONTRACTS BASED ON UNEQUAL RELATIONSHIPS

Legal Capacity

Legal capacity relates to the ability to make binding contracts. Because they may be unable to give true consent, certain kinds of people, particularly children and persons with mental disability, are given special legal protection. At common law, the general rule is that contracts entered into between a minor and an adult cannot be enforced against the minor, but can be enforced against the adult party, unless it is a contract for 'necessaries', beneficial service or it is a voidable contract.

Where the contracting party is mentally impaired through illness or intoxicated such that they are unable to understand the consequences of their actions, and the other party is aware of their state, the contract is vitiated by lack of capacity, and the impaired party may file an action in court to avoid the contract at their option.

Duress

Duress is physical or mental coercion that deprives a person of freewill and thus leaves that person with no practically reasonable alternative other than to accept or kowtow to the contractual terms imposed on him or her.

Since consent to the contract is not genuine, the contract is voidable at the option of the victim. The doctrine of duress permits a court to set aside a contract when one party has been subjected to such coercion that true consent to the contract was actually never given. A contract concluded at gun-point or under compelling threat of physical or mental force for example is voidable.

There are five kinds of threats that are considered to constitute duress in the law of contract. These are namely:

- Actual or threatened physical violence or harm to the individual, his family or property
- Actual or threatened criminal prosecution
- Threat of a lawsuit but only if the threat is made with actual knowledge that the suit would be without any basis
- Threat of subjecting a party to personal, or his family to social, disgrace
- Threat of economic loss to a party, where the party claiming duress can show that the loss may occur because of actions of the one accused of coercion. Where the threatened economic loss is legitimate as illustrated by the case of *Agyemang and Others v. Ayarna and Anor* (1975)[43] a claim of duress will fail.

Agyemang and Others v. Ayarna and Anor (1975)

Facts: The Plaintiffs, who were legal practitioners, sued the Defendants for their unpaid legal fees. The Defendants relied on duress arising from threats by the Plaintiffs to withdraw from appearing as Counsel for the defendants who were involved in a subversion case pending before a military tribunal.

Held: It was held that the plea of duress was not sustainable because it was legitimate for a lawyer to withdraw from a case if his fees have not been paid. That whereas in the instant case, a lawyer and his client had agreed on fees payable and the client had failed to pay the fees, the lawyer was at liberty to commence an action to recover his unpaid fees.

Undue influence

Undue influence arises when one party (party A) takes advantage of another party (party B) by reason of his or her superior position in a close or confidential relationship; notwithstanding that, party A, occupying the superior position of trust, is expected to be acting in the best interest of party B. Examples of such relationships include those between doctor and patient, priest and parishioner, trustee and beneficiary, husband and wife, lawyer and client, etc. To illustrate, the questionable contracts that arise can assume several different forms. For instance:

---

43   1 GLR 149 - 152

- A client obtains judgment in a suit, then is prevailed upon by her lawyer to enter into a loan contract lending a significant portion of the judgment sum to the lawyer under circumstances that indicate that the transaction would not have occurred or arisen but for the dominant position of the lawyer and the client's fear of objecting.

- A dying patient who wills his or her property to his doctor under circumstances that indicate that the transaction would not have occurred or arisen but for the dominant position of the doctor and the patient's fear of objecting.

This is a situation where one party uses coercion or exerts influence to induce another to enter into a contract against his will. The case of *Allcard v. Skinner* (1887), an English contract law case dealing with undue influence, is one of the leading cases in the area of undue influence and unjust enrichment law.

Allcard v. Skinner (1887)

Facts: Miss Allcard was introduced by the Revd. Mr. Nihill to Miss Skinner, a lady superior of a religious order named "Protestant Sisters of the Poor." She had to observe vows of poverty and obedience. Three days after becoming a member, Miss Allcard made a will bequeathing all property to Miss Skinner, and passed on railway stock that she came into possession of in 1872 and 1874. She left the sisterhood in 1879 and in 1884 claimed the return of the stock. She sought to have the transaction set aside on grounds of undue influence.

Held: It was held by the Court of Appeal that although the Plaintiff's gifts were voidable because of undue influence brought to bear upon Plaintiff through the training she had received, she was disentitled to recover because of her conduct and the delay.

Cotton LJ said: "the court interferes, not on the ground that any wrongful act has in fact been committed by the donee, but on the ground of public policy, and to prevent the relations which exist between the parties and the influence arising therefrom being abused."

Lindley LJ said: "What then is the principle? Is it that it is right and expedient to save persons from the consequences of their own folly? Or is it that it is right and expedient to save them from being victimized by other people? In my opinion, the doctrine of undue influence is founded upon the second of these two principles. Courts of Equity have never set aside gifts on the ground of the folly, imprudence, or want of foresight on the part of donors. The Courts have always repudiated any such jurisdiction. ***Huguenin v. Baseley***[44] is itself a clear authority to this effect. It would obviously be to encourage folly, recklessness, extravagance and vice if persons could get back property which they foolishly made away with, whether by giving it to charitable institutions or by bestowing it on less worthy objects. On the other hand, to protect people from being forced, tricked or misled in any way by others into parting with their property is one of the most legitimate objects of all laws; and the equitable doctrine of undue influence has grown out of and been developed by the necessity of grappling with insidious forms of spiritual tyranny and with the infinite varieties of fraud."

Unconscionability

Unconscionability also considers the unequal relationship between the two contracting parties. If both inequality between the parties and an improvident bargain can be established, the contract can be rescinded by the court. If the contract is sufficiently divergent from the community's standards of conduct, it may signal the presence of exploitation and lead to a finding of unconscionablility. The party seeking to have the contract set aside must be able to demonstrate that its terms greatly advantage one party over the other. In short, there must be proof of substantial unfairness.

MISTAKE AND MISREPRESENTATION

MISTAKE

In contract law, a mistake is an erroneous belief about matters of fact that influences the formation of a contract. The word "mistake," as applied in contract law, however, carries a limited meaning than in ordinary parlance. That being so, the courts do not declare a contract void merely because one party or both parties claim to be mistaken about one fact or the other (Dowuona-Hammond).

LEGAL EFFECTS OF MISTAKE

At common law, a mistake operates to negate or sometimes to nullify consent, and to render the contract void ***ab initio.*** As stated earlier, a void contract neither imposes any obligation nor confers any right whatsoever. To have any legal effect, however, the mistake must have existed at the time the contract was concluded.

---

44   14 Ves 273

In equity, a mistake has wider connotation but is less radical in its effect, as these revealing words of Lord Denning in **Solle v. Butcher** (1950)[45] probably show: "A contract is also liable in equity to be set aside if the parties were under a common misapprehension either as to facts or as to their relative and respective rights, provided that the misapprehension was fundamental and that the party seeking to set it aside was not himself at fault." Again, in equity, mistake could be a defense if one is sued in an action for specific performance[46]; mistake can be a basis for rescission[47] and it even entitles the contracting parties to rectification of their written contract[48].

CATEGORIES OF MISTAKE

There are two categories of mistake—mistake of law and mistake of fact. Mistake of law implicates two types of mistake, namely mistake of the domestic law of a country and mistake of foreign law.[49]

Mistake of fact, on the other hand, includes three types of mistake, namely mutual mistake, common mistake and unilateral mistake. The distinction between these three is vital and must be borne in mind. For instance, a mutual mistake arises where the two parties commit different mistakes. With regard to a common mistake, both parties commit the same mistake. In a unilateral mistake only one party commits the mistake.

A.   MISTAKE OF LAW

As already stated, mistake of law may be of two types—mistake of law of the country and mistake of foreign law.

Mistake of Law of the Country

In relation to mistake of law of the country, the maxim, "ignorance of the law is no excuse" applies. The typical citizen or resident is presumed to know the

---

45   (1950) 1 K.B. 671at p 693

46   *Malins v. Freeman* 48 E.R. 537

47   *Sole v. Butcher* (1950) 1 K.B. 671; *Magee v. Pennine Insurance Co. Ltd* (1969) 2 Q.B. 507. Supposing a contract was good at law, a court of equity would often relieve a party from the consequences of his own mistake, so long as it would do no injustice to third parties. In *Torrance v. Bolton* (1872) per James L.J., a court of equity had the power to set aside the contract if it was of the opinion that it was unconscientious for the other party to avail himself of the legal advantage which he had obtained.

48   *Joscelyn v. Nissen* (1970) 2 WLR 509

49   Kuchhal, M.C. (2010) Business Law, 5th Edition, Vikas Publishing House p.76

law and therefore, generally, ignorance of the law does not provide a ground to avoid a contract. No relief can be granted only on grounds that a party was unaware of the law of the country. Thus if A and B enter into a contract based on the mistaken belief that a particular act is barred by the Ghanaian Statute of Limitations, the contract will remain valid and not voidable unless one of the parties committed a "mistake of law" through the inducement, whether innocent or otherwise, of the other party. In that case, the contract may be avoided.

Mistake of foreign law
Mistake of foreign law is on the same footing as mistake of the law of the country, and here the contract can be avoided only in the case of a bilateral mistake.

B. MISTAKE OF FACT

Mutual or Bilateral Mistake
A mutual or bilateral mistake occurs where both parties misunderstood each other and are at cross purposes. There is no true offer and corresponding acceptance of that offer, and therefore no agreement at all. This is because each party understood the contract in his own mistaken way and never actually consented to the exact promise made by the other. If the parties' contract under a bilateral mistake the result is that, that contract is liable to be set aside as being void ab initio.[50] For a bilateral mistake to render a contract void ab initio, the mistake must be mutual in that both parties must have misunderstood each other so as to nullify consent, and the mistake must relate to a fact essential to the agreement.

For example, Dan has two houses to sell, house O and house B. He offers to sell the B. David, not knowing that Dan has two houses, thinks of house O, and agrees to buy it. Here, there is no real consent and the agreement is void.

As stated earlier, the mistake must relate to some fact essential to the agreement. This implies that the fact must be one which goes to the root or heart of the contract. Thus a mistake about the very existence of the subject matter of the contract is a vital mistake. If at the time of the agreement and unknown to the parties, the subject matter had perished or ceased to exist, or if it never had been in existence, then the agreement is void. In **Bell v. Lever Brothers** (1932)[51], A agreed to sell to B a specific cargo of goods supposed to be from England enroute to Bombay. It turned out that prior to the day of the bargain, the ship

---

50   *Peters v. Peters* [1963] 2 GLR 182
51   (1932) A.C. 161

transporting the cargo had been cast away and the goods lost. Neither party was aware of that fact. The court held the agreement to be void.

It was also illustrated in ***Raffles v. Wichelaus*** (1864)[52], where there was a contract for the sale of a certain quantity of cotton arriving per "ex Peerless", and where there were two sailing ships of the same name yet the parties had in mind different ships at the time of entering into the contract. The court held that there was no consensus ad idem and therefore no binding agreement.

Unilateral Mistake

A unilateral mistake involves a mistake of a fact which is important and central to the contract. A unilateral mistake occurs where only one party is mistaken as to the subject matter or terms of the contract. Per Lord Denning in ***Sole v. Butcher,*** "neither party can rely on his own error to say that the contract is a nullity from the beginning, even if it was a mistake which to his mind was fundamental." If the other party is unaware of the mistake, contributed to it and tried to take advantage of the mistake himself, then a Court of law can set aside that contract as void on grounds of mistake.

The application of the objective test could be used to prevent a party who had entered into a contract from setting up his mistake as a defense to a suit brought against him for breach of contract.[53] ***Tamplin v. James,***[54] however, illustrate the principle that if a reasonable man would have understood the contract in a certain sense then in spite of the party's alleged "mistake", that party would be held bound to the contract in that reasonable sense.

A contract may, however, be held to be void, where there is a mistake in the identity of the contracting party. For example, Moses contracts with Morgan, believing that Morgan is Martin. In the well-known case of ***Lewis v. Avery,*** Lord Denning held that the contract can be declared void if the plaintiff believed that the other party's identity was of vital importance, and thus a mere mistaken belief as to identity would be grossly insufficient. Thus in ***Shogun Finance v. Hudson,*** the House of Lords declared that there was a strong presumption in law, that the owner intended to contract with the person physically present before him and that only in extreme cases would the presumption be rebutted.

---

52   2 H & C. 906

53   ***Tamplin v. James*** (1880) 15 Ch. D. 215

54   ***ibid***

Common Mistake

A common mistake arises where, even though the parties believe that they have reached a genuine agreement, both contracted in the rather erroneous belief that some fact, for example the value or quality of particular goods, which is the basis of the contract, is of this value or that quality, when in actual fact it is not true.

MISREPRESENTATION

At common law, a party is generally under no duty to disclose all facts in his possession to the other contracting party before a valid contract can be created between the two of them. Each party must watch out to protect his own interest unaided or without anyone's help. In the sale of goods, the rule *caveat emptor* (let the buyer beware) applies, for the buyer will not be allowed to later avoid the sale by saying that all the facts were not known to him else he would not have entered into that contract.

WHAT WILL AMOUNT TO A MISREPRESENTATION

To amount to an actionable misrepresentation certain criteria must be satisfied:

a.   No obligation to give information

A seller is under no obligation to give information to a buyer about anything that the seller offers for sale unless where the buyer expressly asks questions about what has been offered. The buyer has to find out whatever he wishes to know about whatever he wants to buy.

However, where one party makes a positive false statement which deceives the other party to enter into a contract, then this amounts to what is called a misrepresentation. A misrepresentation is a false statement of fact made by one party to the other party before the contract was entered into, and was intended to induce the other party to enter into the said contract.

b.   Statement of Opinion

A statement of opinion may amount to an actionable misrepresentation where the representor was in a position to know the facts. This is because everyone is entitled to his or her own opinion and no one's opinion is binding on the other. Thus in *Bisset v. Wilkinson,* the contracting parties were holding negotiations for the sale of land. During the negotiations, in the plaintiff's opinion, the land would be able to carry or accommodate 2,000 sheep. In fact, the land could not carry that number of sheep. The plaintiff, therefore, sued for the purchase price of the land since the defendant refused to pay up the money, arguing that the contract could be avoided by him on the grounds of misrepresentation as to the carrying capacity of the land.

It was held that no misrepresentation had taken place since the statement was one of honest opinion and not a statement of fact. (NB misrepresentation must always relate to a categorical statement of fact which is wrong and not an interpretation of the facts since everyone has a right to make his own interpretation of any set of facts and no one person's opinion binds the other.)

c. Statement as to Future Intent
A statement as to future intent cannot amount to a misrepresentation unless the representor had no intention of carrying out the stated intent:

Edgington v. Fitzmaurice (1885) 29 Ch D 459

d. False statement of law
A false statement of law will not amount to an actionable misrepresentation:

Pankhania v. Hackney [2002] EWHC 2441

It must be a statement of fact and not a statement of law since everyone is presumed to know the law. In the case of *Kpeglo v. SCOA Motors Ltd*, the defendants represented that a car which they sold to the plaintiff was new when, in fact, it was not. The car was accepted by plaintiff on hire purchase terms since the plaintiff believed that the car was new. It was held that the plaintiff was entitled to have the contract of hire purchase rescinded (set aside) because of the misrepresentation on the part of the defendants.

e. Silence
Silence will not generally amount to a misrepresentation unless it is a contract of uberrimae fidei (i.e. one of utmost good faith such as an insurance contract or where the representor is in a fiduciary position). In such contracts, a duty exists to disclose all material facts and a failure to do so may give rise to an action for misrepresentation.

Smith v. Hughes (1871) LR 6 QB 597
HIH Casualty and General Insurance Ltd v Chase Manhattan Bank [2003] UKHL

f. Later change of circumstances

If a statement made becomes false because of a later change of circumstances, there is an obligation to disclose the change of circumstances:

With v. O'Flanagan [1936] Ch 575.

g. Inducement/reliance

Once it has been established that a false statement has been made it is then necessary for the representee to demonstrate that the false statement induced them to enter the contract. There can be no inducement or reliance if the representee was unaware of the false statement:

Horsfall v. Thomas [1862] 1 H&C 90

h. Agent checks out the validity of the statement

If the representee or their agent checks out the validity of the statement, they have not relied on the statement. *Attwood v. Small* [1838] UKHL J60

If the representee is given the opportunity to check out the statement but does not in fact check it out, they are still able to demonstrate reliance.

TYPES OF MISREPRESENTATION

A misrepresentation may be classified into two, namely innocent misrepresentation and fraudulent misrepresentation

Innocent Misrepresentation

If a person makes a statement believing that what he says is true but this later turns out to be false, then this amounts to an innocent misrepresentation.

Fraudulent Misrepresentation

The presence of fraud affects the genuineness of consent. A misrepresentation is fraudulent where the party making the statement knows that it is untrue but he still makes it; or makes it recklessly without caring whether it is true or not; or makes it all the same where he himself does not believe the statement to be true.

Four basic elements are necessary to be proved to render a contract voidable:

- *An intention to deceive (usually with knowledge of the falsity)*
- *A misrepresentation of material facts*
- *A reliance by the innocent third party on the misrepresentation; and*
- *Usually damages or injury caused by the misrepresentation*

The above guidelines for ascertaining whether a misrepresentation is fraudulent were outlined in ***Derry v. Peek*** (1889) by Lord Herschell and it is noteworthy that anyone of these guidelines will suffice as proof of fraudulent misrepresentation.

Derry v. Peek (1889)

Facts: In a company prospectus, the Defendant stated the company had the right to use steam powered trams as opposed to horse powered trams. However, at the time, the right to use steam powered trams was subject to approval of the Board of Trade, which was later refused. The Plaintiff purchased shares in the company in reliance of the statement made and brought a claim based on the alleged fraudulent representation of the Defendant.

Held: The statement was not fraudulent but made in the honest belief that approval was forthcoming.

Lord Herschell defined fraudulent misrepresentation as a statement which is made either (a) knowing it to be false (b)without belief in its truth or (c) recklessly careless as to whether it be true or false.

EFFECTS OF MISREPRESENTATION
A misrepresentation does not make a contract void ***ab initio*** (from the onset) but rather, it makes the contract voidable and, therefore, the party that is misled as a result of the false statements can choose to hold the maker of the statement bound to the contract: he may also choose to make the contract void (avoid it or rescind it) on the grounds of the misrepresentation.

REMEDIES FOR MISREPRESENTATION
In relation to fraudulent misrepresentation, the plaintiff may do one of the following:
* The plaintiff may sue the defendant for the tort of deceit
* The plaintiff may affirm the contract (i.e. Treat it as binding) and then sue the defendant for the torts of deceit
* The plaintiff may repudiate the contract or have it rescinded by the court (with or without claiming damages for the tort of deceit)
* The plaintiff can refuse to perform his obligations under the contract and then use the misrepresentation as a defense.

For innocent misrepresentation, the plaintiff may do either of the following:
* The plaintiff may affirm the contract and treat it as binding

• The plaintiff may rescind the contract by notifying the other party and, where necessary, obtaining the court's assistance to secure restitution.

In the final analysis, most well-written contracts endeavor to exclude any representations, warranties or promises made to the other party during the course of the negotiation. In this respect, it is not unusual to find a clause usually towards the end of the Agreement, often headed up "Entire Agreement." The aim of such clauses is to achieve certainty by providing that all of the agreed terms are set in the contract. Regardless of such clauses, a contracting party should still make sure that they are. An important part of such clause may read as follows:

> "The Franchisee acknowledges that he has not relied on any oral or written representations or statements about the System, the Franchisee's Business, the prospects for the same, turnover, profitability or any other matter unless such representations or statements are reduced to writing and annexed to this Agreement and signed by the parties and incorporated herein."

Where such clauses, such as the above are present, a contracting party must make sure that the Franchisor has told him something important on which he could rely and which is one of the main reasons that party is taking the Franchise. In that case, the relevant matter must be written down, signed by both parties, and attached or incorporated into the Agreement. Here is an example: "It is agreed that the Franchisor has represented to the Franchisee that all the Franchisees are earning net profits before tax of at least GHC40,000 per annum. This is of fundamental to the Franchisee's decision to enter into this Agreement."

CONTRACTS BASED ON DEFECTS

Illegality (Illegal by statute and contrary to public policy)
Illegality is a highly complex area of Ghanaian contract law. Illegality deals with criminal conduct prohibited by statute and conduct at odds with public policy.

In some cases, it is relatively easy determining whether an illegal contract exists. For example, a contractual agreement where one part (A) agrees to pay another party (B) GH¢ 1m if B kills C will clearly be considered illegal and void ab initio. In some cases, a contract tainted by incidental illegality might be considered unenforceable rather than void so that proprietary interests might pass notwithstanding the unlawful conduct.

Statutory illegality

Statutory illegality covers contractual agreements which are directly prohibited by statute (e.g., narcotic deals), contracts entered into for an illegal purpose (e.g., to kill), contracts performed legally (e.g., over-speeding whilst driving in the course of performing a contract) and contracts otherwise made void by statute (e.g., certain unfair terms in consumer contracts). Different rules and consequences attach to each.

Contracts contrary to public policy

This type of contracts encompass a broader range of conduct, including contracts prejudicial to the administration of justice, contracts promoting corruption in public life, contracts prejudicing the status of marriage, contracts promoting sexual immorality and contracts in restraint of trade.

It is, however, not always easy to classify these types of contracts, and what constitutes conduct that is contrary to 'public policy' varies with the prevailing morality of the relevant jurisdiction.

Where a conduct is classified as illegal or contrary to public policy, it is generally held to be unenforceable; there are, however, some exceptions to that rule and, in some cases, it may be possible to sever the offending terms and enforce the remainder of the contract.

Writing as a requirement

As a general rule, contracts do not have to be written to be enforceable. Where an oral contract has been entered into, a party to such an agreement must find other ways to prove its existence, such as calling in witnesses.

Where a statute however requires a contract to be in writing, such as contracts of guarantees and contracts concerning land, that requirement must be met. Failure of such a contract to be in writing may render a contract generally unenforceable.

CHAPTER 10 – QUICK REVIEW

Misrepresentations can vitiate a contract. A misrepresentation is a false statement of fact or law addressed to the party misled, which is material, and thus induces the contract. Mere statements of opinion, of intention and puffs, are not statements of fact. A representation does not induce the contract where the representation is trivial, or if the representee was unaware of it or did not allow it to cloud his judgment. Misrepresentations could be fraudulent, negligent or innocent.

Fundamental mistakes in relation to an essential subject matter of the contract could also render a contract as void. Mistake could be common, mutual, or unilateral. Finally, illegality vitiates a contract. As a general rule the courts will not enforce an illegal contract or one which is otherwise contrary to public policy.

11. Performance and Discharge

LEARNING OUTCOMES

What is the legal position when one party fails to perform its obligations? What conditions can legally excuse performance? This topic focuses on how parties to a contract can excuse performance of their legal obligations under a contract. After reading and understanding the contents of this topic, you should be familiar with discharge by performance, discharge by mutual agreement, discharge by breach, discharge by frustration, and the effect of frustration

DISCHARGE OF CONTRACT

To discharge a contract means to terminate the existing contractual relationship between the parties, in which case one or both parties become freed from their future obligations to perform under that contract.[55] A contract that is discharged ceases to operate, and any rights and obligations created by it, grind to a halt.[56]

A discharge can arise through any the following ways— through performance, mutual agreement or consent, by lapse of time, by operation of law, and through breach of terms (condition) and frustration.

DISCHARGES BY PERFORMANCE

Performance refers to the act of doing or complying with terms prescribed by the contract. A discharge by performance occurs where the parties fulfill their obligations within the time and in the manner prescribed. In such a case, the parties are discharged and the contract comes to an end. If only one party performs his obligation, only he is discharged, and he can have a right of action against the other party who is guilty of breach.

To discharge obligations under a contract, a party must perform exactly what was promised. In *Cutter v. Powell* (1795), a ship's engineer undertook to sail a

---

55   Dowuna-Hammond (2011) ibid
56   See *http://220.227.161.86/16817Discharge.pdf*

ship from Jamaica to Liverpool, but died before the voyage was complete. It was held that nothing could be recovered in respect of service; he had not fulfilled his obligation.

Also in **Bolton v. Mahadeva** (1972) the contract was for the installation of a central heating system. The system as installed gave out less heat than it should, and there were fumes in one room. It was held that the contractor could not claim payment; although the boiler and pipes had been installed, they did not fulfill the primary purpose of heating the house. These are examples of 'entire' contracts which consist of one un-severable obligation.

In spite of the rule that performance must be exact, the law will allow payment to be made, on a **quantum meruit basis,** for incomplete performance in the following circumstances:

a. **Where the contract is divisible,** payment can be recovered for the completed part, e.g. goods delivered by installments.
b. **Where the promisor prevents complete performance,** the position of the law is illustrated in **Planche v. Colbourn** (1831). In that case, a writer was allowed payment for the work he had already done when the publisher abandoned the series.
c. **Where the promisee has performed a substantial part of the contract.** Accordingly, in **Hoenig v. Isaacs** (1952), the plaintiff decorated the defendant's flat, but because of faulty workmanship the defendant had to pay £55 to another firm to finish the job. It was held that the plaintiff was entitled to £750 (the contract price) minus the £55 paid to the other firm.

MUTUAL AGREEMENT

Since contracts are created by the parties through mutual agreement, contracts may be discharged through mutual agreement. In real life, the parties could enter into an agreement that may turn out to become unfavorable for both or one of them. If this occurs they may decide to:

a. **Enter into a new contract** – This is known as novation. Novation is the substitution of parties in a contract or the replacement of one contract with another. Where the parties agree to this arrangement a court will give effect to it.
b. **Vary certain terms of the contract** – The parties can opt to amend or vary the contract.

c. **End the contract** – The parties may, on the other hand, simply decide to terminate the contract, with both parties agreeing not to enforce their rights, or one party paying the other to bring obligations to an end.

d. **Substitute a party** – A party who wishes to end his or her continued involvement may, with the consent or concurrence of the other party, assign (i.e. transfer) the contract to a third party.

e. **Occurrence of a 'condition subsequent'**– Discharge by agreement may be in accordance with a term, a 'condition subsequent' in the original contract which provides that the contract ends automatically on the happening of a future event – the 'condition subsequent'.

BREACH OF CONDITION

A breach of contract does not automatically end or discharge a contract. A breach, if sufficiently serious (breach of condition), may allow the innocent party the option of treating the contract as discharged.

WHERE A PARTY REPUDIATES A CONTRACT UNDER A WRONG ASSUMPTION THAT HE IS ENTITLED TO DO SO

There are unique problems whenever a party repudiates a contract under a wrong assumption that he has a right to do so; in that case, the wrongful repudiation can allow the other party to treat the contract as discharged. Thus in *Federal Commerce & Navigation v. Molena Alpha* (1979), the owners of a ship gave instructions not to issue bills of lading without which the charterers could not operate the ship. They wrongly believed that they had the right to do so. It was held that their conduct constituted a wrongful repudiation of the contract which allowed the other party to treat the contract as discharged.

EFFECTS OF TREATING THE CONTRACT AS DISCHARGED

The obligation of both parties to perform any obligation (primary or otherwise) ends from the date of the termination. However, a secondary obligation to pay damages for any losses caused to the innocent party as a result of the breach will come into operation. The innocent party may recover damages to cover both past and future losses (*Lombard North Central v. Butterworth* (1987)).

Although the contract is terminated, it will be taken into consideration in assessing any future losses. In the *Mihalis Angelos* (1971), a ship was due in Haiphong on about 1 July. If it was not there by 20 July, the contract should be cancelled. On 17 July it was obvious the ship could not reach Haiphong by 20 July. The charterers cancelled. It was held to be wrongful repudiation. The charterers had no right to cancel until 20 July. However, only nominal damages were awarded. The court could consult the contract in order to assess damages. The fact that the ship could not have reached Haiphong by 20 July was relevant.

There have been problems, however, with what amounts to an acceptance of a repudiation. In *Vitol SA v. Norelf Ltd* (1996), Vitol telexed a repudiation of a contract of sale to Norelf, who did not respond directly but set out to find an alternative buyer, and ultimately sold the goods to a new buyer. The House of Lords held that these actions by Norelf amounted to an acceptance of an anticipatory breach. Lord Steyn set out three principles which apply to an acceptance of an anticipatory breach:

- Where a party has repudiated a contract the aggrieved party has a choice whether to accept the repudiation or affirm the contract.
- An act of acceptance of repudiation requires no particular form. It is sufficient that the communication or conduct clearly conveys that the aggrieved party is treating the contract as at an end.
- The aggrieved party need not personally, or by an agent, notify the repudiating party's attention, e.g. notification by any unauthorized agent will be sufficient.

ANTICIPATORY BREACH

A party may announce, in advance, that it does not intend to carry out the terms of a contract. This is an anticipatory breach of contract, and may be either:

a.   Explicit, as in *Hochster v. De La Tour* (1853), where a travel courier announced in advance that he would not be fulfilling his contract

b.   Implicit, as in *Frost v. Knight* (1972), where a party disabled himself from carrying out a promise to marry by marrying another person.

EFFECT OF AN ANTICIPATORY BREACH

The injured party has two options:

a)   to sue for damages immediately. He or she does not have to await the date of performance (*Hochster v. De La Tour* (1853)). Or

b)   to refuse to accept the repudiation, affirm the contract and continue to perform their obligations under it.

This is what happened in *White v. Carter Ltd v McGregor* (1962), where the defendants cancelled a contract shortly after it had been signed. The plaintiffs refused to accept the cancellation and carried on with the contract. They then sued for the full contract price. It was held that the plaintiffs were entitled to succeed; repudiation does not automatically bring a contract to an end as discussed earlier. The innocent party has an option either to affirm the contract or to terminate the contract. The rule, however, is subject to two limitations:

a.   The innocent party must be able to fulfill the contract without the co-operation of the other party. In **Hounslow UDC v. Twickenham Garden Developments Ltd** (1971), Hounslow council cancelled a contract. It was held that the defendants could not rely on White and Carter v McGregor because a considerable amount of co-operation from the council was required, and the work was to be performed on council property.

b.   The innocent party must have had a legitimate interest, financial or otherwise, in performing the contract, rather than in claiming damages.

Where a party has affirmed the contract

a.   The party will have to pay damages for any subsequent breach; he cannot argue that the other party's anticipatory breach excused him (**Fercometal SARL v. Mediterranean Shipping Co (1988)**).

b.   There is a danger that a supervening event may frustrate the contract and deprive the innocent party of his right to damages, as in **Avery v. Bowden** (1855).

c.   There is, however, a problem with what amounts to affirmation of a contract.

In **Youkong Line Ltd v. Rendsberg Investment Corp** (1996), the defendants telexed an anticipatory breach of a charter party. The plaintiffs responded by telexing that the cancellation was totally unacceptable and that the charterers were strongly requested to honor their obligations. Eventually, having received no reply from the defendants, the plaintiffs advised them that they were accepting the repudiation, terminating the charter and suing for damages. The defendants alleged that the plaintiffs had in their original telex 'affirmed' the contract and could no longer accept the repudiation. The court held a contract was not affirmed without very clear evidence; in this case, the plaintiffs' first telex was 'a cry of protest'. It tried to persuade the defendants to carry out their obligation but was not clearly an affirmation of the contract. The plaintiffs were therefore justified in later accepting the repudiation.

FRUSTRATION

Frustration occurs where it is established that, due to a subsequent change in circumstances, the contract has become impossible to perform, or it has been deprived of its commercial purpose.

The doctrine has been kept to narrow limits by the courts who have insisted that the supervening event must destroy a fundamental assumption, and by business men who have 'drafted out' the doctrine by force majeure clause.

CIRCUMSTANCES IN WHICH FRUSTRATION MAY OCCUR

a. **The subject matter of the contract has been destroyed, or is otherwise unavailable**
    This occurred in ***Taylor v. Caldwell*** (1863),where a contract to hire a music hall was held to be frustrated by the destruction of the music hall by fire.
    However, the unavailable or destroyed object must have been intended by both parties to be the subject of the contract. In ***Blackburn Bobbin & Co v. Allen*** (1918) where the contract was for the sale of 'birch timber' which the seller intended to obtain from Finland, it was held that the contract was not frustrated when it became impossible to obtain timber from Finland. The subject matter of the contract was birch timber not Finnish birch timber.

b. **Death or incapacity of a party to a contract of personal service, or a contract where the personality of one party is important**
    In ***Condor v. The Barron Knights*** (1966), a contract between a pop group and its drummer was held frustrated when the drummer became ill and was unable to fulfill the terms of the contract. A claim for unfair dismissal can also sometimes be defeated by the defense of frustration where an employee has become permanently incapacitated or imprisoned for a long period.

c. **The contract has become illegal to perform**
    This may be either because of a change in the law, or the outbreak of war. In ***Avery v. Bowden*** (1855) a contract to supply goods to Russia was frustrated when the Crimean War broke out on the ground that it had become an illegal contract – trading with the enemy.
    It has been suggested that the outbreak of war between two foreign states, however, does not render a contract illegal, but may make it impossible to perform. In ***Finelvet v. Vinava Shipping Co Ltd*** (1983), a contract to deliver goods to Basra did not become illegal on the outbreak of the Iraq-Iran war, but was frustrated when it become too dangerous to sail to Basra.

d. **Failure of an event upon which the contract was based**
    In *Krell v. Henry* (1903), the court held that a contract to hire a room overlooking the proposed route of the coronation procession was frustrated when the coronation was postponed. The purpose of the contract was to view the coronation, not merely to hire a room. It was argued that the fact that the hire of the room was a 'one-off' transaction was important. The judge in the case contrasted it with the hire of a taxi to take a client to Epsom on Derby day. This would be a normal contractual transaction for the taxi driver; the cancellation of the Derby would not, therefore, frustrate the contract. In the case of *Herne Bay v. Hutton* (1903), the court refused to hold frustrated a contract to hire a boat to see the King review the fleet when the review was cancelled; the fleet was still there and could be viewed – there was, therefore, no complete failure of the purpose of the contract.

e. **Government interference or delay**
    In *Metropolitan Water Board v. Dick Kerr & Co* (1918) a contract had been formed in 1913 to build a reservoir within six years. In 1915, the government ordered the work to be stopped and the plant sold. It was held that the contract was frustrated.

Leases

It had long been thought that the doctrine of frustration did not apply to leases (see *Paradine v. Jane* and *Cricklewood Investments v. Leightons Investments* (1945)).

However, in *National Carriers v. Panalpina* (1981), the House of Lords declared that, in principle, a lease could be frustrated. In that case, a street which gave the only access to a warehouse was closed for 18 months. The lease for the warehouse was for 10 years. It was held that the lease was not frustrated.

The House of Lords did state, however, that where there was only one purpose for the land/property leased, and this purpose became impossible, then the lease would be frustrated, e.g. a short-term holiday lease.

LIMITS TO THE DOCTRINE OF FRUSTRATION

The doctrine must be kept within narrow limits. It will not be applied:

a. **On the grounds of inconvenience, increase in expense and loss of profit.**
    In *Davies Contractors Ltd v. Fareham UDC* (1956) the contractors had agreed to build a council estate at a fixed price. Due to strikes, bad weather, shortages of labor and materials, there were considerable delays and the

houses could only be built at a substantial loss. It was held that the contract was not frustrated; 'hardship or inconvenience, or material loss' do not themselves frustrate a contract.

b.   **Where there is an express provision in the contract covering the intervening event (i.e. a force majeure clause).**
But a force majeure clause will be interpreted narrowly as in *Metropolitan Water Board v. Dick Kerr & Co* (1918) where a reference to 'delays' was held to refer only to ordinary delays, and not to a delay caused by government decree. A force majeure clause will not be in any case applied to cover trading with an enemy.

c.   **Where the frustration is self-induced**
A contract will not be frustrated if the event making performance impossible was the voluntary action of one of the parties. If the party concerned had a choice open to him, and chose to act in such a way as to make performance impossible, then the frustration will be self-induced and the court will refuse to treat the contract as discharged.
In *Maritime National Fish v. Ocean Trawlers* (1935), the plaintiffs chartered a trawler from the defendants which both knew could only be operated under a government license. The plaintiffs were awarded only three licenses instead of the five they sought. They allocated these to their own trawlers, and returned the hired trawler to the defendants. The court held that the contract was not frustrated since the failure to use the vessel was self-induced.
The rule was confirmed in the *Superservant Two* (1990) where one of two barges owned by the defendant, and used to transport oil rigs, sank. They were, therefore, unable to fulfill their contract to transport an oil-rig belonging to the plaintiff as their other barge (the superservant one) was already allocated to other contracts. The court held that the contract was not frustrated. The plaintiffs had another barge available, but chose not to allocate it to the contract with the plaintiffs. This case illustrates both the court's reluctance to apply the doctrine of frustration and the advantage of using a force majeure clause.

d.   **Where the event was foreseeable**
If by reason of special knowledge, the event was foreseeable by one party, then the party cannot claim frustration. In *Amalgamated Investment & Property Ltd v. John Walker & Sons Ltd* (1977), the possibility that a building could be listed was foreseen by the plaintiff who had inquired about

the matter beforehand. A failure to obtain planning permission was also foreseeable and was a normal risk for property developers. The contract was, therefore, not frustrated.

THE EFFECT OF FRUSTRATION

At common law, the loss lies where it fell, i.e. the date of the frustrating event is all important, anything paid or payable before that date would have to be paid. Anything payable after that date need not be paid. This rule could be very unfair in its operation, as in *Chandler v. Webster* (1904), where the hirer had to pay all the sum due, despite the court holding the contract frustrated on account of the cancellation of the coronation.

In *Fibrosa Case* (1943), the House of Lords moved away from this rule and held that where there was a total failure of consideration, then any money paid or payable in advance would have to be returned. This rule, however, would only apply in the event of a total failure of consideration, and could cause hardship if the other party had expended a considerable amount of money in connection with the contract.

CHAPTER 11 – QUICK REVIEW

A contract is frustrated where, after the contract has come into existence, events occur which make performance of the contract impossible, illegal or something fundamentally different from the contemplation of the parties at the time of the contract.

A contract is not frustrated where the parties have made express provision for the consequences of the frustrating event in the contract, where the frustrating event was forseeable or was 'self-induced'.

A contract which is discharged on the grounds of frustration terminates automatically by the operation of a rule of law, regardless of the wishes of either party.

Any sum paid before the frustrating event is recoverable, sums payable after the time of discharge ceases to be payable and the payee may be entitled to set off against the sums so paid expenses which he has incurred before the time of discharge.

12. Breach of Contract

Violating the Terms

LEARNING OBJECTIVES

What happens when a party cannot perform all its obligations or when it does perform, but does so deficiently? What amounts to a breach of contract? What is the legal position when one party fails to perform his part of the contract in a satisfactory manner? When is a party impliedly in anticipatory breach? At the end of this chapter, you should be familiar with the meaning of breach of contract, types of breach, and legal effects of anticipatory breach.

Once a business is in breach, everything else is now in reactive mode. The contract-breaker is in an unenviable position, since its assets face the liability of costs associated with its default. The business must make both a business and legal decision evaluating the risks of losing in court, the option of negotiating a settlement and drawing a payment plan including assessing whether there is a valuable business relation that can be rescued from possible disaster.

BREACH OF CONTRACT

A breach of contract occurs where one or both parties to a contract fail to comply, either *completely* or *satisfactorily,* with their obligations under the contract. By law and equity, virtually every breach of contract gives the innocent party or non-defaulting party a right to a remedy, among them the payment of damages, or right to terminate or both depending on whether the term breached is a condition or a warranty.

TYPES OF BREACH

Generally, there are two broad types of breach. These are *actual breach* and *anticipatory breach.*

Actual breach occurs on the due date of performance, whiles an anticipatory breach occurs before the due date of performance. In either case, the party in breach renounces his or her obligations or shows an intention not to perform or comply with his or her contractual obligations.

ACTUAL BREACH

An actual breach can take two forms; the first is complete non-performance while the second is defective performance. Complete non-performance occurs where a party without lawful cause fails or refuses to perform his or her obligations as required by the contract on the due date.

In the case of defective performance, the party attempts to perform, but only engages in part-performance or performs his part in an unsatisfactory or defective manner.

ANTICIPATORY BREACH

Anticipatory breach may also take two forms – *express anticipatory breach* (or repudiation) and *implied anticipatory breach* (or repudiation).

Express Anticipatory Breach

Express anticipatory breach occurs where a party declares in advance of the due date of performance that he intends not to perform his side of the bargain. The landmark case of *Hochester v. De La Tour* (1853) is illustrative of the legal effect of an express anticipatory breach.

Hochester v. De La Tour (1853)

Facts: In April, De La Tour employed Hochester to act as a travel courier on his European tour, starting on the 1st of June. On the 11th of May De La Tour wrote to Hochester indicating that he would no longer be requiring his services. Hochester started legal proceedings on 22nd May. In his defense, De La Tour claimed that the Plaintiff, Hochester had no cause of action until the 1st of June.

Held: It was held that Hochester had a cause of action and was entitled to start his action as soon as the anticipatory breach occurred. The effect of breach is that, the innocent party may sue for damages immediately the breach is announced.

Implied Anticipatory Breach

Implied anticipatory breach occurs where a party to the contract does an act which renders the subsequent performance of his own obligations under a contract impossible. This is referred to as implied renunciation. In other words, implied renunciation occurs where the reasonable inference from the party's conduct is that he no longer intends to perform his side of the contract. *Omnium D'enterprises v. Sutherland* (1919) illustrates this position of the law.

Omnium D'Enterprises v. Sutherland (1919)

Facts: In Omnium, the defendants had agreed to hire a shipping vessel to the plaintiff. However, before the hiring period commenced, the defendant chose to sell the ship to someone else.

Held: It was held that the sale of the ship amounted to an implied repudiation of the contract with the plaintiff, and therefore the plaintiff could sue for breach of contract from that date.

As stated earlier, a breach of contract occurs when a party enters into a binding agreement, but then fails or refuses to perform obligations laid out in the contract. In that case, the plaintiff, to succeed, must prove:

a. **The Validity of the Contract**
   The plaintiff will need to prove four conditions in order to show that the contract was indeed legal and binding. In a valid contract, both parties must be in agreement, must be capable of entering into a contract agreement, must receive something of value as a result of the contract and must not engage in any illegal activity. If any of these areas cannot be upheld in court, the contract is not valid and therefore not enforceable.

b. **Agreement over the Terms of the Contract**
   The plaintiff must also prove that he did in fact abide by the terms of the contract. This may be by showing that money was sent to the defendant with the expectation of agreed upon action to follow, or that a certain action was performed incorrectly or inefficiently, according to the terms outlined in the contract. If the plaintiff can show that his actions were in line with the contract that is a step in the right direction for proving a breach of contract.

c. **Failure of the Defendant to meet the Terms of the Contract**
   The plaintiff must show exactly how the defendant failed to perform the terms of the contract. Sometimes this can mean an attempt to interpret the language within the contract and compare that to the actions or inactions of the defendant. While some breaches of contract are easier to show (lack of products delivered or service rendered), any breach should be contrasted with the contract.

d. **Proof of Damages Sustained**
   Finally, the plaintiff must demonstrate that damage occurred as a result of the breach of contract. This could mean lost money, lost clients and a number of other issues. Once all of these issues are presented and proven in

court, the plaintiff will move closer to success in litigating against a breach of contract.

THE LEGAL EFFECT OF ANTICIPATORY BREACH

Repudiation or anticipatory breach does not automatically bring a contract to an end. The repudiation or anticipated breach must be a breach of a condition. In such a case, the innocent party has two options:

a.   The innocent party can choose to treat the contract, if it is a breach of condition, as discharged and bring an action for damages for breach of contract immediately, precisely what occurred in *Hochester v. De La Tour.*

b.   The innocent party can choose, however, to treat the contract as still valid, complete his side of the bargain and sue for payment by the other side, which is what happened in *White & Carter v. McGregor* (1961). In this case, the defendant, McGregor, contracted with the plaintiffs, White & Carter, to have adverts posted on litter bins which were supplied to local authorities. The defendants wrote to the plaintiffs requesting them to cancel the contract. The plaintiffs, however, refused to cancel, but went ahead, produced and pasted the adverts as per the contract. They then approached the defendants for payment. It was held that the plaintiffs were not obliged to accept the defendant's repudiation, but could ignore it, perform their part and claim payment.

In a way, the rule in *White & Carter v. McGregor* (1961) runs counter to the duty to mitigate losses, since it makes the party in breach pay more than the mere profit on the contract. It is thus slightly dangerous not to accept the repudiation where it becomes apparent.

COURSES OF ACTION AVAILABLE UPON BREACH OF CONTRACT

When a breach occurs, the innocent party has various courses of action depending on the circumstances. Some of these options are as follows:

a)   **Repudiation or Rescission**
     The innocent party may treat the contract as repudiated or rescinded and thus refuse further performance. Repudiation or rescission is the refusal of further performance.

b)   **Action for Damages**
     The innocent party is also entitled to damages. The nature and quantum of damages may, however, depend on the loss sustained. Nominal damages are allowed for the infringement of legal rights. Where a loss is sustained

the injured party has to be placed in the same position as if the contract has been performed.

c) **Claim or Sue on a "Quantum Meruit"**

Upon breach of a contract, if the injured party has performed part of his obligation under the contract, he can sue on a *"quantum meruit"* basis and make a claim for the quantum of work already done under the contract. This right to payment is based on an implied promise by the other party arising from the acceptance of an executed consideration.

d) **Sue for Specific Performance**

When there is a breach of contract, the innocent party can sue the contract breaker to carry out his contractual obligation specifically. This is considered as an equitable remedy. Specific performance is a discretionary remedy that may be granted where damages alone do not constitute a fair and just remedy, and where the court can supervise the performance of the act.

e) **Sue for Injunction**

As a last resort, the innocent party can sue to restrain the other party from doing a particular act. Such an order will be given by the court and it is granted where damages would not be an adequate remedy.

Actions which constitute a breach of contract include repudiation of liability under the contract before the due date time for performance, doing acts that disable a party from performing the contract, and complete failure or refusal to fulfill obligations in a contract. Where a party either fails or refuses to perform his duties under a contract, this may amount to repudiation of the whole contract. In such a case the contract becomes discharged by breach.

CHAPTER 12 – QUICK REVIEW

A breach of contract occurs when a party, without lawful justification, a) fails or refuses to perform his obligations under a contract, or b) performs it defectively or c) incapacitates himself from performing. A breach does not automatically terminate or bring a contract to an end. The breach gives to the innocent party a right to claim damages and it may give him the additional right to terminate further performance of the contract.

The innocent party is not obliged to terminate performance of the contract; he can choose to terminate or affirm it. But the doctrine of mitigation requires him to mitigate his losses. The breaching party, however, may be unable to enforce the contract against the innocent party. An anticipatory breach, on the other hand, occurs where one party informs the other party, before the due date for performance, that he will not be able to perform his obligations under the contract. This entitles the innocent party to terminate further performance of the contract immediately.

An innocent party who affirms a contract after an anticipatory breach may continue with performance of his obligations under the contract, even though he knows that performance is not wanted by the other party.

13. Remedies

Damages and Equitable Reliefs

LEARNING OUTCOMES

What remedies are available to an innocent party to a contract in the event of a breach of contract? Under what circumstances will a court order damages? After reading and understanding the contents of this topic, you should understand what damages are, and be able to distinguish between the various types of damages available to an innocent party. Sometimes monetary compensation is insufficient, or is even an unfair remedy. At other times, a Plaintiff who had run to court might himself have acted unfairly against the defendant. This topic examines other remedies, besides compensation, which a court could give an aggrieved party upon breach of contract.

DAMAGES

"Damages" refers to the amount of money to be awarded or given in compensation to an injured party (or plaintiff) who has suffered harm due to an a party's breach of contract, negligence, recklessness, or wrongful action.

As a general rule, a breach of contract entitles the injured party to recover damages (i.e. monetary compensation) for losses suffered. This is a matter of right, and it is a common law remedy for an injured party who has suffered some pecuniary (i.e. financial) loss due to a breach of contract.

Damages often form the main remedy in actions for breach of contract, even though there are other remedies (of which injunctions and specific performance are the two most important reliefs).

In a claim for damages, the object of the court is to place the injured party in the same financial position he or she would have been in had the contract been properly performed.

TYPES OF DAMAGES

There are generally four types of damages that a court of law may award an injured party. These are:

a. General damages

General damages refer to monetary compensation that is paid out to an injured party in the lawsuit for injuries suffered (such as pain, suffering, and inability to perform certain functions) as a result of the breach. General damages cover the loss directly, and are the most common type of damages awarded for a breach of contract.

Let us consider this illustration: Company A delivered the wrong swivel chair to company B, and refused to take it back saying Company B's preferred choice was out of stock. Left with no choice, Company A successfully sued Company B for breach of contract. In this example, Company A is liable to Company B, and the general damages for its breach would include:

- Refund of any amount Company B had prepaid for the furniture to Company A.
- Reimbursement of any expense Company B incurred in sending the furniture to Company A.
- Payment for any increase in cost incurred by Company B in buying the right furniture, or its nearest equivalent, from another seller.

In personal injury cases, general damages can include physical pain and suffering, physical disfigurement, physical impairment, mental anguish, loss of companionship (paid to family members in wrongful death claims), and lowered quality of life.

b. Special damages

Special damages (or consequential damages) compensate the injured party for further losses suffered due to the defendant's actions. Special damages are out-of-pocket expenses that can be determined by adding together all the plaintiff's quantifiable financial losses. Nevertheless these loses must be proven with specificity. These can include repair and replacement of damaged property, loss of wages and loss of earning capacity, medical expenses (past and future) and loss of irreplaceable items.

These are actual losses caused indirectly by the breach. To obtain damages for this type of loss, the injured party must prove that the breaching party knew of the special circumstances or requirements at the time the contract was made. Out-of-pocket costs are costs such as medical bills, repairs and replacement of property, loss of wages and other damages which are not speculative or subjective, but which are directly suffered as a result of the breach of contract, negligence or other wrongful act by the defendant.

c. Exemplary or Punitive damages

Exemplary or punitive damages are requested or awarded in a lawsuit where the defendant's willful acts were plainly malicious, violent, oppressive, fraudulent, wanton or grossly reckless. Examples of acts warranting exemplary damages may include publishing that a company had committed murders when the publisher knew it was not true but hated the company. These damages are awarded both as a punishment and to set a public example. They are designed to reward the plaintiff for the horrible experience suffered.

d. Nominal damages

Nominal damages refer to small amounts of money awarded to a plaintiff in a lawsuit to show that the plaintiff was right, albeit he suffered no substantial harm. The most famous case of nominal damages was when Prime Minister Winston Churchill was awarded a shilling (about 25 cents) in a libel lawsuit he had brought against author Louis Adamic for writing that Churchill had been drunk during a dinner at the White House. The Prime Minister was vindicated, but the jury could not find that his towering reputation had been damaged.[57]

LIQUIDATED DAMAGES AND PENALTY CLAUSES

Where a business agreement or contract provides for the payment of a fixed sum upon breach, it could either be a liquidated damages clause or a penalty clause. Liquidated damages are generally deemed as authentic pre-estimate of the loss expected as a result of the breach. Consequently, the clause containing the said amount is enforceable by a court of law.

A penalty clause, on the other hand, threatens large damages for breach. Normally this amount is extravagant or very large viv-a-vis the expected loss. The case of ***Dunlop Pneumatic Tyre Co v. New Garage Motors*** (1919) illustrates the position of the law in relation to liquidated damages and penalty clauses.

Dunlop Pneumatic Tyre Co v. New Garage Motors (1919)

Facts: The plaintiff supplied the defendant with tyres under a business contract which imposed a minimum retail price. The contract provided that the defendants would pay the plaintiff £5 for every tyre that they sold in breach of the

---

57   *http://legal-dictionary.thefreedictionary.com/Nominal+Damages*

price agreement stated in the contract. The defendants sold the tyres at less than the agreed minimum price, and sought to resist the claim for the £5 on grounds that it represented a penalty clause.

Held: It was held that the provision was a genuine attempt to fix damages for breach, and was not a penalty. Accordingly, it was enforceable.

ASSESSMENT OF UNLIQUIDATED DAMAGES

Where a business contract fails to make any provision for damages, the court will determine the damages payable. This is referred to as unliquidated damages. Two factors must be considered in determining the amount of unliquidated damages payable. These are:

a.   The remoteness of the loss – that is, what losses are being claimed and do the losses arise directly or indirectly from the breach?

b.   The measure of damages that is the worth of the loss.

REMOTENESS OF LOSS

Damages cannot be recovered for losses that are too remote. The losses must be 'within the reasonable contemplation' of the parties.

Thus in *Hadley v. Baxendale* (1854), a mill was closed because of the delay of a carrier in returning a mill shaft. The court held that the carrier was not liable for damages for the closure of the mill since he was not aware that the absence of a mill shaft would lead to this conclusion.

Types of loss recognized

*   Pecuniary loss
*   Pain and suffering consequent on physical injury
*   Physical inconvenience
    In *Watts v. Morrow* (1991) damages were awarded for the physical inconvenience of living in a house whilst repairs were being carried out.
*   Damage to reputation
    Traditionally, these were damages to commercial reputation only.
    In *Gibbons v. Westminster Bank* (1939), damages for injury to reputation were awarded to a trader whose cheque was wrongly dishonored.
*   Distress to plaintiff
    Traditionally, damages for injured feelings were not awarded for breach of contract (see *Addis v. Gramophone Co Ltd* (1909)). However, in recent years, exceptions were developed to this rule. In *Jarvis v. Swan Tours*

(1973), damages for disappointment were awarded against a tour operator who provided a holiday which did not correspond with its description.

Computation of damages

The question that often arises is how much should be paid to an innocent party as damages when a breach of contract occurs. As a general principle, it is the amount which will put the Plaintiff in the position he would have been in had the contract been properly performed. This is described at times as the damages for loss of bargain.

There is some difficulty in computing damages in the building and architectural industry. Nevertheless, theoretically, there are two ways in which compensation can be computed. These are as follows:

a.   The cost of reconstruction or repair of faulty work so that it meets the required specifications, or
b.   The damages could be the difference in value between the building at the time of breach or completion, and its value if it had been completed.

Thus, in **Ruxley Electronics and Construction Ltd v. Forsyth** (1995), the parties entered into a contract for the construction of a swimming pool, whose approximate construction cost was £18,000.00. Even though the contractor provided that the pool was to be 7feet 6inches deep at one end, the actual depth of the pool was only 6feet 9 inches. Fixing the error required a full reconstruction assessed at £21,000.00. It was held by the House of Lords that, as the cost of reinstatement would be out of proportion to the benefit gained, the difference in value only should be awarded as the constructed pool was just as suitable for swimming and diving as one built to the original specifications.

Case Law:
Thus in **Anglia TV Ltd v. Reed** (1972),Reed was engaged to play the leading role in a TV program. The Plaintiffs incurred expenses in preparing for filming. Reed repudiated the contract. Anglia could not find a suitable replacement and had to abandon the project. It was held that Anglia could recover the whole of their wasted expenditure from Reed.

Key Business Tip
If there is no actual loss, the Plaintiff can only recover nominal damages, but then again the law requires the Plaintiff to take steps to mitigate (i.e. reduce) the loss.

Case Law

Thus in **Brace v. Caldar** (1895), Brace was employed for a fixed duration of two (2) years, but after only 5 months the firm, a partnership, was dissolved, thereby prematurely terminating his contract of employment. He was offered identical employment with a reconstituted partnership that was immediately formed to replace the dissolved one, but he refused the offer and sued for the wages he would have earned had his job continued for the agreed two (2) year period. It was held that Brace ought to have mitigated the loss he suffered by his employer's breach of contract. Thus, he could only recover nominal damages, and a notional deduction may be made to reflect taxation.

Methods of limiting damages

- Remoteness rules (losses which the defendant could not foresee)
- Causation rules (losses which the defendant did not cause)
  The breach must have caused the loss as well as having preceded it. The action of a third party may break the chain of causation, if it is not foreseeable. In **Lambert v. Lewis** (1982) a farmer continued to use a defective coupling after he knew it was broken. It was held that the responsibility for paying damages lay with the farmer, not the manufacturer. But, if the intervention was foreseeable, the chain of causation will not be broken.
- Mitigation (losses which could have been avoided)
  The plaintiff has a duty to take reasonable steps to mitigate his loss. In **Payzu v. Saunders** (1919), a plaintiff failed to recover damages when he had turned down an offer of goods at below market price. In Brace v Calder (1985), a dismissed employee had failed to mitigate when he turned down an offer of employment from a partner in his previous firm. The plaintiff need not take 'unreasonable' steps in mitigation. In **Pilkington v. Wood** (1953), it was held unreasonable for the plaintiff to take expensive and uncertain legal proceedings to try to mitigate his loss.
  The plaintiff should not take unreasonable steps which would increase losses. Thus in **Banco de Portugal v. Waterlow** (1932), the court confirmed that damages would not be recoverable for unreasonable actions, but in that case found that the bank's action in compensating persons who had been passed stolen banknotes was reasonable.

Key Business Tip

All parties to a contract have a duty to mitigate their losses. Mitigation may, however, not arise until there has been an actual breach of contract, or an anticipatory breach has been accepted by the other party (see ***White & Carter v. McGregor*** (1962)).

EQUITABLE REMEDIES

Equitable remedies are a distinct category of remedies that can be granted by a court when a breach occurs. The non-breaching party has a right to two types of remedies – legal and equitable. Legal remedies, as discussed in the preceding chapter, allows the innocent party to recover monetary compensation, while equitable remedies are largely actions prescribed by court to resolve the breach or dispute. Thus, a court can order a defendant to perform his or her part of a contract, rather than impose a fine. Examples of equitable remedies include specific performance, rescission, rectification, quantum meruit and injunction.

- **Specific Performance:** This is a decree or court order which requires the party in breach to completely perform their part of the bargain according to the contract. For example, this can include requiring the breaching party to deliver goods or services which have already been paid for. By tradition, specific performance will only be awarded:

i) Where damages are not an adequate remedy, i.e. where the plaintiff cannot get a satisfactory substitute and giving him money is inadequate.

ii) For the sale of land

iii) For antiques, valuable paintings etc, unless bought as an investment, as in ***Cohen v. Roche*** (1927), where the court refused to order specific performance for a contract to buy Heppelthwaite chairs as an investment

iv) Where goods cannot be obtained elsewhere

v) Where damages are difficult to assess, e.g. annuities

vi) Where there is no alternative remedy available.

In ***Beswick v. Beswick*** (1968), damages were not available since there was no loss to Peter Beswick's estate. The court, therefore, ordered specific performance of the promise to pay an annuity to Peter Beswick's widow.

- **Contract Rescission:** This is where the contract that has been breached is rescinded or cancelled. A new contract may be written which more clearly addresses the different needs of each party.
- **Contract Rectification:** This is where an existing contract is reviewed and re-written in a manner that reflects the true intentions of each party more accurately. The remedy of rectification requires that a valid, working contract must first be in existence (otherwise there is nothing to re-write). Rectification is usually prescribed where there was a mistake or misrepre-

sentation in one of the contract terms. A contract may be rectified in whole or in part.

Quantum Meruit: Quantum meruit (is a Latin expression for "as much as he deserved") is the actual value of services performed. Quantum meruit determines the amount to be paid for services when no contract exists or when there is doubt as to the amount due for the work performed but done under circumstances where payment is expected. This may include payment for work where no formal contract exists, or evaluating the amount due when outside forces cause a job to be terminated unexpectedly. If a person sues for payment for services in such circumstances the court will calculate the amount due based on time and usual rate of pay or the customary charge based on quantum meruit by implying a contract existed.

Injunction: An injunction is an equitable remedy in the form of a court order compelling a party to do or refrain from specific acts. A contracting party that fails to comply with an injunction faces criminal or civil penalties, including possible monetary sanctions and even imprisonment. They can also be charged with contempt of court. These are orders directing the defendant not to do a certain act.

Types of injunction
- Interlocutory injunction -This is designed to regulate the position of the parties pending trial.
- Prohibitory injunction - This is an order commanding the defendant not to do something.

Injunctions are also discretionary remedies and are subject to constraints similar to orders of specific performance. However, an injunction will be granted to enforce a negative stipulation in a contract of employment, as long as this is not an indirect way of enforcing the contract.

In *Warner Bros v. Nelson* (1937), an injunction was granted to stop Bette Davies from working for any film company other than the plaintiff. The court believed that she could earn her living otherwise than as an actress, and would not therefore be forced into performing her contract.

In *Page One Records v. Britton* (1968), however, an injunction to prevent the 'Troggs' from appointing another manager was refused. The court considered they did not have the experience to operate without a manager, and an injunction would force them to re-employ the plaintiffs.

The Courts have wide discretion when issuing equitable reliefs. The court will consider several different factors, before granting the relief.

EQUITABLE REMEDIES ARE DISCRETIONARY

Equitable remedies are discretionary. Thus, the following will be taken into account:

- **Mutuality**
  This has both a negative and a positive aspect. It has a negative aspect in that a minor cannot obtain it because it is not available against a minor, and a positive aspect whereby a vendor of land may obtain it although damages would be an adequate remedy, because it is available to a purchaser of land. (But note that in *Price v. Strange* (1978) specific performance was granted to a minor who had already performed all her obligations under the contract.)
- **Supervision**
  The need for constant supervision prevented the appointment of a resident porter being ordered in *Ryan v. Mutual Tontine Association* (1893), but in Posner v Scott-Lewis (1987) a similar order was made because the terms of the contract were sufficiently precise.
- **Impossibility**
  Watts v. Spence (1976) where land belonged to a third party.
- **Hardship**
  Patel v. Ali (1984), where the defendant would lose the help of supportive neighbors.
- **Conduct of the plaintiff**
  Shell (UK) Ltd v. Lostock Garages (1977).
- **Vagueness**
  Tito v. Waddell (1977).
- **Mistake**
  Webster v. Cecil (1861).

CHAPTER 13 – QUICK REVIEW

The aim of an award of damages is to compensate the plaintiff for a loss which he has suffered as a result of the defendant's breach in order to put the plaintiff in the position which he would have been in had the contract been performed according to its terms. The aim is not to punish the defendant. A plaintiff must take reasonable steps to mitigate his loss.

The general rule is that damages cannot be recovered for mental distress suffered as a result of the defendant's breach of contract, except where the plaintiff suffers mental distress and where the object of the term broken is to provide for mental distress.

Specific performance is an equitable remedy which is available within the discretion of the court. Its availability depends, *inter alia,* upon the appropriateness of the remedy on the facts of the case. An injunction is another equitable remedy which may be used in an effort to prevent a threatened breach of contract.

14. Company Law

LEARNING OBJECTIVES

Upon completion of this topic you should be able to explain the meaning and effect of incorporation, compare and contrast the different companies and partnerships, illustrate the effect of separate legal personality and when the veil of incorporation will be ignored, explain the effect of the regulations when registered, and understand the effect of pre-incorporation contracts, explain the role and duties of promoters, company secretary, directors, shareholders etc., describe the statutory books, records and returns that companies must keep as well as explain the rules relevant to winding up operations.

COMPANY LAW

Company law is a branch of civil law concerned with rules and procedures relevant to business formation and governance. It deals with rules of both private and public law. These rules are essential, in that, they promote and enhance participation by the various stakeholders[58] of a company; ensures accountability on the part of certain fiduciaries, notably promoters, directors, officers, receivers, managers, auditors and liquidators; safeguards the investing public and protects employees. The law of business organizations originally derived from English common law and has evolved significantly in the 20th century[59]. Company law is very broad. Our discussion will, however, be concerned with only types of business entities, formation of companies, pre-incorporation contracts, role of directors, promoters, company secretaries, members, and legal issues in the winding-up of a company.

---

58   The stakeholder view of the firm argues that there are several parties and interests involved with a company. These include shareholders, directors, employees, customers, suppliers, financiers, communities, regulators and government bodies, political groups, industry associations and trade unions, even competitors. The nature of who is a stakeholder, however, remains highly contested (Miles, 2011). The theory suggests that if a firm ignores any one of these stakeholders it will have significant problems.

59   wikipedia

TYPES OF BUSINESS ORGANIZATIONS AND COMPANIES

There are several types of business organizations. These are namely, the sole proprietorship, general partnership, limited partnership, limited liability partnership and company.

FORMING A SOLE PROPRIETORSHIP

To form a sole proprietorship in Ghana, it must be registered under the provisions of the ***Business Names Registration Act,*** (Act 151). Under a sole proprietorship the owner 'is' actually the business. He/she owns the assets and is responsible for its liabilities. Besides business registration with the Registrar General's Department, no legal formalities are required to set up this business. It is, however, not an appropriate form of business for large businesses or those involving a significant degree of risk.

FORMING A PARTNERSHIP

To form a partnership in Ghana, it must be registered under the provisions of the ***Incorporated Private Partnerships Act,*** 1962 (Act 152).

A partnership is a relationship which subsists between two or more persons carrying on a business in common with a view to earning or accumulating profit. This form of business organization, like all businesses, could be large, very large or fairly small. Most professional firms (e.g. legal and accountancy firms) find this form of business attractive. The owner 'is' actually the business. He/she owns the assets and is responsible for its liabilities. Besides registration with the Registrar General's Department, no legal formalities are usually required.

FORMING A COMPANY

To form or incorporate a company in Ghana, it must be registered under the provisions of the ***Companies Act,*** (Act 179). Incorporation is conferred by the Registrar of Companies where the Registrar is satisfied with the completed forms filed with the Registrar General's Department.

Under the Ghanaian ***Companies Act,*** (Act 179), twelve (12) kinds of companies may be formed or regulated. These are namely:

1. Ghanaian private company limited by shares
2. Ghanaian private company limited by guarantee
3. Ghanaian unlimited private company
4. Ghanaian public company limited by shares
5. Ghanaian public company limited by guarantee

6.   Ghanaian unlimited public company
7.   External private company limited by shares
8.   External private company limited by guarantee
9.   External unlimited private company
10. External public company limited by shares
11. External public company limited by guarantee, and
12. External unlimited public company

In relation to the above categories of companies, a company that is limited by shares is one which has the liability of its members limited to the amount unpaid on the shares respectively held by them. In contrast, a company that is limited by guarantee is one which has the liability of its members limited to the amount that the members may respectively undertake to contribute to the assets of the company in the event of its being wound up. On the other hand, an unlimited company is one which has no limit on the liability of its members (Section 9 of *Companies Act*).

Under Section 302 (2) an external company is a body corporate that is formed outside Ghana but which has an established place of business in Ghana.

PRIVATE COMPANIES
A private company is a company which by its regulations:

a.   Restricts the right to transfer its shares
b.   Limits the total number of its members and debenture holders to fifty
c.   Prohibits the company from making an invitation to the public to acquire shares or debentures of the company, and
d.   Prohibits the company from making an invitation to the public to deposit money for fixed periods or payable at call, whether bearing or not bearing interest.

Any other company is a public company (section 9 of Act 179).

LEGAL PERSONALITY
In law, the term person (Latin persona) means a legal entity having rights and obligations of its own which the law can enforce. Such a person may be a natural person. The company upon incorporation becomes, a legal entity separate from its shareholders, directors or managers. That is the effect of Section 24 of Act 179 and *Salomon v. Salomon* and Co Ltd (1897) AC 22 at 51. As a corporate body, a company has all the powers of a natural person.

In *Majdoub and Co Ltd v. W. Bartholomew and Co Ltd* [1962]1 GLR 122, the court held that even though a partnership had dissolved and transformed itself into a company with the partners as the shareholders of the company, a judgment awarded against the partners could not be enforced against the company because "a limited liability company is an artificially created body by statute and I think the law is entitled to recognize that artificial existence."

CONSEQUENCES OF INCORPORATION
There are a number of consequences of being a separate legal entity. They include the following:

- The first material consequence is that of limited liability. A company is fully liable for its own debts. If the company fails, the liability of the shareholders is limited to only amounts unpaid on their share capital (or any amount they have agreed to contribute if the company is limited by guarantee).
- The company has capacity to enter into contracts in its own name and therefore can sue and be sued in its own name.
- The company owns its own property.
- The company has perpetual succession, irrespective of the fate of shareholders.
- The management of a company is separated from its ownership.
- The company is subject to the requirements of the Companies Act 1963, Act 179.
- Where the company suffers an injury, it is the company itself that must take the appropriate remedial action (rule in *Foss v. Harbottle* (1843) 2 Hare 461).

LIFTING THE VEIL OF INCORPORATION
Although incorporation creates an artificial veil between the company and its shareholders, under certain circumstances a court can brush aside this veil to the identity of the shareholders. The result of lifting the veil is that the members or directors become personally liable for the company's debts. Under Section 38 of Act 179, where a company ceases to have any members and it carries on business for more than six months, every director of the company at the time shall be jointly and severally liable for the debts of the company incurred during the period.

- Sections 28 and 29 of Act 179- Failure to meet the minimum capital requirement.

- Section 26 of ***Bodies Corporate (Official Liquidation) Act*** - Fraudulent trading.

Judicial Inroads

- **Agency Relationship:** Where an agency relationship is established especially in group companies, the subsidiary company may be treated as the agent of the parent company. The veil of incorporation will, therefore, be lifted to make the parent company liable for the acts of the subsidiary. In ***Kuni v. State Gold Mining Corporation*** [1978] GLR 205, the court held the parent company liable for the acts of the subsidiary. (See also Adams v Cape Industries [1990] CH433.)
- **Sham companies:** The veil of incorporation will be lifted only where 'special circumstances exist indicating that it is a mere façade concealing the true facts'. In ***Jones v. Lipman*** (1962)1 WLR 832, the defendant contracted to sell his land and thereafter changed his mind. In order to avoid an order of specific performance he transferred his property to a company. Held: The veil was lifted to prevent the seller of a house evading specific performance. An order of specific performance was granted against him and the company to transfer the property to the buyer. (See also ***Gilford Motor Co Ltd v. Horne*** (1933)1 CH935.)
- Nationality: in times of war, it is illegal to trade with the enemy. It may be possible to lift the veil of incorporation so as to impute to a company the same nationality as its members. ***Daimler v. Continental Tyre and Rubber*** (1916)2 AC 307

PROMOTERS – ROLE AND DUTIES

A person who is or has been engaged or interested in the formation of a company is a promoter of that company (section 12 of Act 179). Persons acting in a professional capacity in the promotion of a business are not deemed to be promoters. A promoter is under a fiduciary duty to:

- Disclose any interest in transactions to the company and not to make a 'secret profit'.
- Disclose any benefit acquired to an independent board and/or to the shareholders.

If a promoter makes a secret profit, the company may:

- Rescind the contract- but this is not always possible, e.g. if a third party has acquired rights under the contract.

- Obtain damages- but this requires the company to prove loss.
- Recover the profit- the company must prove that the promoter has failed to disclose his profit from a transaction.

PRE-INCORPORATION CONTRACTS

A pre-incorporation contract arises where a person enters into a contract before a company has been registered. By section 13 of Act 179, a pre-incorporation contract may be ratified by the company after its incorporation. Upon ratification, the company becomes bound by and entitled to the benefits of that contract or that transaction as if it has been in existence at the date of that contract or other transaction and had been a party to the contract or the other transaction.

Under Ghanaian law, both corporate and natural persons can incorporate companies (section 8 of Act 179). A minimum of two directors are required, with at least one of them resident in Ghana. To register a company, there is a need to deliver to the Registrar of Companies, a copy of the proposed Regulations. The Registrar will then proceed to register the company, unless he is of the opinion that:

a. Some aspects of the Regulations do not comply with the Companies Act, or
b. The object for which the company is formed is unlawful, or
c. Any of the subscribers is an infant, or of unsound mind, or
d. Any of the directors named in the regulations is incompetent to be appointed as a director under section 182 of the code.

The following information needs to be provided:

- The proposed name of the company.
- Whether the members will have limited liability (by shares or guarantee).
- Whether the company is to be private or public.
- Details of the registered office.

If it is a company limited by shares, the following must be specified:

a. The number of shares.
b. Their aggregate nominal value.
c. How much has been paid up.

If it is a company limited by guarantee, a statement as to the maximum amount each member guarantees to contribute in a winding up. After the registration of the Regulations, the Registrar will issue a certificate under his seal certifying that the company has been incorporated. The fact of incorporation is then gazetted.

THE REGULATIONS

The Regulations contain the rules and procedures by which the company is governed and administered. The Regulations under section 21 of Act 179 constitute a contract between the company and its members (***Hickman v. Kent***); the company and its officers, between members themselves; between officers themselves, and the members and officers. An officer of the company includes a director, company secretary and employees of the company.

COMPANY DIRECTORS (s.179 - s.210)

The term "director" is defined under the Companies Act as a person appointed to direct and administer the business of a company. Company directors are accordingly those persons who are empowered by the Regulations to determine its strategic direction. Now, because in reality a company is a lifeless entity, human intrusion is absolutely required to direct its actions and determine its corporate course.

The directors are clearly those entrusted by the shareholders of the company with the final responsibility for the functioning of the company. While some of the day-to-day running of the company is generally delegated to some level of management, the ultimate responsibility for acts committed in the company's name rests with directors.

But apart from the duly appointed directors, under certain circumstances individuals who are not duly appointed as directors may, in law, be fixed with the duties and liabilities of directors. In this regard, in ***Kwapong v. Ghana Cocoa Board*** (consolidated) (1984-1986)), an Interim Management Committee (IMC) was considered as the de facto governing body of the Defendant. Also in ***Buasiako Co Ltd v. Cocoa Marketing Board*** (1982-1983), the court referred to the three-member IMC as the "directing mind" of the Cocoa Marketing Board.

The principle is that persons, who have not been duly appointed as directors, may nonetheless be saddled with the duties and liabilities of directors if:

a.   They represent (or hold themselves out) to be directors, or
b.   They knowingly allow themselves to be held out to be directors; or
c.   They issue directions or instructions that the duly appointed director are accustomed to acting upon.

Section 179 of Act 179 defines directors as persons who have been appointed to direct and administer the business of the company.

In the Court of Appeal case of ***Commodore v. Fruit Supply (Ghana) Ltd***[60] (1977), the Appeals Court considered whether or not one Attoh Quarshie was a director, and if not, whether the company had held him out as such in transacting business. On the facts, the name of a non-shareholder who had not been appointed a director was printed on the company's letterhead as a director. This person was also allowed to transact business on behalf of the company. The Court held that he was a director and that his acts bound the company unless persons with whom he dealt knew or should have known of the irregularity.

Every company must have at least two directors. The justification for this is to avoid the situation where the affairs of a company are inevitably halted by the demise of the sole director. Sanctions apply to companies that carry on business for more than 4 weeks with less than two directors. There is a prescribed fine per day imposed against the director, members and the company; and there is joint and several liability of any director and all members who are cognizant of this fact for debts and liabilities of the company that are incurred during the default period.

Unless the Regulations hold otherwise, a director need not be a member or shareholder of the company. Where the Regulations require a director to hold a specified share qualification, the director shall obtain the share qualification within two months of his appointment or within any shorter period that is specified by the Regulations.

Types of directors

- #### Managing Director

A managing director is a director to whom other directors have conferred any or all power(s) exercisable by the directors with such terms and restrictions that the board of directors deem fit (section 138 (b)). Section 4 of the First Schedule of the Companies Act defines managing director as "a director to whom it has been delegated some of the powers of the board of directors, to direct and administer the business of the company." The powers entrusted by the board to the MD could be collateral to the board's own powers. The board of directors may nonetheless revoke or vary all or any such powers conferred on the managing director. The managing director has apparent or ostensible authority to undertake commercial transaction on behalf of the directors and/or the com-

---

60   [1977] 1GLR 241

pany. But the managing director does not have the right, unless the same are conferred on him by the Regulation or by a resolution of the board or members in general meeting, to institute legal action on behalf of the company. Instituting legal action is, however, not considered to be part of the ordinary business of a company.

Section 193 (a) of the Act provides that unless the Regulations shall otherwise provide, **"the directors may from time to time appoint one or more of their body to the office of managing director..."** It is customary for a company to have only one managing director but the Act, by the above-noted formulation, permits a company to have several managing directors.

Where a company has more than one managing director, their respective work schedule should be stated. Ashanti Goldfields Company Ltd offers a case in point. Prior to its merger with AngloGold, Ashanti for instance had a managing director for strategy. In that case, it is proper for the overall head of the executive team to be referred to as Managing Director and Chief Executive Officer, i.e. MD & CEO.

For a company to be bound by its Managing Director's actions, the MD should be acting for and on behalf of the company. In some cases, it may not be enough for a person to sign a contract or document as Managing Director. That person should go further and sign for and on behalf of the company. This is because when a signor signs as the MD, it only describes his/her individual capacity or official credential.

The MD must at all times sign for or on behalf of the company. This rule arose in *Promexport International (Ghana) Ltd v. First Ghana Building Society,* [1989-90][61] in which the Court of Appeal was presented with the opportunity to explain the position. In that case, the court indicated that the description of one Raymond Okudjeto as MD does not ipso facto make the MD an agent for and on behalf of the company.

• **Acting Managing Director**

The case of an acting managing director is also important to consider. In law, an acting managing director has all the powers of the substantive managing director. The 1957 case of *West Africa Express (Ghana) Ltd v. Craig* (1963)[62], illustrates this point.

---

61   [1989-1990] GLR 395 at 398-9 (CA)
62   [2001-2002] 2 GLR 231 CC

- **Executive Director (ED):** These are often full-time employees involved in management.[63] EDs perform specific roles under a contract of service and may be distinguished by a special title such as Legal and Regulatory Director, Finance Director or Sales Director.
- **Non-Executive Director (NED):** These are usually part-time, non-employee directors, who bring outside expertise to the board. They contribute an independent view, exert control over executive directors and are subject to the same controls, liabilities and duties of executive directors.
- **Chair of Board of Directors:** This person chairs meetings of the board, acts as spokesperson for the company and has a casting vote.
- **Defacto Director:** these are directors who hold themselves out or allow themselves to be held out as directors of the company though they have not been duly appointed. A de facto director is fixed with the same duties and liabilities as if he was a duly appointed director. The person or the company may be liable to a fine. In **Commodore v. Fruits Supply Ltd** [1977]1 GLR 241, the person was held out by the company as a director and his name appeared on the company's letterhead as a director. The court held that he was a de facto director and his acts were binding on the company. Section 179(5) of Act 179 provides that if a person is described as a director of the company, that person shall be deemed to be held out as a director of that company irrespective of any qualification attached to the name.
- **Shadow directors:** These are persons on whose directions or influence the duly appointed directors are accustomed to act. In **Re Unisoft Group** [1994] BCLC 609 at 620, the court held that where a governing majority of the board is accustomed to act under the directions and instructions of the outsider, it is enough to make him a shadow director.
- **Non-Executive Director:** These are directors who hold themselves out or allow themselves to be held out as directors of the company though they have not been duly appointed. A *de facto* director is fixed with the same duties and liabilities of a duly appointed director.
- **Alternate Director(s.188):** An alternate director is a director who is appointed by a named director. The appointing director (i.e. the "appointer" or the director whose position is being filled) may appoint an alternate director in anticipation of his absence from Ghana or due to his inability to act as director. The appointment of the director must be in writing and

---

63   Section 192

signed by both the appointer and the appointee and lodged with the company. An existing director may also be appointed as alternate director. In that case, he would hold an extra vote for each appointment, but an alternate director cannot appoint another person as alternate director, the rule **delegatus non potestdelegare** applying (a delegate cannot sub-delegate). An alternate director may act for at most 6 months. Section 188 (1) provides that: 'Unless prohibited by the Regulations a director may, in respect of any period not exceeding six months in which he is absent from Ghana or unable for any period to act as a director, appoint another director or any other person approved by a resolution of the board of directors, as an alternate director.'

Minimum number of directors (s.180)
Under section 180 of Act 179, a company is required to have not less than two directors. However, the actual number of directors shall be fixed by the company's Regulations. There is a liability for a company having less than the requisite number of directors (section 180(3)).

Appointment (s.181)
The directors are appointed by shareholders (members) of the company. However, the nominee's prior consent in writing is legally required before his appointment as a director. This is to prevent people's names from being put down as directors without their knowledge and approval.

The Regulations of the company may provide for the appointment of a director or directors by a class of shareholders, debenture holders, creditors or employees of the company by ordinary resolution. The first directors should be named in the regulations. Before a person can be appointed as a director, he should have given his prior written consent. Failure to obtain the consent invalidates the appointment (**Quarcoopome v. Sanyo Electricals** [2009] SCGLR). A casual vacancy may occur through the retirement, resignation, bankruptcy, death or removal of a director. Such vacancies may be filled by the continuing directors of the company even if their number has been reduced below the number required for a quorum. A director's actions are valid notwithstanding that his appointment is defective. But upon his appointment the company must notify the Registrar of Companies within 14 days, usually by filing the prescribed form (i.e. Form 17).

Competence to be appointed director (s.182)

By Section 182 of Act 179, an infant, lunatic, body corporate, undischarged bankrupt cannot be appointed a director of a company. There are other factors, some being industry-specific.

Share qualification requirement

Ordinarily, directors are not required to hold shares in a company. The regulations of a company may however require that a director should hold a certain number of minimum shares. Where the regulations contain such a requirement, then every director is required to acquire those shares within two months after his appointment or within such shorter period as may be required by the regulations.

Removal of Directors (s.185)

Section 185 of Act 179 allows a company by ordinary resolution to remove any director notwithstanding any provision in the regulations or in any agreement with a director. Shareholders have the absolute right to determine who manages their business. *Okudzeto v. Irani Brothers* (1974) GLR

A director cannot be removed at any meeting unless not less than 35 days' notice of the intention to remove him has been given to the company. The relevant director will then be notified and given the opportunity to be heard.

One Director must be present in Ghana (s.189)

At all times, one director of the company must be in Ghana. A breach of this requirement is an offense under the Companies Act; the sanction for it is a fine for everyday the default continued. Apart from this, there is a civil disability attached. The company cannot enforce any action or any legal proceedings or any rights under its Regulations made during the defaulting period when no director of the company was in Ghana. Other parties may, however, enforce their rights against the company.

THE BOARD

The conduct of a company's business is the responsibility of the Board of Directors.[64] The Board is also the proper entity to determine that company's purpose and values. Through the directors (the individuals entrusted with the strategic decisions on the goals and objectives) the Board should determine the strategy to achieve the company's purposes and values.

---

64   Held in *Okudjeto v. Irani Brothers*

Board selection

Board selection is an important strategic undertaking. The Board should be constituted by individuals with experience and integrity, who can inject a blend of knowledge, skill, objectivity, powerful connections and commitment to the Board. Care must be taken to fuse different types of directors,each of which will bring a different asset to the Board of Directors. Executive directors have an intimate knowledge of the workings of the company. Non-executive directors could have a better understanding of the issues facing the entity and useful connections. Independent directors will add to the Board's integrity and experience.

CORE DUTIES OF THE BOARD - KING II

In August 2006, Deloitte published a boardroom brief on Directors.[65] That brief referenced the Code of Corporate Practices and Conduct contained in the King Report on Corporate Governance for South Africa 2002 (called the King II Report). King II advocates that every corporate board has a number of duties, with the following being the most fundamental:

1.   The Board should determine the company's purpose and values.
2.   The Board should exercise leadership, enterprise, integrity and judgment in directing the company so as to achieve continuing prosperity.
3.   The Board should ensure that there are procedures and practices in place to protect the company's assets and its reputation.
4.   The Board should monitor and evaluate the implementation of strategies, policies, management performance criteria and business plans.
5.   The Board should ensure that the company complies with all relevant laws, regulations and codes of best business practices.
6.   The Board should ensure that the technology and systems used in the company are adequate to run the business properly for it to compete through the efficient use of its assets, processes and human resources.
7.   The Board should identify the key risk areas and key performance indicators of the business enterprise in order for the company to generate economic profit, so as to enhance shareowner value in the long term (and stakeholder interest).
8.   The Board should regularly assess its performance and effectiveness as a whole, and that of individual directors, including the chief executive officer.

---

65   Deloitte 'The Duties of Directors: A Boardroom Brief Series Book" Updated and revised(August 2006)

9.   Finally, the Board should ensure that the company has developed a succession plan for its executive directors and senior management.

DUTIES OF DIRECTORS (s.203 – s.208 of Act 179)

Before the enactment of the *Companies Act,* 1963 (Act 179) the duties of company directors were based on common law rules and equitable principles of fiduciary duty (i.e. the legal duty to act solely in another party's interest). At common law, once a person accepted appointment as a director, he became a fiduciary in relation to the company and was obliged to display the utmost good faith towards that company in his dealings on its behalf. This common law rule has, however, been enacted into a statutory law. The duties of directors are addressed in detail in section 203 to section 208 of Act 179.

- Directors have a duty to exercise reasonable care, skill and diligence and to act in good faith in what they believed to be in the best interest of the company (Section 203 of Act 179).

  Section 203 requires that "directors of a company stand in fiduciary or trust relationship towards the company in any transaction with it or on its behalf".

  Case law: *West African Express (Ghana) Ltd v. Craig* (1963)

- **Directors have a duty to disclose interest (Section 207 of Act 179).**

  Section 207 requires that directors who have an interest in a contract or proposed contract to be entered into by the company should declare to the company the extent of their interest at the time it is raised; notice of such interest may be by letter. The notice shall, however, not be effective unless it is given at a meeting of directors, or brought up at the directors meeting where it is given earlier. No director shall be at liberty to enter into a self-interested contract until a resolution of the directors has been passed approving such a contract. Accordingly, an interested director shall not vote on such a resolution.

- **Directors have a collective duty for breach of duty (Section 209 of Act 179).**

  Section 209 requires that a director refrains from knowingly participating in any breach of directors' duty. The section provides that such a director (and any person) is liable with the offending directors to compensate the company for any loss it suffers as a result of the breach, and also account to the company for any profit made by him/her as a result of the breach. Then again the company may rescind any contract or transaction entered into between the director and the company.

- **Directors have a duty to avoid conflict of interest and duty (Section 205 of Act 179).**
  Section 205 requires that directors avoid putting themselves in a position where their duties to the company conflict with their personal interest or duties. As fiduciaries, directors should not place themselves in a position in which their judgments are likely to be biased.
  Case law: ***Addo v. Ghana Cooperative Marketing Association Ltd*** (1968)
- **Directors have a duty to act within their powers.**
  Every director has a duty to act within not outside the company's constitution, and to use his/her powers for the purpose for which they were given. If this rule is not complied with a transaction entered into will be void unless approved or ratified by the shareholders.
  Case law: ***Hogg v. Cramphorn*** (1967)
- Directors have a duty not to make secret profits or take bribes s. 203
  Case law: ***Commodore v. Fruit Supply Ghana Ltd*** (1977)
- **Directors have a duty to exercise independent Judgment (Section 203)**
  Every director has a duty to exercise independent judgment, and a
- Duty not to accept benefits from third parties.

Limitations on Powers of Directors

Their wide powers notwithstanding, directors are proscribed from the following;

a) Directors may not sell, lease or otherwise dispose of the whole or substantially the whole of the company's undertaking or assets (section 202 (1)) (a). Such major transaction require members' concurrence, and this is to protect corporate assets from unscrupulous disposal or undertaking,

b) Directors may not issue new or unused shares, other than treasury shares in the company (section 202 (1) (b)). If directors are given free reign to shares in the company, they may act irresponsibly with the company's reserve-shares. Treasury shares are however exempted because they are shares which previously had been issued and were acquired back and held by the company. Directors are thus given latitude in issuing treasury shares but not new or unissued shares.

c) Directors are not to make voluntary contribution to any charitable or other funds other than pension funds for the benefit of employees of the company or any associated company of any amount total of which in any financial year of the company will exceed the greater of:
   a. A prescribed amount or

b.   2% of the income surplus of the company at the end of the immediately preceding financial year (section 202 (1) (c)).

The rationale for this limitation on the power of directors is that company funds should not be used for voluntary and charitable causes that may boost the directors' respectability to the donees or beneficiaries but not necessarily the company's. Directors are not to issue any new or unissued shares or treasury shares to any director or past director of the company or any associated company or to the director's nominee or to any company controlled by a director (section 202 (2)).

d)   Directors may not exercise the company's power to borrow money or to charge any of its assets where the monies to be borrowed or secured, together with the amount remaining undischarged or monies already borrowed or secured, apart from temporary loans obtained from the company's bankers in the ordinary course of business, will exceed the stated capital for the time being of the company (section 202 (5)). If directors are not so prohibited, the company may be so heavily indebted and encumbered by an over-ambitious, profligate, prodigal or irresponsible board and the company and its members may realize too late that not only is it neck deep in debt but that its existence as a viable company is in jeopardy.

Corporate transactions and limitations on directors' power

A limitation on the powers of directors does not equate with a denial of the powers of the company. In order to undertake the various transactions that directors' powers are limited in undertaking, various additional measures, as described below, must be taken.

i.   An ordinary resolution of the company, signifying the approval of the majority of members of the company rather than a mere directors' decision, is required to undertake the following transactions:

a.   Where the company proposes to dispose off the whole or substantial portion of its undertaking or assets (section 201 (1)).

b.   Where the company proposes to issue a new or unissued shares (other than treasury shares) in the company (section 202 (1)).

c.   Where the company proposes to make voluntary contributions to charitable or other funds in excess of the greater of a prescribed amount of 2% of the income surplus of the preceding financial year (section 202 (1)); and

d.   Where the company proposes to exercise its power to borrow money or charge any of its assets where the money to be borrowed or secured, together with the amount remaining undischarged of monies already borrowed or secured, apart from temporary loans obtained from the company's bankers in the ordinary course of business, will exceed the stated capital for the time being of the company (section 202 (5)).

ii.   In respect of a proposed disposal of the whole or a substantial part of the company's undertaking or assets, the company's ordinary resolution must address the specific transaction proposed by the directors (section 202 (1)). A general or carte blanche resolution will not suffice.

iii.   In respect of a proposed issue of new or unissued shares (other than treasury shares) in a company, the said new or unissued shares shall first have been offered on the same terms and conditions to all existing shareholders or to all holders of the class or classes being issued in proportion as nearby as may be to their existing holdings. There are three components to this edict. The offer must first go to existing shareholders, who have a right-of-first-refusal or pre-emption right. The offer cannot be made first to strangers over the heads of shareholders. Second, the term of the offer to existing shareholders must not be different from the terms subsequently issued. More onerous terms may therefore not be imposed in the offer to existing shareholders and more generous terms subsequently offered to other or vice versa. Third, existing shareholders must be offered the proposed new shares in a number that corresponds with their existing shareholding. Let us demonstrate the proposition that new or unissued shares shall first have been offered on the same terms and conditions to all existing shareholders or to all the class or classes being issued in proportion as nearly as may be to their existing holdings. Dogbe holds 49% of the issued shares in Leele Ltd. He is a shareholder only, but not a director. Mr. and Mrs. Adei are the two directors. The Adeis have between them 51% of the shares, 25% and 26% respectively. The Adei's plan to dislodge Dobge as the single largest shareholder, although he is still in the minority. They therefore propose to issue new shares and plan to buy all of them such that Dogbe's shares will be diluted – reduced from 49% to 15%. In the above scenario, the law requires that Dogbe be offered the opportunity of buying 49% of the proposed shares of Leele Ltd, at the same price and on the same terms as may be subsequently offered.

In early 2008, Cal Bank Ltd. planned to increase its stated capital by the issuance of new shares. In a controversy that saw the resignation of the board chairman and another board member, and a maneuver to remove the managing director, the proposed new shares were offered to existing shareholders in proportion to their shareholding.

Still in respect of proposed issue of new or unissued shares (other than treasury shares) in the company, the company's ordinary resolution authorizing this issue must have been passed less than one year before the issue of the said shares (section 202 (1)). A dated resolution will not suffice.

iv. In respect of the proposed issue of any new or unissued shares or treasury shares to any director or past director of the company or any associated company or to a director's nominee or to any company controlled by a director, this can only be undertaken if the shares shall first have been offered on the same terms and conditions to all existing shareholders or to all holders of the class or classes being issued in proportion to their existing holding or, in the case of a public company, to members of the public (section 202 (2)).

Directors' Duties and Powers

Directors are vested with all powers necessary and incidental to managing and directing the company. Directors are neither agents of the shareholders, and shareholders may not by ordinary, special or even unanimous resolution instruct and direct the directors how to exercise their exclusive power (section 137 (4)). Within their exclusive spheres of authority, directors are autonomous. Directors owe, however, fiduciary, common law and statutory duties to the company. Directors' duties are akin to the duties owed by agents to their principal (section 203 (1)). Such as:

i. To avoid conflict of interest and duty (compare section 205). In *Commodore v. Fruit Supply (Ghana) Ltd* the Court of Appeal held that a director occupied a fiduciary position and therefore was precluded from entering into a binding transaction on behalf of the company in which he himself had a personal interest which conflicted or might conflict with the interests of the company because he had a fiduciary duty to protect the interest of the company.

ii. Not to make secret profits or take bribes. In *Commodore v. Fruit Supply (Ghana) Ltd* the Court of Appeal further held that the director was not entitled to keep the profit of the transaction entered into when conflicted unless the Regulations provided otherwise.

iii. To keep proper accounts. The Court of Appeal further held in *Commodore v. Fruit Supply (Ghana) Ltd* that although the *de facto* director is entitled to 50% of the company's profit, he was at the same time under legal duty, by reason of his fiduciary position, not to have mixed up his share of the proceeds with what was intended for the company. The de facto director was therefore, in law, accountable to the company for all moneys received from the appellant for the company's purposes.

iv.   To take reasonable care in the management of the company's affairs.

In *Cudjoe v. Conte Ltd,* Sarkodee-Addo JSC said (pp. 33–4):

> "Directors occupy a fiduciary position and all the powers entrusted to them are only exercisable in this fiduciary capacity. In the result, the company's assets are impressed with the qualities of a trust fund, so that they may be followed into the hands of an alliance who takes with notice of their ultra vires application. Further, where the directors make a profit as a result of their fiduciary position, they have to account to the company for it."

Both the Regulations and the Companies Act impose duties on directors, among them, to:

- Determine company mission, vision and strategy
- Decide the corporate policies
- Ensure legal compliance
- Appoint and remove key officers from the company such as the company secretary and members of top management
- Set compensations for management
- Propose dividends payable per share
- Ensure financial integrity
- Determine corporate structure

Crucial Duties of Directors:

a)   Before a company commences business, the director shall prepare or cause to be prepared a return in duplicate setting out certain particulars for filing with the Registrar (section 27). These particulars relate to the company's name, authorized business or nature of objects, names and address of auditor; physical and postal address of the company; place where the company's register of members is kept; and for companies with shares, the amount of the stated capital, the number of authorized shares for each class, and the number of issued shares for each class and amount paid thereon.

b)   Before the limited liability commences business, the director shall prepare a declaration that they fulfill the minimum capital requirement (section 28).

c)   Directors shall convene the first annual general meeting (AGM) within 18 months of incorporation (section 149 (1)). After the first AGM, the directors shall convene an AGM every year and in any event within 15months of the last AGM (section 149 (1)).

d)   The directors may convene extraordinary general meetings whenever they think fit (section 150), or if requisitioned by members (section 271 and section 297).

e)   The directors shall cause to be circulated to members and debenture holders every year the following documents (section 124): the company's financial statement (comprising of profit and loss account, balance sheets and any group accounts), the directors' report on the financial statement (section 132) and the auditors' report on the financial statement (section 133).

f)   The directors shall ensure that the company keeps proper books of account, and shall cause full and true account to be kept of moneys received and expended by or on behalf of the company and the matters and things of which sums of money have been received and disbursed. Such books of account shall be in a form sufficient to prepare proper profit and loss accounts and balance sheets (section 123).

g)   The directors shall deliver or make available to the company's auditors the books, accounts, vouchers, and any information or explanation sought by the auditors (section 136 (1)).

h)   Directors may fill a casual vacancy on the board of directors (section 180 (5)). A casual vacancy is one that occurs by any means other than by the expiration of the term of office of the director. A casual vacancy may therefore occur through resignation, removal or death of the director.

i)   The directors shall file or ensure filing with the Registrar various documents, including register of members (section 32 (6)), written contract regarding true value of shares that were not paid for wholly in cash, section 42 (2)), stated capital (section 66 (2)), court orders (section 76 and 77), charges created by the company (section 107 and 111), notice of enforcement of security by appointment of receiver or entry into possession (section 116 (2)), notice of cessation of enforcement of security (section 116 (3)),annual return within 42days of the date that the company's statement, account and report are sent to members and debenture holders (section 122), register of directors and secretary (section 197), return regarding non-Ghanaian (or external) companies (section 303 and 304).

j)   The director shall maintain or cause to be maintained at the registered office of the company various documents, including register of members (section 32 (6)), register of debenture holders (section 96 (2)), register or charges (section 117), register of directors and secretary (section 196), register of directors' holdings (section 215).

k)   The directors shall cause to be established various accounts, including a share deals accounts relating to the redemption or purchase of its shares (section 63).

l)   Every director and former director shall provide the company with notice of matters relating to himself to enable the company prepare particulars of directors' emoluments and pensions (section 128, 129, 130 (4)), particulars of amount due from officers (section 128, 129, 130 (4)), register of directors' holdings (section 215 (6)), statement of information regarding directors' interest in arrangement or amalgamation (section 233 (5)).

m)   In the event of an arrangement or amalgamation, the directors are to provide certain information to members and creditors, including a statement explaining the effects of the arrangement of amalgamation and any material interests of the directors and the effect on the directors' interest arising from the arrangement or amalgamation (section 233).

n)   For public companies, the directors or some of them shall sign and deliver a prospectus in triplicate within 6months before making an invitation to the public (section 275, 279) or a statement in lieu of prospectus within 28 days of incorporation or conversion to a public company (section 274 (1)).

o)   On winding up by way of private liquidation, the directors shall execute an affidavit (or declaration) or solvency to the effect that the directors have made a full inquiry into the affairs of the company and have satisfied themselves that the company will be able to pay its debts and liabilities in full within twelve months from the date of winding up (section 247).

p)   Being vested with the superintendence of the company, it is the directors who may institute various court proceedings on the company's behalf, including bringing an application for a confirmation order regarding the reduction of capital, shares or liability (section 76).

Directors' Meetings and Resolutions

The company's Regulations may set out a provision that relates to directors meetings. The Regulations may amplify or even vary the provisions of the Companies Act (section 200). Directors may meet in Ghana or elsewhere to dispatch business, and/or adjourn their meetings. The directors may delegate any of their powers to committees of directors and impose limits on and set regulations for the committee of directors.

Directors' meeting may be summoned by any director. Alternatively, a director may requisition the secretary to summon a meeting, in which case the secretary shall summon a directors' meeting. Directors who are absent from Ghana are not required to be served with notices of directors' meetings.

The quorum for directors' meetings is two, unless the Regulations provide otherwise. A quorum is always required, both for the commencement as well as for the continuation of the directors' meetings to conduct the general business of the company. However, the continuing directors are exempted from fulfilling the quorum requirement if the remaining number of directors is below the quorum and the continuing directors seek to increase their number or summon a general meeting.

The directors may elect one of them to be chairman and determine the period he is to hold office, but if no chairman is elected by the board, or the chairman is late for the board meeting by more than 5minutes, the directors present may choose one of their fellow directors to chair the meeting.

Attendance and voting by proxy are prohibited at directors' meetings. Matters are decided at meetings by majority vote; and should there be a tie, the chairman has a second or casting vote. A second vote occurs when the chairman voted the first time, resulting in a tie. A casting vote occurs when the chairman did not vote the first time but a tie resulted. In either case, when there is a tie, it is the chairman who breaks the tie and determines the matter by his vote.

Provision is made for directors to decide matters without the necessity of attending a board meeting. As such, a resolution in writing, signed by all the directors for the time being entitled to receive notice of a meeting of the board of directors, shall be valid and effectual as if it had been passed at a meeting of the directors duly convened and held (section 200 (j)).

Types of resolutions

A meeting can pass two kinds of resolutions. Ordinary resolutions are carried by simple majority (more than 50% percent) of valid votes cast. Special resolutions require a 75% majority of valid votes cast.

THE COMPANY SECRETARY – ROLE AND RESPONSIBILITIES

Oddly, one of the key roles in corporate governance that has received relatively less attention is that of Company Secretary. Section 190 of the *Companies Act,* (1963) Act 179, requires all companies incorporated in Ghana to appoint a Secretary.[66] The Company Secretary is an officer of the Company,[67] sharing certain legal and other responsibilities with the directors.[68] The obligatory nature of the requirement for Ghanaian companies contrasts profoundly with the English law position, where, apart from listed companies, private companies are no longer enjoined to have a Company Secretary, less so if they do not want to, unless so required explicitly by provisions in their own Articles (the Regulations).

---

66   The relevant provision s.190 provides that:

(1)   Every company shall have a secretary and if any company shall carry on business for more than six months without a secretary the company and every officer of the company who is in default shall be liable to a fine not exceeding five hundred pounds for each day that the company continues to carry on business without a secretary after the expiration of such six months.

(2)   Anything required or authorized to be done by or to the secretary may, if the office is vacant or there is for any other reason no secretary capable of acting, be done by or to any assistant or deputy secretary or any other officer of the company appointed by the directors to be acting secretary.

(3)   Unless the Regulations shall otherwise provide, the secretary shall be appointed by the directors for such term, at such remuneration and upon such conditions as they may think fit, and may be removed by them, subject however to his right to claim damages from the company if removed in breach of contract.

The appointment of the secretary may be by the board of directors, or members in a general meeting or any other person if permitted by the Regulations. The Secretary may be a body corporate, member-secretary, non-member-secretary, executive secretary or professional secretary.

67   See First Schedule 2 of the *Companies Act*

68   The First Schedule 2 of the Companies Act places the secretary on substantially equal terms to that of corporate directors, at least in regard to their duties, as officers of the company. In simple terms, company secretaries are required to discharge their duties as officers of the company to the same standard as the directors.

The Companies Act does not state any precise duties of the company secretary or recite any powers or qualifications of the secretary. In publicly traded companies, at least, anecdotal evidence suggests that the position has more often than not been held by lawyers, accountants or chartered secretaries. In an article by Professor Adams, reference is made to a KPMG and Chartered Secretaries of Australia (CSA) survey of technical backgrounds of company secretaries in 1997 and 1999; which found that increased regulation of the commercial sphere has made employment of board secretaries with a legal background a more attractive option.

APPOINTMENT
The first company secretary would usually be appointed along with the first directors of the company. Subsequently, notice of appointment of succeeding company secretaries would have to be given to the Registrar; this is done by filing Form 17, executed by one or more of the existing Directors. The company secretary provides support to the chairman and the board of directors, ensuring that regulatory and statutory requirements are met.

CORE DUTIES OF THE COMPANY SECRETARY
The duties and responsibilities of the company secretary can vary from company to company. This notwithstanding, the duties usually include, among others, the following — (a) maintenance of statutory registers (b) convening and attending board meetings and general meetings (c) drafting resolutions of directors and shareholders (d) undertaking corporate statutory filings (e) the maintenance of statutory books (f) corporate compliance review and (g) custody of corporate seal, among others. These duties should be regarded by the Company Secretary as overarching duties for which compliance is mandatory.

MAINTAINANCE OF STATUTORY REGISTERS
Company secretaries are responsible for registry functions within the company; the maintenance of statutory registers, which includes the register of members, register of company charges, register of directors and secretary, registrar of debenture holders, etc., have accompanying sanctions for non-compliance.

Register of Members (Section 32)
Section 32 requires every company to keep in Ghana register of its members or shareholders. This register must show the following true particulars:

i.   name and address of each member

ii.   statement of shares held by each member with distinguishing numbers

iii.   amount paid on each share

iv.   date of entry on the Register, and

v.   date of cessation of membership.

Section 32 (5) requires every company to send to the Registrar for registration notice in the prescribed form of the place where its register of members is kept and every company shall within 28 days of any change in the place at which the register is kept notify the Registrar of it or in default pay a fine for each day of the default. Members of the company may inspect the Register free of charge. However, non-members may within ten days inspect the Register upon payment of a minute fee.

Register of Directors and Secretaries (Section 196)

Every company is also required to maintain at its registered office a register of Directors (including substitute directors but excluding alternate directors) and Secretaries both past and present. The Register must contain the names (and former names where applicable), the residential address, business occupation if any, and the particulars of any other directorships held. The Company Secretary must, however, notify the Registrar within twenty-eight (28) days of any alteration to particulars on its Register. If a company defaults or fails to file a form 17 notification of a change among its directors or secretary that default will render the company and every officer of the company in default, liable to a fine for each day the default continues.[69] In practice, this requirement often suffers non-compliance. The names of directors must be exhibited on the company's letterhead, but are oftentimes not. Anecdotal evidence suggests that the reason for non-compliance is because the Registrar is perceived as weakened by lack of resources and, thus, often incapable of any serious monitoring and enforcement.

Register of Directors' Holdings (Section 215)

Section 215 of the *Companies Act* also requires every company to maintain a Register showing each director's interests in shares and debentures. The task of opening the register falls on the Company Secretary. It is the duty of the Company Secretary to enter this information within twenty-eight (28) days of such acquisition. When a publicly-listed company receives notification from a director, it must, before the end of the following day, notify the Ghana Stock Exchange

---

69   See s. 197 (4)

which may publish the information. The Register of Directors' Holdings must be produced at the commencement of any general meeting and kept opened and accessible during the pendency of the meeting to all persons in attendance, and to be made accessible at the company's office to the members and auditors free of charge.

Register of Charges (Sections 107 and 117)
Sections 107 and 117 require every company to register with the Registrar all charges created by the company within twenty-eight (28) days of its creation. The repercussions of non-registration of the company charges are stern. This is because unless registered, the charge is void as security on the company's property. This however does not imply that the company is not liable for the repayment of any money that was to have been secured by the unregistered charge. The Act points out that when a charge becomes void, the money secured thereby immediately becomes payable despite whatever contrary intentions may have been stated in any contract.

STATUTORY FILINGS
Companies cannot merely issue a letter to notify the Registrar that the firm has changed or wishes to change the address of its registered office or that alterations have occurred among the directors or secretaries or their particulars. Every company must file specific statutory forms set out in the ***Companies Prescribed Forms Instrument,*** 1963 (LI 289) and submit them within a stipulated time frame. As indicated supra, the Company secretary must inform the Registrar of any significant changes in the company's structure or management, for example of appointment or resignation of any director or directors.

BOARD AND SHAREHOLDER MEETINGS
The responsibility to arrange meetings and notify the directors, members and auditors falls on the Company Secretary. This involves the issue of proper notices, preparation of agenda, circulation of relevant papers, the taking and production of minutes to record the business transacted and the resolution passed. For example he or she must ensure that the company provides at least twenty-one days written notice of an Annual General Meeting (AGM) and fourteen days written notice of a meeting which is neither an AGM or a meeting to pass special resolution. The Company Secretary must ensure that the company fulfils its obligation to supply copies of the final accounts to members, debenture holders and any person who is entitled to receive notice of general meetings at least

twenty-one days prior to the meeting. Debrah rightly observes that a company may provide in its Regulations for a period longer but not shorter than the twenty-one days stipulated by law. It is instructive to note that members may call any meeting described as a general meeting if they so decided and it will be a meeting properly so-called despite a shorter notice. Also, members holding 95% of the shares may also call a meeting at shorter notice where the holders of the 95% constitute a majority in number of the shareholders. It is the Company Secretary who would administer adherence to all these provisions of the Act.[70]

BOARD AND SHAREHOLDER RESOLUTIONS

Companies make decisions by resolutions. Under section 176 of the Act, certain resolutions have to be filed with the Registrar within twenty-eight days of their passage. Examples of such resolutions include all special resolutions, and all resolutions to which the required proportion of a class of shareholders have given their written consent to but which would otherwise have required a special resolution of the class. The compliance behavior of even listed companies with these requirements remains a matter of conjecture.

MINUTES TAKING

The Company Secretary must be abreast with the law and procedure relevant to calling and holding meetings. The tasks associated with meetings may be categorized into preparation for the meeting, procedures for holding meeting and voting, minutes taking and preparation of procedural irregularities. A Company Secretary must be adept at procedural requirements involved in holding a meeting, inclusive of the rules of debates, the procedure relating to periods of notice, the required quorums and majorities needed to pass different types of resolutions, the tabling of motions and amendments, taking of polls, elections and ballots, so as to be able to assist the chair.

CORPORATE RECORDS

Public companies, in particular, have an obligation to ensure that people entitled to do so can inspect company records. For example, members of the company and members of the public, i.e. non-shareholders are entitled to a copy of the company's Register of Members. Members of the company are also entitled to inspect the minutes of its general meetings and to have copies of these minutes for a minimal fee.

---

70   Op cit

COMPANY SEAL AND DOCUMENTS

The Company Secretary is responsible for official custody and use of the company seal. He is also responsible for creating and maintaining the company's registered office as the address for its official communications, ensuring that all the company's business stationary bears its name, registered number, country of registration and registered address. The Company Secretary must also ensure the security of the company's legal documents, including its Certificate of Incorporation and Regulations. He must institute or decide on company policy for document filing and retention.

REGULATORY COMPLIANCE

Section 122 of the Act makes the filing of annual returns a statutory duty failure of which the company is liable to the payment of penalties and prosecution. Further under section 261, the Registrar can strike the names of delinquent companies off the register, and thereafter publish same in the gazette and dailies. For serious companies, non-compliance could carry considerable regulatory and reputational harm. Other documents which must be filed include the financial statements detailing assets and liabilities, director's report and the auditor's report, among others.

CORPORATE ADVISORY DUTIES

The company secretary provides advisory services to the board members about the company generally.

COMMON LAW DUTIES OF THE COMPANY SECRETARY

The company secretary is subject to a number of duties at common law and equity in addition to any other duties. At common law, the Company Secretary has a duty to act in good faith; that is, to act in the best interest of the company and not exploit his or her position to make gains at the expense of the company. The Secretary must also exercise due care and skill. If not, in certain cases, he/she could be held liable for losses resulting from negligent performance of those duties. As an employee of the company, the company secretary is obliged to follow instructions, and not at liberty to use the company's records, such as trade secrets or lists of customers which are classified as confidential, for his or her own purposes.

The Company Secretary is chief administrative officer of the company. In **Panorama Developments (Guilford) Ltd v. Fidelis Furnishing Fabrics Ltd**[71] the Secretary of the Defendant Company entered into a number of contracts for the hire of cars. The cars were ostensibly to be used to collect important customers from Heathrow Airport, but the Secretary used them for his own private purposes. Counsel for the Defendants cited a passage of Lord Esher MR in the 1887 case of **Barnett Hoares v. South London Tramways.** The Learned Judge had said that "a secretary is a mere servant; his position is to do what he is told and no person can assume that he has any authority to represent anything at all". However, on appeal to the Court of Appeal it was held that the Defendant Company was liable. Lord Denning, sitting in the English Court of Appeal, stated as follows, "…times have changed. A Company secretary is a much more important person nowadays than he was in 1887. He is an officer of the company with extensive duties and responsibilities…. He is no longer a mere clerk…. He is entitled to sign contracts connected with the administrative side of a company's affairs, such as employing staff and ordering cars and so forth."

LISTING-RELATED DUTIES OF THE COMPANY SECRETARY
Generally, listing on the Stock Exchange carries with it a regime of tenuous new obligations. These obligations arise out of the protective duty which the Stock Exchange itself imposes due to its inherent duty to protect investors and the public. To meet this duty, and maintain the respect and quality of the market, Stock Exchange rules oftentimes require listed entities to adhere to Listing Rules and to provide timely information so that investors can make well-informed decisions. Listing Rules aim to ensure continuing obligations to ensure that all information that has the ability to impact the prices of securities when the information gets into the public domain are made available.

Disclosure issues
Their timely disclosure is vital if investors are to retain confidence in the stock market. Part VII of the Listing Regulations of the Ghana Stock Exchange lists matters which have to be publicly disclosed within a specified time, some immediately and others by a specified deadline. Under Part VII public announcements are mandatory in the following situations:

---

71   (1971) 2 QB 711, (1971) 3 All ER CA

a. significant acquisitions or disposals
b. major developments in the company's business activities, such as new products, contracts or customers
c. decisions to pay dividends
d.   issues of securities and changes in the company's capital structure and financial statements of fully audited annual returns
e. a change in directors or a change in the functions or executive responsibilities of a director; and
f. changes in the interests of major shareholders and directors.

Where a company is listed on more than one Stock Exchange, special procedures could apply to ensure that announcements are made simultaneously to all the Exchanges on which they are listed.

Assisting specialist committees

Board accountability and performance is a recurring issue. The creation of specialist sub-committees at board level is becoming normative. Sub-committees may include the audit committee, compensation committee, corporate governance committee, finance committee, regulatory, compliance & government affairs committee, among others. The responsibility for ensuring the efficient implementation of such procedures rests with the Company Secretary.

CHAPTER 15 – QUICK REVIEW

The essence of a company is that it has a legal personality distinct from the people who create it. Legal personality continues regardless of changes in management. The company is formed by the process of 'incorporation'. Once incorporated, a company has both legal personality and legal capacity.

A company is protected by the 'veil of incorporation' and the identity of the members is only ascertainable when the 'veil' is lifted (**Salomon v. Salomon** [1897] AC 22). The company directors and shareholders may contract with it (**Lee v. Lee's Air Farming Ltd** [1961] AC 12). Directors and shareholders do not incur liability for the company's defaults, nor are they entitled to its property. Directors owe their duties to the company – **Percival v. Wright** [1902] 2 Ch 421. Directors have fiduciary duties (duties to act in good faith). Their duties are not to make secret profit, to act for a proper purpose, to act with care and skill, and to have regard in the performance of their functions, to the interests of employees as well as members.

15. The Law of Agency

Structuring Business Activity

LEARNING OUTCOMES

This topic examines the nature of agency, its creation, duties and termination – how the agency authority is acquired and defined. After reading this topic, you should be able to define the role of the agent and offer examples of such relationships, paying particular attention to partners and company directors; creation of agency relationship, capacity of agents, rights and duties of agents, agent's authority, the undisclosed principal and settlements between agent and principal and termination of agency. You should be able to also define the authority of the agent, explain the potential liability of both the principal and agent, among others.

Nature of Agency

Agency arises when a person is authorized to act for another person in the making of legal relations with a third party. The agent is a person who is entrusted with another person's business. Take companies for example. They are, in reality, just lifeless artificial persons. All their acts must necessarily be done for them by natural persons; these natural persons are referred to as agents of the company. A company's officer is an agent of that company. It can be seen that the function of an agent is to act on behalf of his principal in establishing contractual relations between that principal and third parties. For obvious reasons, agency is a necessary part of commercial life.

When an Agent makes a contract for the principal, the rights and obligations under the contract continue with the principal and the third party; the agent has no rights or liabilities under that contract. In law, however, the relationship could be far more complicated than that, as the principal could be jointly and severally liable with his agent for torts (that is, civil wrongs) committed by the agent within the scope of his authority.

TYPES OF AGENTS

Partners who run a practice together, company directors, promoters, factors (i.e. mercantile agents such as car dealers, etc.), brokers (e.g. stock brokers, insurance brokers, etc.), auctioneers and commercial agents are examples of agents.

FORMATION OF AGENCY

The relationship between principal and an agent is a consensual one. No one can claim to be another person's agent unless he has that other person's consent. The consent may be express or implied.

Express Agreement

This is where the agent is expressly appointed by the principal; this may be done orally or in writing. An agent who is expressly appointed by the principal has actual authority of the principal to act on his/her behalf.

Implied Agreement

An agency relation may be implied by the conduct of the parties or by the relationship. For instance, if an employee's duties include making contracts for the employer, then they are, by implied agreement, the agent of the employer for this purpose.

Ratification of the Agent's act

An agency relationship may be created retrospectively. This happens where the agent has no authority but purports to make a contract with third parties on the principal's behalf and the principal later ratifies expressly or impliedly what the agent has done.

Conditions for ratification:
- The principal must have existed at the time the contract is made by the agent
- The principal must have the legal capacity at the time the contract is made
- Ratification must take place within a reasonable time
- The ratification of the contract must be done in its entirety
- The ratification is communicated to the third party clearly

FORMATION OF AGENCY AGREEMENT WITHOUT CONSENT

An agency may be created, or an agent's authority could be extended, without express content. This happens by estoppel, when a principal holds out a person to be his/her agent, and when there is an agent of necessity.

Implied agreement

An agency that is created by implied agreement could result in an agent assuming even more implied authority than what the principal might have consented to.

Agent by estoppel

An agency relationship could be formed by implication where a principal holds a person as an agent to third parties, even though neither the principal nor the agent agrees to formally form such a relationship. In that case the principal is estopped from denying the agent's ostensible authority, thus the name, "agent by estoppel."

Agent of necessity

On certain rare occasions, in emergency situations, it becomes crucial for a person to take action on behalf of another. In such situations, that person becomes an agent of necessity.

CAPACITY OF AGENTS

An agent must have contractual capacity. It is not necessary for someone to have full contractual capacity in order to be the agent of another person; a minor (one under the age of 18) can effectively bring about contractual relations between his principal and a third party.

However, a minor can only appoint an agent to make a contract on his behalf if the contract is one which he could validly make himself, e.g. a contract to buy necessaries.

Since the agency relationship is a personal one, the death, mental incapacity or bankruptcy of either the principal or the agent (assuming the agent is unfit to continue his duties) brings the contract to an end and notice of such event to the other party is immaterial.

In *Young v. Toynbee*[72] a solicitor started legal proceedings on behalf of a client. The client was later certified insane. Ignorant of this, the solicitor continued to act for him and took certain steps on behalf of the client in the litigation. It was held that the solicitor as agent was liable to the third party for breach of warranty of authority, i.e. purporting to have an authority which he no longer had by reason of his principal having become insane.

---

72   (1901)1 KB 215

AUTHORITY OF THE AGENT

If an agent acts within the scope of his or her authority, any contracts they make is binding on the principal and third party. The extent of the agent's authority may be express, implied or ostensible. It is important to note that implied and express authority are both forms of actual authority.

Express authority

This type of authority is explicitly given to the agent to perform specific tasks. It is created by words, either in writing or orally. No particular form is required but the agent may be appointed by a deed, called a Power of Attorney.

Implied authority

Without express authority, authority may be implied from the nature of the agent's activities. The agent cannot contravene the principal's express instructions.

Ostensible authority

The ostensible or apparent authority of an agent is what the principal represents to third parties. In that regard, an agent with implied or express authority can be held to have much broader authority.

Ratification of authority

Where A has no authority but purports to contract with a party third on the principal's behalf, the principal may later ratify the contract and the ratification then relates back to the making of the contract by the agent.

Kelner v. Baxter (1866) LR 2 CP 174

In this case, the promoters of a hotel attempted to enter into a contract on behalf of the hotel – a yet unformed company. It was held that the company could not ratify the contract after the incorporation and accordingly the promoters, as agents, were personally liable on the contract.

- The principal must have legal capacity to make the contract, i.e. it is not possible for minors to ratify a contract even though it was made in their name.
- Contract was made expressly on behalf of principal, i.e. an undisclosed principal cannot ratify a contract.
- Ratification must be done within a reasonable period of time.

- Principal must adopt the whole of the contract, i.e. he/she cannot pick and choose which parts of the contract to adopt but they must accept all of its terms.

Agency of necessity
The master of a ship, in times of emergency, may contract for provisions and urgent repairs and bind the owner of the ship to such a contract.

THE RIGHTS AND DUTIES OF AGENTS
Common law implies a number of rights and obligations as between an agent and his principal. These are implied terms of the agency agreement and are subject to express terms of the agreement.

Rights of Remuneration
An agent is only entitled to remuneration if that has been agreed with the principal. However, even if there is no express agreement that the agent should be paid for services, the court may imply a term giving him a right to remuneration.

Right of Indemnity
Subject to any express terms in the agency agreement, an agent has a right to claim from his principal an indemnity against all expenses or loss incurred in acting on the principal's behalf.

Rights of Lien
An agent who is entitled to claim an indemnity and remuneration or both from his principal may exercise a lien on any goods belonging to the principal which are in his lawful possession as an agent until his claims are met.

Duty to obey instructions of his principal
Whether an agent is acting gratuitously or not, if he proceeds to carry out the agency, he must do so as agreed and comply with his principal's lawful instructions and is liable in damages to his principal if he does not. An agent does not commit any breach of duty if the principal gives an order in such uncertain terms as to be susceptible of two different meanings and the agent bona fide accepts one of them and acts upon it.

To exercise duty with care and skill
Even a gratuitous agent must exercise duty of care and skill. The duty of an agent to exercise due care and skill could come into conflict with his duty to obey his

principal's lawful instructions. Normally, if an agent obeys his principal's lawful instructions, he will not be liable even though following those instructions is against the principal's best interest.

Duty not to delegate duty

Unless expressly or impliedly authorized by the principal to delegate the work to another person, an agent owns a duty to act personally. Where the principal expressly gives authority to delegate, delegation is, of course, permissible. If he is in contravention of this duty, the principal is not bound by any contract signed on his behalf by the sub-agent, and the agent is liable for breach of duty.

Duty to avoid conflicts of interest

When acting for the principal, an agent must not allow his own personal interests to come into conflict with the interests of his principal. If the agent has any personal interest that might conflict with his principal's interest, he must disclose it and the principal must consent to the agent continuing to act for him. If the agent breaks this duty, his principal may set aside any transaction effected by the agent and claim any profit made by the agent.

Duty not to make secret profit

Similarly, any agent who uses his position as agent to acquire a benefit for himself is in breach of his duty of good faith.

Duty not to take a bribe

A bribe is a secret profit; it is a payment to agent by a third party who knows the agent is acting as an agent, the payment being kept secret from his principal. Once a bribe is established there is an irrebutable presumption that it was given with an intention to induce the agent to act favorably to the payer.

Duty not to misuse confidential information

It is a breach of good faith if the agent uses information, acquired while acting as agent, for his own personal advantage or for the benefit of a third party. This applies even after the agency ceases.

Duty to account

There is a duty on the agent to keep proper accounts of all transactions he enters into on his principal's behalf, and to keep the money involved in the agency apart from his own.

TERMINATION OF AGENCY

Termination by act of parties

- The parties to an agency contract may at any time mutually agree to bring it to an end. There is normally a right in both the principal and the agent unilaterally to revoke the agency contract at any time before the agency has been completely performed by giving notice.
- Revocation requires no formality so that even a deed containing a power of attorney can be revoked orally. However, such unilateral withdrawal or revocation of agent's authority may be a breach and the principal can be made liable in damages to the agent for such breach.

Termination by operation of law

In Toynbee where a Solicitor started legal proceedings on behalf of a client, and the client was later certified as insane and yet the Solicitor continued to act for him in litigation, it was held that the Solicitor agent was liable to the third party for breach of warranty of authority, i.e. purporting to have an authority which he no longer had by reason of his principal having become insane.

CHAPTER 15 – QUICK REVIEW

An agency relationship is a fiduciary relation which results from the consent by one person to act on behalf of another.

An agency relationship could be based on express or implied agreement that the agent will act for the principal, or by a confirmation by the principal of an act performed or entered into on his or her behalf by another, or by estoppel or by operation of the Law. The agent may possess express authority or Implied Authority: actual authority, apparent authority. Agents owe duties to the principal such as a duty of loyalty, obedience, accountability, performance, and notification. The principal also has duties to the agent, among them, a duty of compensation, reimbursement, indemnification, cooperation, and a duty to provide safe working conditions.

Agency relationships may, however, terminate by the act of the parties, operation of law, death or incompetence, impossibility of performance, bankruptcy of the principal or agent.

16. Sale of Goods Law

The regulation of sales in commercial life

LEARNING OBJECTIVES

What is the role of law in the sales and marketing process? How does the law affect sales? If a truckload of sugar is destroyed by fire in mid-delivery, who owns the goods, and who therefore bears the loss if they are destroyed? If goods are to be paid for within 30 days of sale, does the 30 days begin upon delivery or at some earlier point in time? Who owns a completed custom-built machine that is yet to be delivered? Could possession of goods without ownership confer obligations or rights?

After studying this chapter, you should have a meaningful understanding of the meaning of sale of goods, the rights of the seller and buyer in a contract of sales, the legal obligations associated with sales, the rules on transfer of property and risk in goods sold, among others.

SALE OF GOODS LAW

The law governing sale of goods is a specialized branch of the law of contract. It is governed by statute, and where statutory law is inadequate, by the common law rules of contract.

In Ghana, the primary statute governing sale of goods transactions is the ***Sale of Goods Act,*** 1962, (Act 137).[73] Section 80 of the Act permits Common law and Customary law rules, but only to the extent that they are not inconsistent with provisions of the Act.

Meaning of Sale of Goods

Section (1) of Act 137 defines a sale of goods transaction as:

"A contract whereby the seller agrees to transfer the property in goods to the buyer for a consideration called the price, consisting wholly or partly of money."

---

73   The Act also applies to contracts made on behalf of the Republic.

A sale agreement is thus, first and foremost, a contract. In a contract for sale of goods, there are three main ingredients:

a) the subject matter must be goods (as defined within the Act), over which
b) the seller has title or ownership, and which
c) he or she agrees to transfer for a consideration from the buyer which must fully or partly be monetary in nature.

By virtue of Section 1(4) of the Act[74], a contract of sale may or may not be subject to a condition precedent, subsequent or absolute. This means that the parties can subject their contract of sale of goods to certain mandatory terms. For instance, they can agree that the price of the goods would be subject to the prevailing interbank exchange rate.

CONTRACT FOR SALE OF GOODS

A contract for the sale of goods is a contract in which a seller agrees to transfer ownership of goods to a buyer for a consideration called price. This consideration may be fully or partly money. (See *Nanor v. Auto Parts* (1992) 2GLR 273.)

A contract for the sale of goods may be oral (that is by word of mouth), written or could be inferred from the conduct of the parties. An oral contract is relatively less time consuming and less costly. Its obvious disadvantage is that it may be relatively difficult to prove the terms of such a contract in times of dispute over the existence and scope. The common law rules of contract in relation to capacity govern contracts for the sale of goods in Ghana.

What is not a contract sale of goods

Not every contract involving goods is a sale transaction. As a general rule:

a) Where the transfer of ownership of goods is in return for payment or consideration in the form of goods, the transaction is not a sale transaction, but a barter
b) Where the ownership of goods is transferred for free, the ensuing transaction is not a sale transaction but a gift
c) Finally, where goods are given out to a particular person for a particular purpose at the end of which the goods are to be returned to the owner, the ensuing transaction is not a sale transaction but a bailment.

---

74   This Section provides expressly that "A contract of sale may be absolute or conditional."

Contractual capacity

To form a valid and enforceable contract, however, both parties must have capacity. Persons aged 21 years who have a sound mind have legal capacity to contract. Companies and Partnerships equally have legal capacity to contract. However, where one of the parties to the sale contract is a minor, the goods in respect of which the contract is formed must be "necessaries" in which case, the infant must pay a reasonable price. Under section 2(3) "necessaries" are defined as "goods suitable to the condition of life of the person to whom they are delivered and to his actual requirement at the time of delivery."

DEFINITION OF GOODS

The Act defines goods to mean movable property of every description. Immovable property such as land and buildings and interest in land are not goods. However, crops or plants and other things attached to or forming part of land which can be severed before sale may be described as goods.

Types of goods

The *Sale of Goods Act* categorizes goods into unascertained, ascertained and future goods.

Unascertained goods

These are goods which the parties have not identified and agreed upon, before the formation of the contract, as goods which they intend to buy or sell.

Ascertained goods

These are goods which the parties have clearly identified and agreed upon, before the formation of the contract, as goods which they intend to buy or sell. Ascertained goods are clearly marked, and identification can take several forms including registration. Registration can render goods specific. In this regard, a registered vehicle may be identified by specific registration number, and therefore can be termed as an identified good.

Future goods

These are goods that do not yet exist at the time of the contract. Such goods are yet to be manufactured, grown or acquired.

Price

Price is the consideration for the transfer of goods under a contract of sale, which may be money or partly money. Price may be fixed and agreed to by the parties themselves or determined by a course of dealing between the parties, but where none of this apply, then the buyer must pay a reasonable price.

OBLIGATIONS OF THE SELLER

a) **Obligations of the seller to deliver the contract goods**

The Act provides that "in a sale of Specific goods, the fundamental obligation of the seller is to deliver those goods identified and agreed upon with the buyer." This implies that for ascertained goods, a seller commits a fundamental breach if he fails to deliver the goods which have been identified and agreed upon under the contract.

b) **Obligations of the seller to deliver the right quantity**

Every seller has a duty to supply the right quantity, which is the quantity agreed upon under the contract. The rules are that:

- Where the seller delivers less than the quantity contracted for, the buyer has a right to either accept the quantity delivered or reject it.

- Where the seller delivers more than the contract quantity, the buyer may not reject all the goods delivered by reason only of the excess quantity. The buyer may accept only the quantity contracted for. He can, however, sue the seller and recover the cost (if any) involved in separating the excess goods from what he accepted. On the other hand, he may choose to accept all the goods delivered and pay the contract price for the excess goods.

- Where the seller delivers both contract type goods and non-contract type goods less than the contract quantity, the buyer may reject all the goods delivered. However, he may rather choose to accept all the goods delivered and pay a reasonable price for the non-contract goods. Otherwise, he may accept the contract goods and reject the non-contract goods and sue for the cost (if any) of separating the contract goods from non-contract goods.

- Where the contract goods are either of the right quantity or more than the contract quantity, the buyer may not reject all the goods delivered: he may accept all the contract goods and where the contract goods exceed the contract quantity, he should pay the contract rate for the excess he may accept only the contract quantity and reject the excess contract goods and the non-contract goods and sue for the cost (if any) of separating the accepted goods from delivered goods paying the contract rate for the excess contract goods, if any, and a reasonable price for the non-contract goods. The only time that the buyer can reject is when the goods are less than the contract quantity.

c) **Obligations of the seller in relation to existence of the goods**

By virtue of section 9 "in a contract for sale of specific goods there is an implied condition on the part of the seller that the goods are in existence at the time when the contract is made." There is also an implied warranty that the seller will have a right to sell the goods.

d) **Obligations of the seller where goods are sold by sample**

The legal obligation of a seller where goods are actually sold by sample is provided for under section 8 (ii) of the *Sale of Goods Act, 1962.* The section provides that "in a sale of unascertained goods the fundamental obligation of the seller is to deliver to the buyer goods substantially corresponding to the description or sample by which they were sold."

Section 12 provides that where the contract is one of sale by sample (whether or not the sale is by description as well as by sample) then the seller is under a legal duty to supply goods which substantially match the sample.

e) **Obligations of the seller in relations to quality**

There is also an implied condition that goods supplied by the seller to the buyer are free from any material defects not declared or known to the buyer before or at the time the contract was made.

Where the goods involved are not of the type normally supplied by the seller in the ordinary course of his business, the parties can, in the agreement, provide that this condition will not apply. The implied condition under section 13 (i) (a) will not also apply in each of the following cases:

i. Where the buyer examined the goods in respect of defects which should have been revealed by reasonable examination.

ii. Where the buyer, in the case of sale by sample, has examined the sample for defects which could have been discovered by a reasonable examination of the sample.

iii. Where the seller does not normally sell that type of goods in the ordinary course of business and the defect is of a kind that he could, by reasonable examination, have been aware of it. The rule case of *Thornett v. Beers* (1919) applies.

Thornett v. Beers (1919) K B p 486

Facts: B wanted to purchase a quantity of vegetable glue from S. He went with S to the warehouse where the goods, which were in barrels, were stored for the purposes of inspection. Every facility was offered to B for inspection but being pressed for time, B did not have any of the barrels opened. He merely looked at the outside of the barrels and said that he believed that the glue was of the right quality. When the glue was delivered, it was found to be defective (not of merchantable quality).

Held: It was held that B had examined the glue and that since the examination could have led to the discovery of the defect, then the implied condition did not apply.

Where the defect is such that the buyer could not have discovered it through reasonable examination, the implied condition would still be applicable, and it is irrelevant whether the buyer examined the goods or not.

Godley v. Perry (1960) 1 WLR

Facts: In *Godley v. Perry* (1960) 1 WLR, a father bought a catapult for his son. When the boy first used it, it broke. There was evidence that the defect was not discoverable on first examination.

Held: It was held that the seller was liable.

f) **Obligations of the seller in relations to fitness for intended purpose**

In Ghana, sellers of goods sold have a legal duty to supply goods which are reasonably fit for their intended purpose(s). Under the ***Sale of Goods Act, 1962*** where the goods are of a description normally sold by the seller in the ordinary course of his business and the buyer expressly or by implication makes known the purpose for which the goods are required, there is an implied condition that the goods supplied are reasonably fit for that purpose. Where, for example, a buyer specifies that he wants to buy a particular type of computer but does not indicate its memory size and speed, then the implied condition would not apply if the seller delivers any type. By virtue of section 13 (2), however, the implied condition as to fitness of goods may be avoided by the parties if they provide a contrary provision in the agreement; in that case the exclusion clause must be brought to the notice of the buyer before the contract is executed, only then can the seller exclude his or her liability.

Where by the usage of the trade there are established warranties and conditions as to quality and fitness for particular purposes in respect of goods sold in a particular trade, these warranties and conditions would apply. Note that under section 13 (5) a seller's obligation as to quality and fitness of goods sold cover not only the goods themselves, but also extend to even the boxes, tins, bottles or other containers in which the goods are delivered. The case of ***Geddling v. Marsh*** (1920) I KB 668 is very illustrative of this rule.

Geddling v. Marsh (1920)

Facts: B bought a drink from S. After she had consumed the contents and was replacing the bottle in the crate, the bottle exploded and injured her.

Held: It was held that the seller was in breach because the duty as to quality and fitness extended to the bottle. That the goods must be reasonably fit for the intended purpose means that the seller must supply the right specifications where: the buyer made known to the seller the real purpose of the goods and the buyer was clear and precise in his offer.

The other obligations that arise include:

- Obligations of the seller who sells in the ordinary course of business
- Obligations of the seller who does not sell in the ordinary course of business
- Obligations of the seller in relation to the right to sell
- Obligations of the seller where goods are sold by description

Duties of the buyer under a contract of sale of goods

The buyer of goods in Ghana has two primary legal obligations. These are:

(a) to pay the price of the good(s), and
(b) to accept delivery of the goods sold.

Unless the parties agree otherwise, provisions as to time for accepting delivery are not a condition of the contract. Similarly, unless there is a contrary intention, the buyer is not under any legal obligation to accept delivery by installment.

TRANSFER OF PROPERTY AND RISK IN GOODS

Transfer of property

Transfer of property or ownership of goods is very fundamental to sales transactions as it has an impact on a number of business concerns, especially risk transfer.

Transfer of property means the transfer of title or ownership in the goods from the seller to the buyer. The type of goods, however, determines the rules governing transfer of property. There are, as stated earlier, three classifications of goods, namely:

- Specific goods
- Unascertained goods
- Goods delivered on sale or return basis (specific or unascertained).

Rules on Transfer of property in Specific goods

As a general principle, property in specific goods passes at any time the parties intend it to pass. This implies that in the absence of any stipulation by the parties as to when property will pass, property is deemed to pass at the time when the goods are delivered.

Unascertained goods

As a general principle, property in unascertained goods passes only when the goods have been ascertained. Ascertained is defined to cover the setting aside, the separation, earmarking or final preparation, before the goods are delivered to the buyer. At common law it has been held that where ascertainment has not taken place a buyer could be liable for stealing. The case of ***R v. Tideswell*** (1905) illustrates this point.

R v. Tideswell (1905)

Facts: T was in the habit of going to G's company to buy various unascertained goods. In collusion with H, T obtained more goods ascertained for him than he was actually entitled to – as in, T was entitled to 10 tons of the goods but he made it weigh eleven and half tons. Subsequently, T was charged with the difference of one and half tons. He contended that the property in its entirety (eleven and half tons) passed to him the moment the goods were ascertained and that he could not accordingly be charged with stealing.

Held: It was held that only 10 tons passed to him on ascertainment. Accordingly, the one and half did not. Therefore, he was liable.

Section 26 (3) Goods sold "on sale or return basis"

Transfer of property in Goods sold "on sale or return basis" passes under the following conditions unless a contrary intention appears:

- Where the buyer signifies his approval.
- Where he does an act adopting the transaction and
- Where the buyer neither signifies his approval nor adopts the transaction but merely retains the goods without giving notice of his rejection. If time has been fixed for the return of the goods, property passes on the expiration of such time. Where no time has been fixed, then property passes within a reasonable time.

Section 27 Transfer of Risk

Risk refers to loss, damage, or deterioration to the goods which form the subject of the contract of sale. In practical terms, the risk remains with the seller at the beginning of the contract by transfers to the buyer. A number of rules apply:

- **Rule 1**
  When a contract of sales occurs, risk in the goods is transferred to the buyer at a date or time when the goods are ascertained or passed, regardless of whether the goods are ascertained or unascertained.

- **Rule 2**
  Where no such intention is evident, risk in the goods is transferred at the same time as the property in the goods passes from the seller to the buyer.

- **Rule 3**
  Where delays occur in delivery of the goods, rules 1 and 2 will generally be inapplicable. In cases of delay, the party responsible for the delay bears the risk for the loss, damage or deterioration which might not have occurred but for the delay. Thus in **Stern v. Vickers** [1923] S sold 120,000 gallons of spirits out of 200,000 gallons stored in a tank to B. S issued a delivery order to B but did not act on the order for some time such that the spirits deteriorated, although the spirits would not have deteriorated had B acted on time. It was held that B was liable for the deterioration. Pothiers L J observed, "if I sell you a horse and make default in delivery and it is struck by lightning in my stable, the loss falls on me because the accident will not have occurred if I had made the delivery. However, if the horse dies of a disease which would have killed it anyway, then I am not liable."

- **Rule 4**
  Where any of the parties is in possession of the goods, that party is expected or has a liability to take reasonable care of the goods. Accordingly, where any loss, damage or deterioration directly attributable to his failure to exercise reasonable care occurs, he would be liable although under rules 1, 2 and 3, the other party would have been responsible.

NEMO DAT RULE – TRANSFER OF TITLE BY NON-OWNERS

The Caveat Emptor Rule

The caveat emptor rule (or 'let the buyer beware' principle) requires the buyer of goods take heed to see that the title he is buying or acquiring is a good one. This is a common law rule which is applicable to the sale and purchase of goods contracts (e.g. land). If the buyer pays the consideration (money) he cannot, as a general rule, recover it back after the deed has been executed (signed), unless the transaction is vitiated by fraud, or by force of some covenant in the deed which has been broken. The buyer, if he fears a defect of title, has it in his power to protect himself by proper covenants, and if he chooses or fails to do so, the law may not come to his aid.

In the case of a buyer of goods for sale, the buyer must beware that the goods may contain defects and imperfections which, after the sale and exchange of money has taken place, may be final, and not subject to refunds should defects be found later.

Protection of the rights of the buyer (the consumer) is enshrined in various Acts. Some of these Acts include the *Food and Drugs Act,* (1992) PNDCL 305 as Amended by the *Food and Drugs (Amendment) Act,* 523, 1996; the *Public Utilities Regulatory Commission (Energy Commission) Act,* 1997 (Act 541) and the *National Communication Authority Act,* (Act 769). Recent consumer protection laws have thus limited, however, the full implications of this buyer beware rule.

The NemoDat Quod Rule

Allied to the caveat emptor rule is the *'nemodat quod non habet'* rule, which literally means that "no one gives what he does not have." By virtue of this legal rule, the purchase of a good from a person who has no ownership right to it also denies the purchaser of any ownership title, usually except a bona fide purchaser, for value without notice. The actual owner or party with a valid and full title can recover the goods from the third party (purchaser). The real owner can also maintain an action against the seller for wrongful sale.

In Ghana, Section 28 of the *Sale of Goods Act, 1962* re-states the nemodat rule that "where goods are sold by a person who is not the owner of it and who does not sell them under the authority or with the consent of the owner, the buyer acquires no better title than the seller had". S 28 (3) provides, however, three exceptions to this rule: (a) it does not affect the operation of the doctrine of estoppels or (b) any power of sale which may be conferred by or (c) under any enactment or a contract of pledge or otherwise.

Sale under an enactment or common law

Section 28 restates the general common law position that in a contract of sale of goods, a non-owner cannot confer a valid title on a buyer. Except that Section 28 (2) also provides that a non-owner of goods can confer a valid title, where such non-owner sellers obtained possession under contract of a pledge or a power of sale under a statute or non-owners who are clothed with an ostensible or apparent authority to sell by the real owners.

Under Section 29 a buyer who acquires a voidable title (i.e. a title which is defective) may nonetheless obtain a good title if he gave value for it, acted in good faith without notice of the defect in the title of the rascal, before his title was avoided by the real owner.

Disposition by Mercantile Agents

Section 30 states the applicable rules on a disposition by a mercantile agent. The definition of a Mercantile Agent as provided for in Section 81 is "a person having, in the ordinary course of his business, authority to sell goods or to consign goods for sale or to buy goods or to raise money on the security of goods" As such an independent contractor, a servant or a mere shopkeeper is not a mercantile agent.

Rule 1(Section 30 (I))

Where the goods were sold to C in the ordinary course of K's business, C obtains good title so long as the original owner B consented to K's possession of the goods even though he did not consent to K's sale of the goods.

Rule 2 (Section 30 (II))

This rule provides that where at the time of disposition the mercantile agent's consent had been withdrawn, in that he had been ordered to return the goods, but he continues to have documents of title to the goods, C can still acquire a valid title if he has no notice of the withdrawal of consent.

Rule 3 (Section 30 (III))

This third rule provides that where a mercantile agent obtains documents of title as a result of having been given possession of the goods, he would be deemed to have possession of the goods.

Rule 4 (Section 30 (IV))

The fourth rule is that in a dispute over whether or not there was any consent, the burden of proof is on the real owner to prove that he did not give the mercantile agent his consent.

Rule 5 (Section 30 (V))

This fifth rule is that whenever the mercantile agent succeeds in conveying title to the purchaser but it turns out that the sale itself was a wrongful one, the agent will be liable to the true owner for damages for the wrongful sale.

Section 31 provides for situations where there is a disposition of goods by a seller who still has possession of goods that have already been sold. Now if the owner of goods sells them first to X, but remains in possession of them after the sale, then a subsequent sale and delivery of the same goods to Y would defeat X's ownership under the first sale, provided however, that Y bought the goods in good faith without notice of the earlier sale to X.

Under Section 32 where the buyer obtains possession of the goods with the seller's consent although there is a term in the contract that ownership of the goods would remain in the seller, the buyer could pass on a good title in the goods to an innocent third party. These various exceptions, notwithstanding, the nemodat rule remains critical in sales transactions as none of the exceptions mentioned above could operate successfully where the buyer has adequate notice.

Remedies available to an unpaid seller

An unpaid seller is a party:

*   to whom the whole of the purchase price has not been paid or
*   to whom a negotiable instrument has been given by a buyer as payment negotiable instrument has, however, been dishonored.

An unpaid seller has two main rights or remedies against the buyer:

1.   **Real rights which are of four types:**
*   a lien on the goods
*   a right of stoppage in transit
*   a right of resale
*   a right to recover possession.
     The unpaid seller can choose to exercise the first three rights whether or not property in the goods has passed to the buyer. The fourth right can only be exercisable when the goods have been delivered, but property has not passed.
2.   **Personal rights which include two legal rights:**
*   a legal right to sue for the price when property in the goods has passed to the buyer who has wrongfully refused to abide by the terms of the contract

or where property has not passed and the buyer has refused to pay the seller on the due date.

- a legal right to sue for damages for wrongful non-acceptance. Here, damages may be obtained for foreseeable loss (that is profit that could reasonably be foreseen by the buyer at the time of the contract).

3. **Right of lien on Goods**

    Under Section 36 and 37 the seller may retain possession of goods which are already in the sellers' own possession – this is the right of lien on goods. However, a seller cannot exercise this right if he had earlier agreed to deliver the goods before payment, or if he had granted credit to the buyer unless there is accompanying evidence that the buyer has gone bankrupt.

    A seller can still exercise a right of lien if part of the goods was still outstanding unless he has undertaken or promised to waive that right. The use of a right of lien does not rescind or terminate the contract. On the contrary, the contract will continue in effect, except where:

- the seller allows the buyer to obtain possession.
- the seller himself waives the right
- the seller delivers to a carrier or bailee for onward transmission to the buyer.

Stoppage of goods in transit

Where the goods are not in the seller's possession but are in transit, a right of lien (seizure) may still be exercised if there is obvious evidence that the buyer is bankrupt. The goods, however, cease to be in transit the moment a carrier or bailee of the goods informs the buyer of the arrival of the goods and the buyer accepts. Where the buyer fails to accept the goods and the carrier delivers only part of the goods then the seller can seize by taking actual possession of the goods. Where, however, the lien is being effected by notice, the seller must make sure that the carrier's principal instructs their agent or servant accordingly before the goods are wrongly delivered to the buyer.

Rights and Duties of Carrier and Seller

A carrier's freight charge generally has priority over a seller's right of stoppage. Accordingly, where a seller exercises a seller's right of stoppage the seller must inform the carrier about what the carrier must do with the goods, and if re-delivery is required the seller must arrange to pay for the extra expense.

Loss of the right
The right of stoppage will be lost if the seller agrees either to a resale or disposes the goods to a buyer, and the buyer disposes the goods such that a third party acquires a valid title under the nemodat rule.

Insurance Cover
Where the goods are insured, the seller will be paid for any loss if damage occurs.

Right of Resale
A seller can exercise a right to resell the goods which he has retained by virtue of the exercise of his right of lien or stoppage in transit, but the following conditions must be present:

- the goods must be of a perishable nature
- the buyer should have repudiated the contract and the seller should have accepted this
- the seller should have given notice to the buyer of his intention to sell the goods and the buyer had failed to follow up.

Right to recover possession
The seller's right to recover possession of goods delivered to a buyer may arise where property in the goods has not yet passed to the buyer, or where a provision in the contract confers a right of repossession on the seller after a breach by the buyer, or where the buyer breaches a fundamental obligation by failing to pay for the price under the terms of the contract.

RIGHTS OF THE BUYER
The buyer has both personal and real rights. A buyer's real right consists of a right to reject the goods where the seller is in breach of a fundamental obligation or breach of a condition or where the contract of sale was induced by means of a fraudulent misrepresentation by the seller. In the case of innocent misrepresentation, the buyer can only reject the goods if he acted timeously and where restitution is impossible.

The buyer is under no duty after rejection, to send the goods to the seller. However, he must grant the seller access to them.

Section 52 provides for waiver. Here, a buyer's right to reject the goods is waived if he had already accepted the goods, as in if:

- he actually informs the seller that he accepts the goods, or if

- he does not within a reasonable time after delivery inform the seller that he rejects them and
- where after rejection the buyer wrongfully refuses to place the goods at the seller's disposal.

In law, the buyer has two types of personal rights:

- he has a right to sue the seller in an action for damages for non-delivery.
- or in an action for damages for breach of a condition or a warranty.

Personal rights of an unpaid seller

Generally, personal rights refer to rights in personam. Here, an unpaid seller can take two legal actions against the buyer. He or she can sue for the price of the goods sold or sue for damages for non acceptance of the goods.

Under Section 46 (1) an unpaid seller may sue the buyer for the price of the goods when the property has already passed. There are, however, some exceptions where the property has not fully passed. One possible scenario is where the seller delivers only part of the goods and the buyer accepts that part. In that case, the seller may only sue the buyer for a proportionate part of the price in spite of the fact that in such cases of part delivery, the buyer may maintain an action against the seller for damages under Section 5.

CHAPTER 16 – QUICK REVIEW

The Sale of Goods Act applies to all contracts for the sale of goods. Among other things, it provides four main protections for buyers. The seller must have the right to sell the goods, goods sold by description must correspond to the description, goods must be of satisfactory quality, in goods sold by sample, the goods must correspond to the sample in quality.

17. Business Torts

TORT OF NEGLIGENCE

What remedies are available to persons who suffer economic loss or physical and emotional harm as a result of the intentional or careless acts of others? What happens if a newly established mine releases toxic chemicals into nearby streams or water bodies, causing illnesses to local inhabitants?

If a person gets hurt in some way by another person or another company's negligence, carelessness, or malice, tort law may allow the injured person to seek justice and financial compensation. This chapter is mainly concerned with these questions and concerns.

After studying the chapter, you will be able to:

• define a tort and show how it differs from a contract
• explain the elements of negligence
• discuss defenses to an action in negligence
• demonstrate how businesses can manage potential tort liability

THE NATURE OF TORT LAW

Definition

The word 'tort' is originally derived from Latin and means 'crooked' and from French meaning 'wrong'. A tort is a type of civil wrong. It is a breach of legal duty or an infringement of another person's legal right which gives rise to a claim for damages (i.e. financial compensation). The law of torts is a segment of law that addresses cases involving civil wrongs.

Torts and Crime

The term crime denotes an unlawful act punishable by a state. It denotes an act, default or conduct prejudicial to the community, the commission of which, by law, is punished by fine, imprisonment or death.

Differences between crime and tort

a. A crime is an offense against society made punishable by the state while a tort is a wrong against a private person.

b.   The main purpose of criminal law is to protect public interests while the object of the law of torts is to provide redress for persons who have suffered an injury.

c.   Tort is a civil wrong and therefore involves civil action. It is governed by civil procedure, while crimes are prosecuted, and are governed by the criminal Procedure Code 1960, (Act 29).

d.   With tort, the offending party is made to financially compensate the innocent party, with crimes the offending party may be fined, imprisoned, etc.

e.   With tort, the claimant is the plaintiff whilst in the criminal case the claimant is the complainant, represented by the State.

Differences between Torts and Contracts

Tort-based claims differ from contract-based claims. Virtually no contractual relationship needs to exist for a claim in tort to succeed. For example, in a claim for personal injury arising from a fatal road accident, the disputing parties need not have had any previous relationship – as the claim would arise from negligence as opposed to breach of agreement.

If, however, a tort occurs whiles there is a contractual relationship, the claimant has to choose the remedy most appropriate, and in that case, there are two options.

a)   First, if the claim is brought under breach of contract, the award of damages is intended to place the claimant back in the position he would have been had the contract been performed properly.

b)   If the claim is brought under tort, the award of damages is intended to place the claimant in the position he would have been in had the tortious act never occurred.

Limitations period

•   For contracts, the limitation period is 6 years from the date of breach
•   For torts, the limitation period is six years, but three years for personal injury

Elements of a Tort

In order to receive financial compensation from an injury, four elements must be in place:

a)   The presence of a duty of care. This is the duty to take all reasonable precautions to prevent the injury of other persons around you.

b) The breach of duty. The defendant must have failed in his or her duty. An example may be a property owner who did not maintain his or her property, or a motorist who failed to drive safely.

c) An injury occurred. You received a physical, mental, or emotional injury.

d) The breach of duty caused the injury. There must be a causal link between the breach of duty and your injury.

If all of these four elements are in place, the claimant may be entitled to financial compensation. To succeed, the loss suffered must not be "too remote." This means it must be a direct consequence of something the defendant did/or did not do.

Types of Tort

Nuisance

The tort of nuisance allows a claimant to sue for acts that interfere with their use and enjoyment of land. The tort of nuisance is divided into private and public nuisance.

Private nuisance

The law recognizes that owners of land and those in rightful possession have a right to reasonable comfort and quiet enjoyment (convenience) while in occupation. A private nuisance is a continuous, unlawful and indirect interference with the use or enjoyment of land, or of some right over or in connection with it

Public Nuisance

Public nuisance is a class of common law offense in which the injury, loss or damage is suffered by the whole community as a whole rather than by individual victims. Examples include a mining company that pollutes a stream, the keeping of diseased animals or shooting of fireworks in the street.

Public nuisance is only actionable as a tort if the claimant(s) have suffered damage over and above other members of the public. Remedies include damages and an injunction to restrain further repetition of acts of public nuisance.

Trespass to Land

Trespass to land occurs where a person directly enters upon another person's land without permission, or remains upon the land, or places or projects any object upon the land. This tort is actionable per se without the need to prove damage. In contrast, the tort of nuisance is an indirect interference with another

ELEMENTS OF A TORT

TORT LAW

The segment of law that addresses cases involving civil wrongs: if you have been hurt in some way by someone else's negligence, carelessness, or malice, tort law may allow you to seek justice and financial compensation.

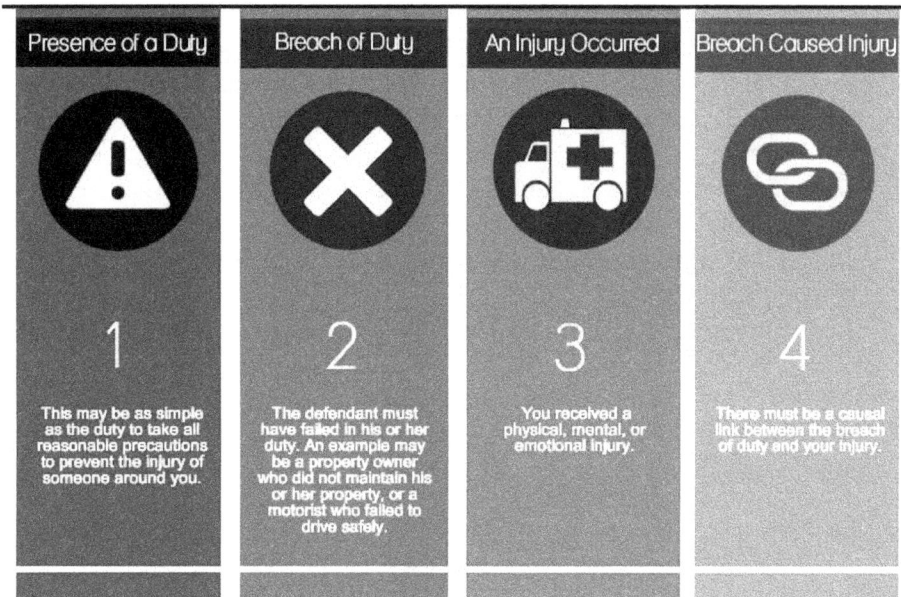

Presence of a Duty	Breach of Duty	An Injury Occurred	Breach Caused Injury
1	2	3	4
This may be as simple as the duty to take all reasonable precautions to prevent the injury of someone around you.	The defendant must have failed in his or her duty. An example may be a property owner who did not maintain his or her property, or a motorist who failed to drive safely.	You received a physical, mental, or emotional injury.	There must be a causal link between the breach of duty and your injury.

If all of these elements are in place, you may be entitled to financial compensation.

GHS

person's use and enjoyment of land and as a rule requires proof of damage to be actionable.

Trespass to Person

Trespass to the person consists of three torts, namely assault, battery and false imprisonment.

a)   An assault is an act which intentionally causes another person to apprehend the infliction of immediate, unlawful force on his person. The claimant must have reasonably expected an immediate battery.
      Stephens v. Myers (1830) 172 ER 735
      Facts: The defendant made a violent gesture at the plaintiff by waiving a clenched fist, but was prevented from reaching him by the intervention of third parties.
      Held: The defendant was liable for assault.

b)   A battery is the actual intentional infliction of unlawful force on another person. It was stated in ***Cole v. Turner*** (1704): 'The least touching of another in anger is a battery'.

c)   False imprisonment is the unlawful imposition of constraint upon another's freedom of movement from a particular place. This tort protects a person from restraint and does not give a person absolute freedom of movement. Thus, if there is a reasonable escape route there will be no false imprisonment.

Negligence

In ***Alhassan Kotokoli v. Moro Hausa,*** Edusei J preferred the meaning of negligence as follows: "Negligence means more than heedless or careless conduct; it properly connotes the complex by the person to whom the duty owed."

Liability for another person's injuries is by and large predicated on the legal theory of negligence. Whether a person has been negligent, and can be forced to bear at least some of the financial cost of another person's injuries depends on the answers to four basic questions:

a)   Did X have a duty to the injured person? (That a duty of care was owed)

b)   If so, did X breach that duty? (That the defendant breached that duty)

c)   Did breaching the duty cause the injuries? (That the injuries were caused by the breach)

d)   Finally, did the injured person suffer damages? (That the injured person suffered damages)

Duty of Care

The first element of negligence is the legal duty of care. This concerns the relationship between the defendant and the claimant, which must be such that there is an obligation upon the defendant to take proper care to avoid causing injury to the plaintiff in all the circumstances of the case.

The origins of duty of care can be found in cases such as *Donoghue v. Stevenson* (1932), where a woman successfully showed that a manufacturer of ginger beer owed a duty of care, where the production of the ginger beer was negligently produced.

This case laid down the principle that a manufacturer owes a duty to consumers and users of his products not to cause them harm.

In this regard, catering houses, chop bars, etc., for example, clearly owe a duty to their customers and the people who come in contact with their food. It is essential to avoid any dispute that these businesses take the upmost care in preparing food and delivering services which was agreed upon.

The "Neighbour Principle"
Donoghue v. Stevenson [1932] AC 562

Facts: The facts involved Mrs Donoghue drinking a bottle of ginger beer in a café in Paisley, Renfrewshire. A dead snail was in the bottle. She fell ill, and she sued the ginger beer manufacturer, Mr Stevenson.

Held: The House of Lords held that the manufacturer owed a duty of care to her, which was breached, because it was reasonably foreseeable that failure to ensure the product's safety would lead to harm to consumers.

This case was a foundational decision in English tort law. It created the modern concept of negligence, by setting out general principles whereby one person would owe a duty of care to another person.

Lord Atkin defined those to whom we owe a duty of care in terms of the "neighbour principle" – in his very famous words:

> "The rule that you are to love your neighbour becomes in law, you must not injure your neighbour and the lawyer's question, 'who is my neighbour?'receives a restricted reply. You must take reasonable care to avoid acts or omissions which you can reasonably foresee would be likely to injure your neighbour. (Foreseeability) Who, then, in law is my neighbour? The answer seems to be—persons who are so closely and directly affected by my act (Proximity) that I ought rea-

sonably to have them in contemplation as being so affected when I am directing my mind to the acts or omissions which are called in question."

There are a number of recognizable situations in which the courts recognize the existence of a duty of care. Examples include:

- employer to employee
- one road user to another
- manufacturer to consumer
- doctor to patient
- solicitor to client
- teacher to student

Pure Economic or Financial loss

Negligence which causes no physical or psychiatric harm, but causes economic loss to a person or company is termed pure economic loss. There are limits in place on the recovery of pure economic loss. Pure economic loss is monetary loss which is unconnected to physical injury to a person or damage to a person's property. Where the economic loss is connected to physical injury or damage to property, then it is termed as consequential economic loss. The development of pure economic loss stems from the case of *Hedley Byrne & Co Ltd v. Heller & Partners Ltd.*

Hedley Byrne & Co Ltd v. Heller & Partners Ltd.

Facts: In this case, Hedley Byrne, an advertising agency, approached Heller & Partners for a credit check on a third company, Easipower Ltd, before carrying out advertising orders on their behalf. Heller & Partners reported that Easipower Ltd was credit-worthy, and in reliance on this statement, Hedley Byrne placed advertising orders for them. When subsequently Easipower Ltd was declared bankrupt, Hedley Byrne took legal action against Heller & Partners, alleging they had been owed a duty of care when consulting for a credit reference. Whilst Hedley Byrne did not succeed in their claim,

Held: The House of Lords recognized that such a duty may be owed, where a relationship of reliance exists between two parties.

Breach of Duty of Care

Breach of duty in negligence may be found to exist where a defendant breaches the duty of care – bearing in mind that a defendant is liable if and only if the claimant can show that the defendant was at fault. The claimant must show that the defendant failed to meet the required standard of care expected of him by law. To be successful, the claimant must therefore not only prove that a duty of care existed, but also the duty was breached by the defendant; that the defendant's conduct does not measure up to the requisite standard of care.

Standard of Care

The requirements of the standard are closely dependent on circumstances of the case. Whether a standard of care has been breached is determined by the court, and is usually phrased in terms of the reasonable person. It was famously described in *Vaughn v. Menlove* (1837) as whether the defendant "proceeded with such reasonable caution as a prudent man would have exercised under such circumstances."

Once it has been established that the defendant owed the claimant a duty of care, the claimant must also demonstrate that the defendant was in breach of duty. The test of breach of duty is generally objective (that is, the defendant is expected to meet the standard of a reasonable person).

Vaughan v. Menlove (1837) 3 Bing N.C. 467

The objective test can be variable and may depend on the circumstances of the particular defendant or the situation. For example: An amateur footballer is not expected to meet the standard of a footballer in the first division:

PROFESSIONAL ADVICE AND NEGLIGENT MISSTATEMENTS

Factors a Court will consider

In deciding whether a defendant has taken reasonable care, a court will examine the surrounding circumstances; in so doing a number of factors will affect the court's decision.

a.   **The likelihood of harm**
     People must guard against reasonable probabilities but they are not bound to guard against fantastic possibilities. The general principle is that the law requires a person to take reasonable care. He or she must guard against the consequences of his actions which are reasonably foreseeable.

b.   **The seriousness of harm**
     A reasonable man will guard against the possibility of serious harm as the case of *Paris v. Stepney Borough Council* shows.

Paris v. Stepney Borough Council

Facts: The defendant employers knew the plaintiff had only one good eye. He was not provided with goggles for his work and was injured at work when a splinter entered his one good eye blinding him.

Held: It was held that although it would not have been negligent to fail to provide goggles for normally sighted employees, the employer had been negligent in not providing them for the plaintiff because the consequences for him of injury to his eye were serious than they would be for a fully sighted employee.

c. **The value of the defendant's conduct**

The likelihood of causing grave injury will be balanced against the social value of the defendant's conduct. A risk, which would not ordinarily have been justified, might be justified by circumstances, for example an emergency requiring prompt action. The case of ***Watt v. Hertforshire County Council*** illustrates this principle.

Watt v. Hertforshire County Council

Facts: The plaintiff was a fireman. He was called out with his colleagues to an accident where a woman lay trapped beneath an overturned vehicle. A heavy jack was needed to shift the vehicle but the fire brigade did not have a suitable vehicle to convey it. The jack was therefore carried onto a lorry with the plaintiff and several colleagues holding it. The plaintiff was badly damaged when the jack slipped during the journey and he sued in negligence.

Held: The Court of Appeal held that the claim ought to fail although it might ordinarily have been negligent to transport the jack unsecured in this way. The risk was justified by the need to protect life and limb.

Proof of carelessness

The burden of proof rests with the plaintiff to prove each and every element of his case on a balance of probabilities. In negligence cases, he must prove that it is more likely than not that the defendant failed to exercise reasonable care. To do so satisfactorily, the plaintiff may call a medical expert witness to explain what the defendant did and what the generally accepted practice in the particular profession is.

RES IPSA LOQUITUR

Res ipsa loquitur (RIL) is a Latin expression which means that "the facts speak for themselves." Where RIL applies, the contention is that the facts themselves raise an inference of negligence. Accordingly, the plaintiff ought to succeed unless the defendant can adduce contrary evidence to refute the inference. What must a plaintiff show in order to rely on the rule?

Firstly, a plaintiff who intends to rely on IRL must prove two conditions. He must prove that the accident was caused by something under the defendant's exclusive control. If the defendant is, however, able to show that a third party could have interfered with the cause of the accident, the plaintiff's case may collapse. As a result, it was held that IRL would not apply where, for instance, the plaintiff fell out of a moving train through a door, which was not properly locked. A passenger could have tampered with the door between the time of the train leaving the station and the accident.

Secondly, the plaintiff must show that the accident would normally not have occurred but for negligence on the part of the defendant. Accordingly, in a product liability claim like **Donoghue v. Stevenson,** for example, a consumer might contend against the product manufacturer "snails do not ordinarily come sealed in ginger beer bottles. Please explain how this happened."

It can also apply in medical negligence claims against professionals where a patient may contend, "While I was in your hands something has been done to me which has wrecked my life. Please explain how this came to pass".

On the part of the defendant, he or she may deny that the maxim applies by showing that he was not in sole control of the thing which caused the harm or that the accident could have occurred without negligence.

He can show how the accident came to happen, that he took all reasonable care to avoid it or if he does not know how it happened, that he had taken all reasonable care. In other words, that he had a foolproof system to guard against misfortunes of the kind that occurred. In these cases, the legal and evidential burden on a defendant is a heavy one as illustrated by **Henderson v. Henry E Jenkins & Sons and Evans.**

Henderson v. Henry E Jenkins & Sons and Evans

Facts: The brakes on a lorry owned and operated by the defendants failed and it was discovered that the failure was caused by loss of brake fluid from a hole in a corroded brake pipe. The plaintiff relied on res ipsa loquitor. For their part, the defendants showed that they had inspected the lorry in accordance with the manufacturer's instructions and advice of the Ministry of Transport and that removing the pipe could only have discovered the hole.

Held: It was held that the defendant had failed to disprove negligence. That they should have demonstrated that nothing had happened during the life of the vehicle to warrant suspicion that the pipe might have been damaged.

DEFENSES IN NEGLIGENCE
The following defenses can apply.

a. **Inevitable Accident**
    It is a potent defense if the accident was one, which could not have been avoided by any care, precaution, provision or forethought that a reasonable man could have taken as held in *Stenley v. Powell* (1891).
    Stenley v. Powell (1891)
    Facts: The plaintiff and the defendant were both members of a shooting party. A pellet which had been fired in a proper manner by the defendant wounded the plaintiff but had glanced off a tree almost at right angles.
    Held: It was held that the accident was inevitable and the defendant not liable.

b. **Act of God**
    It is a good defense to show that the harm complained of is actually the direct result of natural causes without human intervention even though this does not mean that human activity must have been completely absent. *Nicholas v. Marsland* (1876) is an illustrative case.
    Nicholas v. Marsland (1876)
    Facts: This case was an action under the rule in *Rylands v. Fletcher.* The defendant constructed a series of artificial pools by damming a natural stream. The pools were constructed and were adequate generally. However, they were destroyed by a storm of quite exceptional magnitude, leading to damage to the plaintiff's bridges.
    Held: It was held that no one had been negligent and the accident was due entirely to an act of God.

c. **Contributory negligence**
    It is a good defense to a negligence claim to demonstrate that the plaintiff is himself or herself at fault and partly the author of his or her own misfortunes.

d. **Volenti non fit injuria (voluntary assumption of risk)**
    As a general rule, a person cannot be heard to complain of an injury to a risk which he had either expressly or impliedly consented to. Such an injury is not actionable as a tort. In other words, the plaintiff will be taken

to have excused the defendant by consenting to what would otherwise be a tort. Therefore, a patient who consents to a surgical operation cannot thereafter sue his surgeon, even though the operation would otherwise be technical battery.

e. **Limitation Act**
   The Limitation Act, 1972 (NRCD 54) provides that an action in tort must be brought within 3 years of the date on which the right of action accrued. In the case of libel and slander, the action must be brought within two years. What this means is that claims commenced in breach of this statutory period are statute-barred and not actionable.

f. **Ex turpicausa non oritur action**
   The maxim ex turpicausa non oritur action applies if it would be an affront to public conscience to grant the plaintiff the relief he seeks. The courts have been slow to allow a plaintiff to succeed in claims where he has been injured whilst engaged in an illegal or immoral act. For instance, the defense would apply if two robbers went to loot a bank safe by resorting to deadly explosives and one of the robbers was injured because the other negligently used too much explosive.

PROFESSIONAL ADVICE

The law of tort recognizes a special relationship between professionals (e.g. accountants, lawyers, doctors etc.), their clients, and those who rely on their work. The law in such circumstances recognizes a duty of care situation when professionals act in an expert capacity, a professional being someone engaged in an occupation requiring the exercise of special knowledge, education and skill.

Where negligence takes the form of words, the resulting tort is called negligent misrepresentation or misstatement (an incorrect statement made carelessly). The professional who, therefore, gives poor advice to a client, who, as a result, suffers injury (e.g. financial loss, or even greater physical harm) not only faces liability for the tort of negligent misstatement but also for breach of contract. Providing incompetent advice is thus both a tort and a breach of contract and the case of *Hedley Byrne & Co Ltd v. Heller and Partners Ltd* (1963) is illustrative of this.

Hedley Byrne & Co Ltd v. Heller and Partners Ltd (1963)

Facts: D, a bank gave a reference to C (another bank) regarding the financial responsibility of a customer, expecting the bank to act on it. The reference was given "without responsibility." The second bank acted on the reference and suffered financial loss as a result. They sued D for negligence.

Held: The law will imply a duty of care when a party seeking information from a party possessed of a special skill, trusts him to exercise due care, and that party knew or ought to have known that reliance was being placed on his skill and judgment. However, since here there was an express disclaimer of responsibility, no such duty was, in any event, implied.

PRODUCT LIABILITY

Manufacturers have a responsibility to create safe products that will not cause harm to consumers. When they fail to do so, they may be held responsible for injuries or illness caused by the dangerous product.

In terms of product liability, the doctrine of privity is swept aside, and a manufacturer is legally subject to liability for his or her negligence. His or her liability also extends to all those who are foreseeably expected to suffer injury as a result of a defective product or dangerous condition. In short, a person injured by a defective product can sue the manufacturer for negligence even if he or she had purchased the product from someone else – the effect of this rule is immediate and sweeping.

A person injured by a product can base his or her claim for damages on a range of different legal theories: negligence, breach of warranty, or even strict tort liability.

Negligence claims are governed by tort law discussed earlier in this chapter, and so probably it needs no rehearsal. **Warranty claims,** on the other hand, are governed by contract law, also previously discussed under the law of contract – as a quick recall, a warranty is a promise, claim, or representation made about the quality, type, number, or performance of a product by the manufacturer or the seller. In general, the law assumes that a seller always provides some kind of warranty concerning the product he or she sells and that the seller should be required to meet the obligation created by the warranty. **Strict product liability** is liability without fault for an injury proximately caused by a product that is defective and not reasonably safe. In establishing strict liability, the injured plaintiff need only prove that: (1) the product was defective, and (2) the product defect was the cause of the injury. In other words, the focus at trial is on the product, not the conduct of the manufacturer, because it does not matter whether the manufacturer took every possible precaution. If the product was defective and caused an injury, the manufacturer is liable.

CHAPTER 17 – QUICK REVIEW

Tort law defines when a person may be held liable for an injury caused to another. Legal injuries include emotional, economic, or reputational injuries as well as violations of privacy, property, or constitutional rights.

Intentional torts,such as a trespass to land, is committed when an individual intentionally enters the land of another without lawful excuse. It is actionable per se, even if no actual harm is done. Also actionable are economic torts which follow common law rules on liability on interference with economic or business. The tort of nuisance involves denial of quiet enjoyment to owners of real property. The tort of negligence is discussed. This tort involves a failure to exercise the care that a reasonably prudent person would exercise in like circumstances. It involves a breach of a duty of care, an obligation imposed on an individual requiring that they adhere to a reasonable standard of care while performing acts that could possibly harm others, and therefore the need to pay damages – a monetary value on the harm done, following the principle of *restitutio in integrum,* "restoration to the original condition".

Under product liability, product manufacturers, distributors and sellers could be held responsible for the injuries caused by their products. Generally, a product's liability claim is based on a design defect, a manufacturing defect, or a failure to warn. This topic is closely associated with negligence, breach of warranty and consumer protection. Several defenses exist such as: contributory negligence – a defense based on negligence of the plaintiff wherein the plaintiff's actions caused the event which drew the suit – or volenti non fit injuria, which isLatin for, "to a willing person, no injury is done."Or even ex turpicausa non orituractio – "From a dishonorable cause an action does not arise".

18. Employment Law

LEARNING OBJECTIVES

At the end of this chapter you should be able to distinguish between employees and the self-employed, explain the nature of the contract of employment and give examples of the main duties placed on the parties to such a contract, distinguish between wrongful and unfair dismissal, including constructive dismissal, explain what is meant by redundancy, and discuss the remedies available to those who have been subject to unfair dismissal or redundancy.

EMPLOYMENT LAW

The rules governing employment relations in Ghana derive from several sources, chief among them– the 1992 Constitution, Case law, Statutory law (e.g. the *Labour Act,* 2003 (Act 651), the *Labour Regulations,* 2007 (LI 1833), the *Persons with Disability Act,* 2006 (Act 715), the *Workmen's Compensation Act,* 1987 (PNDCL 187), *Factories Offices and Shops Act,* 1970 (Act 328), *The National Pensions Act,* 2008 (Act 766), the *Internal Revenue Act,* 2000 (Act 592))as well as international law — the International Labour Organization Conventions (ILO) among others.

Generally, employment rules fall into two categories – voluntary and legal. Voluntary rules include rules arising from private agreements that derive from, among others, collective bargaining, arbitration, conciliation, mediation, and grievance and discipline handling. They also include voluntarily accepted standards of good employment practices such as those advocated by the Institute of Human Resource Practitioners. Legal rules include statutory law, the common law of contract and of tort, case law, and international standards such as the International Labour Organization's (ILO) international standards.[75]

---

75   The ILO, established in 1919, is an agency of the United Nations, charged with setting internationallabor standards. The ILO is a tripartite body comprising representatives of government, employers and workers.

Who is an employee?

An employee is any person who works under a contract of service, as opposed to a contract for services. A person who works under a contract for services is a self-employed person (or independent contractor).Such a person is not an employee. This distinction is important because, while employees are protected by common law and statutory law, no such protection is offered to self-employed persons.

Test of employment

A number of tests are used by the courts to determine whether or not a person is an employee or self-employed; these include the control test, the integration test and the economic reality test.

Control test

Employees are subject to control by their employer as to how, where and when they do their work. In Walker v Crystal Palace Football Club (1910), it was held that a professional football player was an employee, on the grounds that he was subject to control in training, discipline and method of payment.

Integration test

Under the integration test, a person is regarded as an employee if his or her work is an integral part of the business and not merely an accessory to it.

Economic reality test

Here, the courts take into consideration all the surrounding factors of the employment situation. The test involves determining whether the person who is performing the work is doing so as a person within the business or on his own account. The relevant factors that are then considered include, among others:

a) control
b) provision of his own equipment
c) whether he hires his own helpers
d) degree of financial risk he undertakes
e) degree of responsibility he bears for investment and management
f) the extent to which he has an opportunity of profiting from sound management in the performance of his task
g) whether there is a regular method of payment
h) whether the person works regular hours, and also
i) whether there is mutuality of obligations.

In *Ready Mixed Concrete (South East) Ltd v Minister of Pensions & National Insurance & Others* (1968),the driver of a lorry had a contract with a company under which he drove his own lorry only on company business, obeyed instructions of the foreman and wore company colors. It was held that although the employer exercised some control over his work, the other factors were inconsistent with a contract of service. In particular, the fact that he owned his own equipment and was operating at his own financial risk to a degree meant he was an independent contractor.

Temporary or casual workers

There are significant problems in determining the status of temporary or casual workers, as the case of *O'Kelly v. Trusthouse Forte Plc* (1983) illustrates.

O'Kelly v. Trusthouse Forte Plc (1983)

Facts: A winewaiter was called a 'regular casual' because he was given work when it was required in the banqueting hall. He had no other employment and it was generally accepted that he would be offered work in preference to others when work was available, and that he would accept such work when offered.

Held: He was an independent contractor because there was 'no mutuality of obligation' in that the company was under no duty to offer him work and he was under no duty to accept it.

Home workers or outworkers

There are also problems with home workers or outworkers. Generally, such people will be paid by the number of pieces they produce and will supply their own equipment. Their position is ambiguous and many consider themselves to be self-employed, but the law does not always take this view.

Nethermere (St Neots) Ltd v. Taverna and Gardiner (1984)

Facts: Two women sewed trousers at home for a company. They informed the company when to deliver materials and when to collect completed garments. Rarely did they refuse work. However, they gave adequate warning each time they were indisposed and did not wish to take on work. They submitted time sheets and were remunerated at the same rate as the workers in the factory. The company relied on their work and provided the sewing machines they used.

Held: The women were employees because, by the giving and taking of work over a continuous period of time, the parties had built mutuality of obligation (i.e. the company to provide work and the women to accept it).

Contract of employment

Normally, a contract of employment consists of:

- Express terms
- Terms implied by the courts
- Terms implied by statute.

Express terms

Express terms are those terms which are agreed upon by the parties themselves, regardless of whether the agreement is written or oral. *The Labour Act,* (Act 651) requires an employer to provide an employee with express terms of employment, inclusive of details such as:

- pay rates and interval
- job title
- place of work
- length of notice
- details of disciplinary and grievance procedures
- date of commencement of employment.

Terms implied by the courts

The courts have power to imply various terms into an employment contract.

Terms implied by statute (Labour Act)

DUTIES OF THE EMPLOYEE

1. **A duty to obey lawful and reasonable orders**
   Pepper v. Webb (1968)
   Facts: A gardener refused to plant the plants where instructed by the employer.
   Held: He was in breach of a duty of obedience and coupled with the fact that he was rude and surly, it justified his summary dismissal.
2. **Duty of mutual co-operation (or the duty to perform the work in a reasonable manner)**
   As a general rule, it is the duty of the employer to give lawful instructions and that of the employee to obey same – this is usually described as a duty of mutual co-operation. The courts have interpreted the duty to obey lawful and reasonable orders as also a duty not to frustrate the commercial aims of the employer. An illustrative case is the case of *Secretary of State for Employment v. ASLEF* (1972).

Secretary of State for Employment v ASLEF (1972)

Facts: Railway workers 'worked to rule', i.e. obeyed the British Rail rule book to the letter. This resulted in considerable delays in the train service.

Held: There was an implied term that each employee, in obeying instructions, would not do so in a wholly unreasonable way which had the effect of disrupting the service he was there to provide.

3.   **Duty to exercise reasonable care and skill**

An employee is under a duty to act with reasonable care in the performance of his duties. The standard of care will, however, depend on the circumstances of each case. In law, it is generally accepted that a single act of negligence, unless it is gross negligence, will not justify summary dismissal. These notwithstanding, there are certain occupations, such as that of airline pilots, where a single act of negligence in the performance of essential duties could warrant a dismissal.

An extension of this duty of care is a duty to indemnify the employer for any damages which he has had to pay as a result of his vicarious liability for the employee's negligence; the case of **Lister v. Romford Ice & Cold Storage Ltd** (1972) illustrates this principle.

Lister v. Romford Ice & Cold Storage Ltd (1972)

Facts: an employee negligently ran over another employee with a fork-lift truck.

Held: He was liable in damages to his employer for breach of contract.

4.   **Duty of good faith – a duty to give honest and faithful service**

An employee cannot appropriate and use the employer's property as his own — he must account to his employer for all money or properties which he receives in the course of his employment. A good case in point is **Sinclair v. Neighbour** (1967).

Sinclair v. Neighbour (1967)

Facts: An employee secretly borrowed from the shop till. He repaid the money the next day.

Held: He was in breach of the duty of good faith and, since this was a serious breach of contract, the employer was justified in summarily dismissing him.

The employee may do other work in his own time. The law, nevertheless, imposes a duty not to do spare time work which competes with that of his employer and may cause his employer damage.

5. **Duty not to disclose trade secrets to third parties or misuse confidential information acquired during employment**

    An employee is under a legal duty not to disclose the trade secrets of his employer to a third party or to misuse confidential information acquired in the course of his employment. This implied duty may continue even after the employment has terminated. Thus, an employee who uses or sells trade secrets, like chemical formulae, or list of customers and who sells them for his own purposes, is in clear breach. The case of ***Hivac Ltd v. Park Royal Scientific Instruments Ltd*** (1946) is illustrative of this principle.

    Hivac Ltd v. Park Royal Scientific Instruments Ltd (1946)

    Facts: Two employees of a company which manufactured sophisticated components for hearing aids worked at the weekends for a rival company.
    Held: An injunction was granted as there was potential for misuse of the secret information.

6. **Duty to render personal service**

    Employees may not delegate the performance of their work to someone else unless they have their employer's express or implied permission to do so.

THE LABOUR ACT – ACT 651

Rights of Employees under the Labour Act

The rights of employees under Act 651 include the right to:
*   Work under safe, satisfactory and healthy conditions.
*   Receive equal pay for equal work without distinction of any kind.
*   Have rest, leisure and reasonable limitation of working hours and period of holidays with pay as well as remuneration for public holidays.
*   Form or join a trade union.
*   Be trained and retrained for the development of his or her skills.
*   Receive information relevant to his or her work.

Duties of Employees under the Labour Act

The statutory duties of employees under the labor law include the obligation to:
*   Work conscientiously in the lawfully chosen occupation.
*   Report for work regularly and punctually.
*   Enhance productivity.
*   Exercise due care in the execution of assigned work.
*   Obey lawful instruction regarding the organization and execution of his or her work.

- Take all reasonable care for the safety and health of fellow workers.
- Protect the interests of the employer; and
- Take proper care of the property of the employer entrusted to the worker or under the immediate control of the worker.

DUTIES OF EMPLOYERS - Section 9 (Act 651)

1. **Duty to pay reasonable remuneration**
   This will be implied in the absence of any express provision regarding the employees pay or earnings.

2. **Duty to indemnify the employee**
   It is the duty of the employer to indemnify the employee where the employee has incurred a legal liability or expenses while acting for or on behalf of the employer.

3. **Duty to provide a safe system of work**
   An employer is under a statutory duty to take reasonable care for the health and safety of his employees. Section 118 of the *Labour Act* makes this mandatory. Breach of this duty may expose an employer to significant liability (often in negligence). At common law, this implicates careful staff selection and supervision to ensure that the work environment, plant and materials are safe.

   Laws providing guidance include the *Factories, Offices and Shops Act, 1970,* Act 328; the *Mining Regulations,* 1970 LI 665; and the *Workmen's Compensation Law,* 1987 (PNDC 187) which relate to compensation for injuries caused by accidents suffered at the workplace. Where an employer has not acted unreasonably or negligently, he has no common law liability (*Latimer v. AEC Ltd*).

   Latimer v. AEC Ltd (1953)

   Facts: Following flood damage, the employer carefully sprinkled sawdust over a factory floor to prevent employee slippage until the floor could be properly cleared. A small patch remained uncovered and L slipped and was injured.

   Held: It was held that the employer has not acted unreasonably or negligently and had no common law liability.

   Duty to give reasonable notice of termination of employment
   In practice, this implied duty rarely arises since most contracts of employment contain express provisions stating the exact length of notice or stating that the contract is to be for a fixed term. Also, there are statutory minimum periods of notice.

Duty of mutual co-operation

The employer has a duty not to behave in a manner calculated to damage the relationship of trust and confidence, e.g. by abusively reprimanding an employee.

Provision of work

There is no general common law duty to provide work. However, such a term may be implied under the business efficacy test (e.g. where failure to provide work would deprive the employee of a benefit contemplated by the contract). For example, if the contract expressly provides for remuneration on a piecework or commission basis, it may be possible to imply a duty on the employer to provide sufficient work to enable the employee to earn a reasonable sum. Similarly, where the employee is skilled and needs practice to maintain those skills, there may be an obligation to provide a reasonable amount of work.

William Hill Organisation Ltd v. Tucker (1998)

Facts: T worked as a senior dealer (one of only five authorized to do so) operating in the field of spread betting. He served notice to terminate his contract in order to work for a competitor. WH insisted that he remain on the payroll for the notice period, but stayed at home 'on garden leave'. T sought to start his new job immediately, arguing that WH was in breach of contract in refusing to allow him to work.

Held: WH was in breach by not providing work because T had particular skills which must be exercised to maintain them.

Provision of a reference

There is no duty to provide a reference but, if one is provided, it must be truthful, as shown in:

Spring v. Guardian Assurance (1994)

Facts: The dismissed employee worked as a representative for a company, Guardian Assurance, but was dismissed after its sale. He applied to work for an insurance company, Scottish Amicable. Guardian provided a bad reference in respect of the claimant who then claimed damages for negligent misstatement. The reference was, the judge said, "so strikingly bad as to amount to ... a 'kiss of death' to the claimant's career in insurance."

Held: The defendants did owe the claimant a duty of care in providing a reference, knowing that a bad one might damage his prospects of employment, and that they were in breach of that duty.

Rights of the Employer under the Labour Act (Section 8 of Act 651)

The statutory rights of employers under the **Labour Act** include the right to:

a) employ a worker, discipline, transfer, promote and terminate the employment of the worker

b) formulate policies, execute plans and programs to set targets

c) modify, extend or cease operations and

d) determine the type of products to make or sell and the prices of its goods and services.

Duties of the Employer under the Labour Act (Section 9 of Act 651)

The statutory rights of employers under the labour law include the right to:

- provide work and appropriate raw materials, machinery, equipment and tools.

- pay the agreed remuneration at the time and place agreed on in the contract of employment; or collective agreement or by custom without a deduction except deductions permitted by law or agreed between the employer and the worker.

- take practicable steps to ensure that the worker is free from risk of personal injury or damage.

- to health during and in the course of the worker's employment or while lawfully on the employer's premises.

- develop the human resources by way of training and retraining of the workers.

- provide and ensure the operation of an adequate procedure for discipline of the workers.

- furnish the worker with a copy of the worker's contract of employment and

- keep open the channels of communication with the workers; and protect the interests of the workers.

AN OVERVIEW OF THE LABOUR ACT 2003 (ACT 651) AND EMPLOYMENT PRACTICE IN GHANA[76]

---

76   This synopsis of employment law in Ghana is credited with thanks to an article by Jane Hodges, DIALOGUE, ILO and Dr. Anthony Baah, Head, Research and Policy Department, Ghana Trades Union Congress. Accessed at *http://www.ilo.org/ifpdial/informa-tion-resources/national-labour-law-profiles/WCMS_158898/lang--en/index.htm1/31/2015 4:50:48 PM* and also to Lex Mundi, and to Rosa Kuduazi and AminaKuguah, both of Bentsi-Enchill, Letsa and Ankoma *http://www.lexmundi.com/images/lexmundi/PDF/*

The *Labour Act* (Act 651) of 2003 consolidated various previously scattered legislations. It also introduced new provisions reflecting various ILO Conventions ratified by Ghana. The Act applies to all categories of employers and employees in Ghana except staff of the Armed Forces, Police Service, Prisons Service and the Security Intelligence Agencies. The main provisions of the Act include the establishment of public and private employment centers, the protection of employment relationship, general conditions of employment, employment of persons with disabilities, employment of young persons, employment of women, fair and unfair termination of employment, protection of remuneration, temporary and casual employees, unions, employers' organizations and collective agreements, strikes, establishment of a National Tripartite Committee, forced labor, occupational health and safety, labor inspection and the establishment of the National Labour Commission.

The Constitution guarantees every person the right to work under safe, satisfactory and healthy conditions, as well as a right to receive equal pay for equal work. Workers are guaranteed a right constitutionally to rest, leisure, reasonable limitation of working hours and periods of holidays (inclusive of public holidays) with pay. The right to form or join trade unions is guaranteed under both the Constitution and the *Labour Act* and any form of forced labor is proscribed.

Requirements - Employment Contract

Section 12 of Act 651 requires that every contract of employment for a period of six months or more within a year or for a number of working days equivalent to 6 months or more within a year, be secured by a written contract. The contract must state rights and duties of the parties, names of parties, date of first appointment, job title, pay (including overtime rates), hours of work, holidays, sickness and work-related injury entitlements, social security or pension scheme, termination notice, disciplinary rules/grievances, and must be signed and dated by both parties. These particulars are provided in Schedule 1 of the Act.

Special provisions relate to temporary and casual workers, which is the subject matter of Part X of the *Labour Act.* A contract of employment for a casual worker need not be in writing, but casuals have a right to the minimum wage for each day worked, to overtime and medical facilities. Temporals are also entitled

---

Accessed at1/31/2015 5:59:30 PM, credit is also due MyWages.Org.Ghana at *http://www. mywage.org/ghana/home/labour-law/employment-security/notice-and-severance/termination-of-employment*

to the minimum wage, hours of work, rest periods, paid public holidays, night work and sick leave, regardless of any terms agreed by the parties.

Subject to more favorable provisions that may be negotiated in a collective bargaining agreement (s.19), the grounds for termination (s.15) include:

- termination by mutual consent of the parties
- termination by the worker on grounds of ill-treatment or sexual harassment
- termination by the employer where the worker dies before the end of the employment period
- termination by the employer where the worker is medically certified to be unfit for the job
- termination by the employer where the worker is unable to do the job because of misconduct; and
- termination by redundancy (s. 65).

A notice of termination must be in writing, and may follow a scale. Where a contract is for more than 3 years, the law requires 1 month's notice; where the contract is for less than 3 years, 2 weeks' notice or two weeks' pay in lieu of notice; or where the contract is on a weekly basis, 7 days' notice. **If the parties signed an "at will" clause in the contract, then the contract could be terminated at the close of any day at will.** Notwithstanding notice requirements, either party may buy out of an employment relationship by paying to the other a sum equal to the amount that would have accrued under the notice period.

Section 57(8) prohibits dismissal of female employees due to absence from work as a result of maternity leave. Section 50 protects the employment of a person who suffers a disability where such a worker could be found employment within the same institution or a corresponding job in the same institution. Where no such job can be found, the employer may terminate by notice.

Where an offending employee who has been warned in writing commits a similar offense within six months of a prior warning, an employer can lawfully terminate the employee without notice.

Hours of work

Sections 33 to 39 of the *Labour Act* cover hours of work. A maximum is 8 hours a day or 40 hours a week, except in cases expressly noted in the Act. Provision is made for paid overtime, and the Act permits unpaid overtime in certain exceptional circumstances "including an accident threatening human lives or the very existence of the undertaking". Under section 40, workers on continuous workdays are entitled to a rest period of at least 30 minutes counted as normal hours of work, but where the normal hours of work is split into two, the break should not be less than one hour's duration and is not counted as part of the normal work hours.

Leave
Sections 20 to 32 cover annual leave with pay (which is 15 working days in every calendar year of continuous service, being not less than 200 days in any particular year).

Equality
Both the Constitution and the *Labour Act* prohibit employment discrimination founded on race, sex, ethnic origin, creed, skin color, religion, social or economic status.

Part VI provides protection to working women while Part V protects workers with disability. Section 46 offers special incentives for the employment of persons with disability, and Section 53 emphasizes training and retraining to enable employees cope with any aspect of the job. Section 68 espouses equal pay for equal work. Workplace sexual harassment is criminalized in Ghana. Under Section 175, the offense is defined as "any unwelcome, offensive or inopportune sexual advances or request made by an employer or superior officer or a co-worker to a worker, whether the worker is a man or a woman."

Maternity
Section 57 covers maternity leave (of at least 12 weeks, with extension under certain circumstances) and nursing pauses of one hour during working hours for a nursing mother to nurse her baby, up to the time the infant child attains one year.

Minimum age and protection of young workers
In Ghana, the minimum age of entering the labor market is 16 years. Section 58 to 61 of the Act prohibits the employment of young persons in hazardous work, which includes work likely to expose a young person to physical or moral hazard. A young person is defined as of or above 18 years of age but below 21 years.

Trade unions and employers' organizations

Sections 79 to 95 of the Act cover formation, registration and free internal administration of unions and employers' organizations. Two or more workers employed in the same institution may form a union, and two or more employers may similarly form or join an employers' organization. Section 79(2) prohibits certain types of workers from exercising the right to form trade unions (e.g. policy-making managerial staff). An employer who engages in anti-union discrimination is liable for unfair labor practices (Section 127); similarly interference by employers in the formation of a union or in union affairs is prohibited (Section 128). Reasonable facilities and time must be afforded to officers of a trade union, but trade union officers may not engage in union activities during working hours without the consent of the employer. These organizations must be independent of political parties. They must keep proper books and abide by simple financial rules. To enjoy the benefits of the Act, they must satisfy rules for registration with the Chief Labour Officer, who must maintain a register of trade unions and employers' organizations. Any change of name and amalgamation must also be registered with the Chief Labour Officer.

Expatriate Staff

All expatriates require work permits. A work permit may be obtained within 4 weeks at an approximate cost of US$500, and all expatriate employee contracts must be registered with the Internal Revenue division of the Ghana Revenue Authority.

Termination of Employment

A contract of employment may be terminated in any of the following circumstances:

* By mutual agreement
* By the employee on grounds of ill-treatment or sexual harassment
* By the employer upon the death of the employee
* By the employer if the employee is found upon medical examination to be medically unfit
* By the employer if the employee is unable by reason of sickness, redundancy (Section 62 (3)), accident, incompetence (Section 62 (a)) or proven misconduct (Section 62(3)

Unfair termination under the Labour Act

Termination of employment may be unfair if it is based on any or some of the following reasons:

- That the worker has joined or intends to join or has ceased to be a member of a trade union or intends to take part in the activities of a trade union.
- That the worker seeks office as, or is acting or has acted in the capacity of a worker representative.
- That the worker has filed a complaint or participated in proceedings against the employer involving alleged violation of this Act or any other enactment.
- The worker's gender, race, color, ethnicity, origin, religion, creed, social, political or economic status has been discriminated against.
- In the case of a woman worker, due to the pregnancy of the worker or the absence of the worker from work during maternity leave.
- In the case of a worker with a disability, due to the worker's disability.
- That the worker is temporarily ill or injured and this is certified by a recognized medical practitioner.
- That the worker does not possess the current level of qualification required in relation to the work for which the worker was employed which differs from the level of qualification required at the commencement of his or her employment.
- That the worker refused or indicated an intention to refuse to do any work normally done by a worker who at the time was taking part in a lawful strike unless the work is necessary for the maintenance of plant and equipment.

Remedies for unfair termination

The affected employee can petition the National Labour Commission, and if it is established that the termination was unfair, the Commission may order the employer to re-instate the worker from the date of the termination of the employment, or place the employee in a reasonably suitable work under the same terms and conditions enjoyed by the worker before the termination, but then also the Commission can order the employer to pay compensation to the affected employee.

Legal obligations upon terminating an employee

Under Section 18 of the *Labour Act,* when a contract of employment is terminated the employer is required to pay to the employee:

- any remuneration earned by the employee before the termination.
- any deferred pay due to the employee before the termination.
- any compensation due to the employee in respect of sickness or accident.
- in the case of a foreign contract, the expenses and necessaries for the journey and repatriation expenses in respect of the employee and accompanying members of his or her family in addition to all of the payments specified above; and
- where an employer terminates the employment of an employee without giving him notice, the employer is required to pay the employee a sum equal to the amount of remuneration which the employee would have received.

Workman Compensation

Employers in Ghana are generally liable for personal injury sustained by an employee by accident arising out of and in the course of the employment contract.

The *Workmen's Compensation Law,* 1987 (PNDCL 187) and the *Workmen's Compensation (Calculation of Compensation) Instrument,* 1994 (L.I. 1594) govern the issue of financial compensation and calculations payable by employers to employees in respect of injuries sustained by them in the course of their duties.

Employers are not liable to pay compensation where the accident causing the injury to the worker is attributable to the employee having been at the time thereof under the influence of drugs or alcohol, or in respect of any incapacity or death resulting from a deliberate self-injury. However, an employee who acts in breach of statutory or other regulation relating to his employment, or who acts without the instructions of his employer at the time an accident happens, is not deemed to be acting in the course of his employment. Where a corporate employer goes into liquidation or receivership, or where the holder of a debenture secured by a floating charge goes into possession, the rights of the employer company as against any insurer of its liability is transferred to and vested in any workman entitled to compensation; and that workman has the same rights and remedies, and is subject to the same liabilities under the policy, as the employer company.

Employees' Social Security and Pension

Employers are obliged to pay 5.5% of employee salary (whether or not the salary was actually paid to the employee) and added to it the employer's contribution of 13% of the employee's monthly salary. These two contributions are then to be held in trust for and on behalf of the employee and remitted by the employer in accordance with the Pensions Act.

CHAPTER 18 – QUICK REVIEW

The *Labour Act,* (Act 651) covers a wide range of issues involving rights and obligations owed by employees to employers and vice-versa. The Act covers discipline and grievance procedures, working time regulations, ensuring that employees do not work in excess of the legal maximum and granting them sufficient holidays. It covers redundancy, including entitlement to statutory redundancy payments, the right to be treated fairly in all employment decisions, and parental rights involving such things as maternity leave.

19. Mortgages

Regulation of Securities and charges

How can a company secure loans that it lends out? Of what essence is the creation of charges over a borrower's assets? This chapter looks at mortgage transactions, which are creditor arrangements giving lenders rights to realize certain assets of a borrower in the event a secured loan is unpaid.

A lender's rights usually involve four remedies – suing the borrower, taking possession of the mortgaged asset, selling it or having it sold, and foreclosure (terminating the mortgagor's interest in the asset). At the end of this chapter, you should have an understanding of, the mode of creation of a mortgage, the changes brought by the Mortgages Act, registration requirements for mortgagees, remedies of a mortgagee, distinction between a second mortgage and a sub-mortgage, and the collateral registry.

MORTGAGE

A mortgage may be defined as a contract charging immovable property as security for repayment of a debt and any interest accruing thereon or for the performance of some other obligation for which it is given. It is thus a credit arrangement where title to land is security for a loan.

Mortgagor and Mortgagee Relations

The person who borrows money and signs a mortgage deed promising repayment under the transaction is referred to as the mortgagor, whiles the lending party who signs the mortgage as security for payment is referred to as the mortgagee.

Once created, a mortgage acts as an encumbrance on the property charged, but does not operate to change ownership, right to possession or other interest in the property charged. The bank or mortgagee becomes the legal owner, but the mortgagor remains the equitable owner. The mortgagor, however, has an equity of redemption — the right to have legal ownership restored to him or her upon full repayment of the loan.

THE MORTGAGES ACT 1972 (ACT 96)

Necessity of writing

In Ghana, a mortgage is not enforceable unless it is expressed in writing, and signed by the mortgagor or his agent, or is otherwise, as provided under Section 3 (1), excused from the requirement of writing by the operation of the rules of equity, including the rules relating to fraud, duress, hardship, unconscionablility and part performance, or is excused from the necessity of a writing by an enactment, in the case of a customary law transaction.

Registration of Mortgages

The instrument evidencing the mortgage may thereafter be registered with the *Land Registry Act,* 1962 (Act 122). In *Asare v. Brobbey* (1971) the Court of Appeal held that a mortgage deed, which was not registered under Section 24 of the *Lands Registry Act,* 1962 (Act 122) at the time of the exercise of the power of sale became ineffective and invalid to pass good title to a purchaser of the property.

Requirements of Mortgages

Section 3 (3) states that in order to be acceptable for registration, a mortgage must meet the following conditions:

a) it must state the name and address of each mortgagor and each mortgagee
b) it must state the nature of the mortgagor's interest in the property and the extent to which that interest is subject to the mortgage
c) it must identify the mortgaged property by reference to its location and boundaries or to a previously registered writing describing that property, and
d) where the mortgage secures the payment of money, the date on which payment is due, the principal sum of money lent or to be lent, or if the sum of money to be lent is indeterminate then the mortgage instrument must say so, and if further advances are to be made and secured by the mortgage the instrument must say so.

Personal liability of mortgagor

Section 6 makes a mortgagor personally liable, as well as liable on the mortgage security, for the performance of any act secured by the mortgage.

Land Title documents

The mortgagee is entitled under Section 10 to possession of all the mortgagor's title documents which relate exclusively to the mortgaged property. Priorities among mortgagee or charges are considered in order of time, with the first in time having priority over later ones.

Where a person redeems a mortgaged property by repaying his debt, or performing his obligations under the mortgage, he shall be entitled to require the mortgagee to issue a written discharge to that effect. That is, a document testifying that the mortgaged debt has been paid off by the mortgagor.

Remedies of a mortgagee

Under Section 15, where a mortgagor fails to fulfill his obligation under the mortgage, the mortgagee may:

a) sue the mortgagor on any personal covenant to perform, that is on breach of his solemn promise to repay the debt
b) realize the mortgagee's security in the following manner
i. Apply to court for the appointment of a receiver on default or
ii. The mortgagee, if it can be done peacefully, can enter and take possession of the mortgaged property
iii. Apply for a judicial sale

Under Section 18, where a Court orders a judicial sale, it may make an order for a conveyance, or a vesting order, necessary for giving effect to the sale, and may authorize the Registrar or any other officer of the Court to execute, on behalf of the mortgagor and the mortgagee who requested the judicial sale, a conveyance granting the interest of the mortgagor and mortgagee in the mortgaged property to the purchaser at the judicial sale.

A purchaser at such a judicial sale shall by law take title to the mortgaged property free of any interest, but subject only to the interest which had priority to that mortgage.

The National Mortgage Financing and Guarantee Scheme Act, 1976 (Act 23)

A financial institution which opts for or holds a mortgage executed under this scheme is not obliged or required to commence a court proceeding in order to exercise its rights under the mortgage.

Act 23 provides detailed rights of mortgagees in a manner that suggests that in default, a bank has a right to proceed with a direct sale of the mortgaged asset without going to court or making any application to the court for an order to do so. Under Act 23, a mortgagee financial institution can:

- Appoint a Receiver
- Take possession of the mortgaged asset
- Sell the property by public auction, or by private contract after giving reasonable notice of the sale to the mortgagor and any second or other mortgagees of whom it has notice.

Exemptions

Where, however, at least 75% of the total loan sum has been paid by the borrower, the financial institution is precluded by law from

a.   Enforcing any right to recover possession of the asset, or
b.   Exercising its right of sale, or
c.   Any other court action.

Second Mortgages and Sub Mortgages

Second Mortgage: Besides creating a first mortgage, a second or even third mortgage is still legally possible using the same mortgaged property. To illustrate, let us consider the following example - A mortgaged property is worth GH₵ 10, 000,000.00 but is mortgaged for GH₵ 2, 000, 000.00 in this case there is a residual equity of GH₵ 8, 000, 000.00 remaining in the property. If it suits him the borrower (Mr B) will be at liberty to enter into a second agreement with the same financier or another bank for an additional loan of say GH₵ 3,000,000.00.

If Mr B actually approaches another bank, that second bank would immediately realize that there is a prior borrowing outstanding, as Mr B will be unable to furnish any title deeds (because it is in the possession of the first bank). The second bank may, however, be content to grant the loan against the same security or property held by the first bank.

Sub Mortgage: A sub-mortgage is a mortgage for a mortgage. To illustrate, let us consider this other example – Mr B mortgages his property to Mr C for GH₵ 10, 000,000.00. Later Mr C needs to borrow GH₵ 3,000,000.00. He can obtain it by calling in Mr B's loan or mortgage, however, he can approach his Bank, Bank X and borrow the money from the Bank against the security of Mr B's mortgage. In this case, the original mortgage would become the head mortgage and the newly-created mortgage with Bank X against Mr B's mortgage is a sub-mortgage with Mr C as the sub-mortgagor and Bank X as the sub-mortgagee.

The Collateral Registry

The Bank of Ghana in February 2010 established the Collateral Registry, located in Accra. The Registry is not only web-based; it is also the first movable and immoveable asset secured transactions registry (STR) in Africa.

Operations of the Registry

The Registry itself is a body established under the ***Borrowers and Lenders Act,*** (Act 773, 2008), with a mandate to mainly register secure loans (otherwise known as charges) and collaterals which borrowers have used to obtain credit facilities from lenders. Among its functions the Registry registers (a) charges and collaterals (b) Registration of Amendments, and (c) Responds to search requests. For the purposes of registration of charges, an amount of five hundred Ghana Cedis (GH¢500.00) and upwards is payable.

The Twenty-Eight Day [28] Rule

The ***Borrowers and Lenders Act,*** (Act 773, 2008) requires borrowers or lenders to register charges or collateral with the Collateral Registry within twenty eight days [28] following their date of creation. Under the Act, an unregistered charge is of no effect as security for the borrower's obligations for repayment of the credit, and the money becomes immediately payable regardless of any provision in the credit agreement to the contrary.

Benefits of the Registry

Since its establishment to the end of March 2013, a total of 40,096 charges or secured loans, with 104,308 collaterals were registered. Prior to its establishment, commercial lenders had an ineffective means of searching for prior charges, if any, on properties presented to them for credit. The result was numerous and unending litigations in courts as well as substantial rate of non-performing loans recorded in the books of lenders. Similarly, members of the general public who wish to procure properties also had no effective means of ascertaining whether or not property which they intend to procure had been used as collateral for a credit facility.

CHAPTER 19 – QUICK REVIEW

A mortgage is a contract charging immovable property as security for repayment of a debt. It is therefore the security interest of the lender in the property. This could entail restrictions on the use or disposal of the property. These restrictions could include, for example, requirements to purchase insurance, or pay off outstanding debt before selling the property.

Mortgage lending may be used to finance private ownership of residential and commercial property. A mortgaged agreement that is breached may be foreclosed or repossessed. Foreclosure or repossession is the possibility that the lender has to foreclose, repossess or seize the property under certain circumstances essential to a mortgage loan; without this aspect, the loan is no different from any other kind of loan.

20. Intellectual Property Law

LEARNING OUTCOMES

This chapter considers the nature of intellectual property and how the law controls unfair competition. At the end of the chapter, you should understand, among others, the rights that are attached to intellectual property as a business asset, how intellectual property is acquired and also how it is protected to safeguard commercial interests.

Introduction

In Ghana, many companies have an inadequate understanding of their business's intellectual property rights (IPRs), and those that do, still fail to take legal steps to protect all their intellectual property rights (IPRs) at home and abroad. Anecdotal evidence suggests that businesses are rarely informed of how to protect or enforce their IPRs.

What are Intellectual Property Rights (IPRs)?

Intellectual Property Rights (IPRs) are rights pertaining to creations of the human intellect that individuals, companies, or other entities may invest in and lay claims to. Examples of intellectual property are:

- Advertising jingles
- Business and marketing plans
- Distinctive names given to products
- Recipes and formulas for making products
- Manufacturing processes
- Logo designs and
- Methods of extracting minerals

IPRs give the owner exclusive rights to control the use of the creation for a certain period of time. Laws governing IPRs are thus intended to stimulate innovation and creativity, ensure fair competition, while protecting consumers.

Types of IPRs
The main types or categories of IPRs are:

- Copyrights and related rights
- Trademarks (including geographical indications)
- Patents
- Industrial designs, integrated circuit designs and plant varieties, and
- Trade secrets

Importance of IPRs to Business Entities
IPRs enable businesses that register and protect them to, among others:

- Reap profits from its ideas and creations and from licensing its rights
- Preserve a market niche and thereby compete effectively with larger companies
- Establish and grow its reputation and goodwill in the marketplace
- Enhance the worth of a small business in the eyes of investors and financing institutions
- Raise the value of a small business in the event of a sale or merger

IPR Registration is an important legal means of asserting ownership of an IP and acquiring required protection. Beyond registration, licensing agreements between the commercial owners of IP and users of the IP are equally vital.

IP Laws enacted by Parliament[77]
In broad strokes, Ghana has enacted legislation that ensures legal protection for Intellectual Property Rights (IPRs). The current IPRs laws in force in Ghana are:

- *Copyright Act,* 2005 (Act 690) (2005)
- *Layout-Designs (Topographies) of Integrated Circuits Act,* 2004 (Act 667)
- *Trade Marks Act,* 2004 (Act 664) (2004)
- *Geographical Indications Act,* 2003 (Act 659) (2003)
- *Industrial Designs Act,* 2003 (Act 660) (2003)
- *Patent Act,* 2003 (Act 657) (2003)
- Copyright Regulations 2010

---

77   *http://www.wipo.int/wipolex/en/profile.jsp?code=gh*

International Conventions and Agreements

Below is a summary table of the World Intellectual Property Organization (WIPO), World Trade Organization and the United Nations administered treaties:

- Beijing Treaty on Audiovisual Performances
- Marrakesh Treaty to Facilitate Access to Published Works for Persons Who Are Blind, Visually Impaired or Otherwise Print Disabled
- Nairobi Treaty on the Protection of the Olympic Symbol
- Patent Law Treaty
- Singapore Treaty on the Law of Trademarks
- Washington Treaty on Intellectual Property in Respect of Integrated Circuits
- WIPO Performances and Phonograms Treaty (February 16, 2013)
- Hague Agreement Concerning the International Registration of Industrial Designs (September 16, 2008)
- Protocol Relating to the Madrid Agreement Concerning the International Registration of Marks (September 16, 2008)
- WIPO Copyright Treaty (November 18, 2006)
- Patent Cooperation Treaty (February 26, 1997)
- Second Protocol to the Hague Convention of 1954 for the Protection of Cultural Property in the Event of Armed Conflict
- United Nations Convention on Contracts for the International Sale of Goods
- Convention on the Rights of Persons with Disabilities (August 30, 2012)
- Optional Protocol to the Convention on the Rights of Persons with Disabilities (August 30, 2012)
- Agreement for the establishment of the Global Crop Diversity Trust (September 6, 2006)
- International Plant Protection Convention (October 2, 2005)
- WHO Framework Convention on Tobacco Control (February 27, 2005)
- Kyoto Protocol to the United Nations Framework Convention on Climate Change (February 16, 2005)
- International Treaty on Plant Genetic Resources for Food and Agriculture (June 29, 2004)
- Stockholm Convention on Persistent Organic Pollutants (May 17, 2004)
- Cartagena Protocol on Biosafety to the Convention on Biological Diversity (September 11, 2003)

- International Covenant on Economic, Social and Cultural Rights (December 7, 2000)
- United Nations Convention to Combat Desertification in Those Countries Experiencing Serious Drought and/or Desertification, Particularly in Africa (March 27, 1997)
- United Nations Framework Convention on Climate Change (December 5, 1995)
- Agreement establishing the World Trade Organization (WTO) (January 1, 1995)
- World Trade Organization (WTO) - Agreement on Trade-Related Aspects of Intellectual Property Rights (TRIPS Agreement) (1994) (January 1, 1995)
- Convention on Biological Diversity (November 27, 1994)
- United Nations Convention on the Law of the Sea (November 16, 1994)
- Protocol (I) Additional to the Geneva Conventions of 12 August 1949, and relating to the protection of victims of international armed conflicts (December 7, 1978)
- Protocol (II) Additional to the Geneva Conventions of 12 August 1949, and relating to the Protection of Victims of Non-International Armed Conflicts (December 7, 1978)
- Convention concerning the Protection of the World Cultural and Natural Heritage (December 17, 1975)
- Universal Copyright Convention of 6 September 1952, with Appendix Declaration relating to Article XVII and Resolution concerning Article XI (August 22, 1962)
- Protocol 1 annexed to the Universal Copyright Convention as signed at Geneva on 6 September 1952 concerning the application of that Convention to works of stateless persons and refugees (May 22, 1962)
- Protocol 2 annexed to the Universal Copyright Convention as signed at Geneva on 6 September 1952 concerning the application of that Convention the works of certain international organizations (May 22, 1962)
- Protocol 3 annexed to the Universal Copyright Convention as signed at Geneva on 6 September 1952 concerning the effective date of instruments of ratification or acceptance of or accession to that Convention (May 22, 1962)
- Convention for the Protection of Cultural Property in the Event of Armed Conflict (October 25, 1960)

- Protocol to the Convention for the Protection of Cultural Property in the Event of Armed Conflict (October 25, 1960)
- Convention (I) for the Amelioration of the Condition of the Wounded and Sick in Armed Forces in the Field (February 2, 1959)
- Convention (II) for the Amelioration of the Condition of Wounded, Sick and Shipwrecked Members of Armed Forces at Sea (February 2, 1959)
- Convention (IV) relative to the Protection of Civilian Persons in Time of War (February 2, 1959)
- Convention on International Civil Aviation (June 8, 1957)
- Agreement on the Importation of Educational, Scientific and Cultural Materials (March 6, 1957)

Regional IPR Treaties
- Charter for African Cultural Renaissance
- Swakopmund Protocol on the Protection of Traditional Knowledge and Expressions of Folklore within the Framework of the African Regional Intellectual Property Organization (ARIPO)
- Cultural Charter for Africa (September 19, 1990)
- Harare Protocol on Patents and Industrial Designs Within the Framework of the African Regional Industrial Property Organization (ARIPO) (April 25, 1984)
- Lusaka Agreement on the Creation of the African Regional Intellectual Property Organization (ARIPO) (February 15, 1978)

COPYRIGHT

Copyright is an intangible property right granted by statute to the author or originator of a literary or artistic production of a specified type. In Ghana, the *Copyright Act* of 2005 (Act 690) and Copyright Regulations of 2010 are two legislations enacted to protect copyright holders.

The purpose of copyright is to protect particular expressions of an idea, not the idea itself. Copyright law aims at preventing the copying of created works and is the foundation for commercial businesses involved in, among others, art, publishing, music and software since copyright provides the basis for their salable products. Copyrights can be registered with the copyright office.

Copyright infringement in Ghana

Copyright is believed to be the most infringed IPR by volume in Ghana[78]. The

---

78   IPR Toolkit – Ghana, Statement from Ambassador Donanld Teitelbaum

Copyright Office, in concert with the Ghana Police Service and Customs Excise and Preventive Service (CEPS), undertake periodic sweeps. The **Copyright Act,** passed in March 2010, created and specified the powers of a Copyright Tribunal, established a levy on devices used for reproduction of copyrighted material and specified the procedures for copyright filings. Infringing parties are subject to civil and criminal penalties.

TRADEMARKS
A trademark is a sufficiently distinctive mark, device, motto, or implement that a manufacturer stamps, prints, or fixes to products so that they can be identified on the market and their origin made known. In other words, a trademark is a source indicator.

At common law, a person who uses a distinctive symbol or mark to identify a business or goods was protected in his or her use of that trademark. In Ghana, the **Trade Marks Act,** 2004 (Act 664) is the primary legislation offering statutory protection to registered trademark holders. Registration of trademarks is done by the Trademarks Registry at the Registrar General's Department.

TRADE NAMES
Whereas a trademark applies to products, the term trade name is used to indicate part or all of a business name, regardless of whether the business is a sole proprietor, partnership, or company.

A trade name may be protected as a trademark if the trade name is also the name of the company's trademarked product – like Pepsi Cola or Coca-Cola. Unless the trade name is also used as a trademark or service mark, a trade name cannot be registered. A trade name is directly related to a business and its goodwill.

Trade names are protected under common law, but only if they are unusual or fancifully used. Thus in the US case of **Safeway v. Suburban Foods,**[79] the word "Safeway", for instance, was held sufficiently fanciful to obtain protection as a tradename for a grocery chain. Competition law (anti-trust law) gets in here – competition law is law that seeks to promote market competition by regulating anti-competitive conduct.

In Ghana, **the Protection Against Unfair Competition Act,** 2000 (Act 589) or the PAUC Act provides protection against unfair competition. The PAUC Act entitles right-holders to civil remedies when a party purposely causes confu-

---

79   130 ESupp. 249 (E.D. Va 1955)

sion, damaged goodwill or misleads the public. Under Section 1 of the PAUC Act, any activity which causes or is likely to cause confusion with respect to another's enterprise, activities, products or services offered by that enterprise, constitutes an act of unfair competition. Under Section 2, the confusion may be caused with respect to:

a)   a trademark, whether registered or not
b)   a trade name
c)   a business identifier other than a trademark or trade name
d)   the presentation of a product or service; or
e)   a celebrity or well-known fictional character.

Trademark infringement

Trademark infringement is the most infringed IPR by value in Ghana.[80] Upon registering with the RGD, right-holders are granted the right to exclusive use of the trademark and the capacity to institute legal action against violators. Infringing parties are subject to both civil and criminal penalties.

PATENTS

A patent is an exclusive right granted under the **Patent Act,** 2003 (Act 657) to an inventor, the right-holder, to use the patent. Under Act 657 a person who makes, exports, offers for sale or is selling or using a patented product or process without the lawful consent of the right-holder commits an infringement, and is subject to civil and criminal penalties.

Exclusions from Patent Protections

a)   **Things that receive exclusive protection under other areas of the law** – for example, computer programs (like software, apps, etc.), may not be patentable, as they receive protection under copyright law. They may, however, receive patent protection as part of a broader patent as, for instance, a computerized method of controlling the operations of a plant.[81]
b)   Things that do not meet the definition of a patent – for example, scientific principles and abstract theorems are 'discoveries' as opposed to inventions and therefore not patentable.[82]

---

80   IPR Toolkit Supra
81   David Vaver, Intellectual Property Law (Toronto: Irwin Lawn, 1997) at p.129
82   David Vaver, Supra

c) Things that are for policy reasons unpatentable – for example, methods of surgical treatment are not patentable so are illicit objects. Can a mobile app be patented? The simple answer is "yes". This is because it is a component of the methods of interaction – the process running on a mobile phone that connects to a remote server containing data that either stores the data or processes it to be used on the mobile phone. In other words, it is what makes the mobile phone function in a particular way. The code that runs the software, however, cannot be patented, but can be copyrighted.

INDUSTRIAL DESIGNS

Section 1 of the *Industrial Designs Act,* 2003 (Act 660)defines industrial design as:

a) a composition of lines or colors, a three-dimensional form or a material, whether or not associated with lines or colors, or

b) a textile design (that is, an industrial design where the composition, form or material gives a special appearance to a product of industry or handicraft and can serve as a pattern for a product of industry or handicraft).

According to Vaver (1997), industrial designs are also generally taken to mean a visual shape, configuration, pattern or ornament, or any combination of these that, in a finished article, appeals to and is judged solely by the eye.[83] Examples include the shape and ornamentations applied to toys, vehicles, furniture, textiles and household utensils. Computer generated icon display, cellular phones, tablets, etc., may all be registered as industrial designs. To be registerable, industrial designs must be new or novel and original. However, under Section 4, an industrial design which is contrary to public order or morality is not registerable. Infringing parties are subject to civil and criminal penalties.

Domain Names

A domain name is simply an internet address. It is a unique address of a website. Domain names are controlled by various organizations that act as registrars. Generic domain names such as .com, .org, and .biz are controlled by the Internet Corporation for Assigned Names and Numbers (ICANN), a US Non-Governmental Organization. Sometimes conflict develops when a number of organizations are laying claim to a domain name containing a particular word. For

---

83 Martin Kratz, Canada's Intellectual Property Law in a Nutshell (Scarborough, ON, Carswell, 1998) at 63

example, the following companies – Imperial Air, Imperial Tobacco, Imperial Soap, and Imperial Oil – would all have a legitimate interest in a domain name containing the word "Imperial".

Protecting Intellectual Property
Businesses and individual right-holders can protect their inventions, trademarks or designs across borders through WIPO.

Anti-Infringement Measures
a) Register trademarks, patents and industrial designs, etc. with the RGD prior to market entry – Right-holders planning on entering the Ghanaian market should develop a comprehensive IPR strategy before entering the Ghanaian Market.

b) Register Copyrights with the Copyright Office prior to market entry.

c) Take legal action (including applications for Anton Pillar Orders) to prevent unauthorized use of IPRs.

d) Approach CEPS and Commercial Crimes Unit of the Criminal Investigations Department to establish relationships, education, and information on differentiating between fake and authentic goods.

e) Approach Food and Drugs Board and Ghana Standards Board regardless of whether the goods are imported into or manufactured in Ghana, and provided they are health-related, medical, pharmaceutical, etc., then establish enforcement relations and goods registration.

f) Consider public relations campaigns.

g) Involve NGOs involved in IPR enforcement and advocacy.

h) Engage a local IPR Lawyer.

i) Consider the useof Non-Disclosure Agreements, MoUs, Confidentiality agreements, Licensing at an early stage, etc.

IPR Enforcement System – Ghana
A number of governmental agencies are charged with IPR enforcement in Ghana. These include:

a) The Registrar-General Department (RGD)

b) The High Court

c) The Customs Division of the Ghana Revenue Authority (Formerly Customs Excise and Preventive Service (CEPS))

d) The Commercial Crime Unit of the Ghana Police Service

e) The Food and Drugs Board (FDB), and

f)   The Ghana Standards Board (GSB)

IPR Enforcement System – WIPO

The World Intellectual Property Organization (WIPO) is an agency of the United Nations, with 188 member states that provides intellectual property services, policy, information and cooperation. Its mission is to lead the development of a balanced and effective international intellectual property (IP) system that enables innovation and creativity for the benefit of all.

The International Patent System enables patent owners to obtain patent protection in multiple countries by filing a single international application. The PCT system postpones the major costs associated with international patent protection, provides IP owners with a strong basis for making a patenting decision and is used by the world's major corporations, research institutions and universities.

The International Trademark System enables applicants to register trademarks in multiple countries by filing one international application. This can be done through the Madrid system,the benefit of which are that the trademark applicant saves time and money, covers over 90 countries and enables the trademark owner to manage and renew their marks through one centralized system. The International Design System enables design owners to register their industrial designs in multiple countries with a minimum of formalities and expense through the Hague system, which replaces multiple registrations with just one, lets applicants register up to 100 industrial designs with one form, makes management of registered designs easier — record changes or renewals through a single step.

CHAPTER 20 – QUICK REVIEW

Intellectual property (IP) law deals with the formulation, usage and subsequent commercial exploitation of original creative labor. Generally, IP law covers and protects confidential information, patents, copyright, passing off, design rights and provides remedies for breach. An action for breach of confidence may cover personal and technical trade secrets. A patent is a monopoly right in an invention. A copyright, on the other hand, is essentially a negative right which prevents others from making copies of the work of an author. The concept of passing off is different. It is based on the rule that a trader must not sell his goods under the pretense that they are the goods of another trader. As a result of the serious economic interests involved, there are several agencies apart from the courts that enforce IP rights.

21. Land Law

LEARNING OUTCOMES

This chapter provides an overview of land law in Ghana. At the end of the chapter, you should understand, among others, the various types of lands in Ghana, the types of interest that may be acquired in land, the characteristics of leases, the requirements of due diligence and the basic issues surrounding drafting, review and registration of leases in Ghana.

TYPES OF LAND HOLDING

The dominant form of land ownership in Ghana is customary or traditional land holding. About 80% of the land belongs to traditional owners. The other lands are public lands and private lands acquired out of the traditional land holding.

Public lands, form the remaining 20 percent, and this comprises state and vested lands. **State lands** refer to land acquired by the state from its allodial owners. **Vested lands** refer to land owned by the state and customary authorities in a form of partnership i.e. split ownership.

TYPES OF INTERESTS IN LAND

Customary freehold

The customary freehold is an interest that individuals or groups hold in a piece of land, which is owned by a larger traditional community – the allodial owner – of which the interest holders are members or subjects. It is an interest that is transferrable to successors of the individuals or subgroups until there are no successors.

Common law freehold

The Common law freehold is similar to the customary freehold. The difference, however, is that this interest can be acquired by both strangers and members of the community that owns the land. A stranger in this respect refers to a Ghanaian who is not a member of the land-owning community. It is important to note that the 1992 Constitution by article 267 (5) forbids the creation of freehold interests in stool land in Ghana.

Foreigners

Foreigners are restricted in respect of the type of interest they can hold. A foreigner cannot hold a freehold interest in land or a lease exceeding 50 years. If a person who is not a Ghanaian buys a freehold interest in land it would be converted to a 50 year lease.

A leasehold/lease is an interest in land that has a specified start and end date, subject to payment of annual ground rents and covenants.

There are two other interests or tenancies in the Akan speaking areas. These are the *"Abunu"* and *"Abusa"* systems.

LEASES IN GHANA

A lease is an interest in land created to last for a fixed period. Every lease therefore has generally a stated date for commencement and expiration. In Ghana, a lease may be as short a period as one (1) year or as long as 99-year lease, although in exceptional some leases have been longer. For instance, the Tema Development Corporation's interest in Tema lands was created for 125 years, commencing in 1956. A person who creates a lease is referred to as the Lessor and the person to whom a lease is granted as the Lessee.

CHARACTERISTICS OF A LEASE

Definite period - A lease must be created for a definite period, with a clearly stated start and end date, which must not be in doubt. This implies that the lessor is entitled to repossess the leased property (and whatever is built on it) when the lease expires.

Exclusive possession - A lease must also give exclusive possession of the subject land to the lessee.

DUE DILIGENCE, DRAFTING AND REVIEWING LEASES

It has been admitted in several studies and published literature, that although the land tenure system in Ghana, is relatively settled, it is still fraught with challenges. First and foremost, land boundaries in Ghana are not properly demarcated, as a result there are instances where two or more stools could claim ownership of a parcel of land. If a purchaser does not engage a qualified lawyer to do the appropriate due diligence, there is the possibility of buying a piece of disputed land from one feuding faction only to have the other faction showing up and claim the same land, thus landing you squarely in the middle of the dispute.

In drafting or reviewing a lease, close attention must be placed on applying for a search report, informal enquiries from owners of adjourning property, and check for any litigation or disputes. The draft deed must include:

- Names of the parties of the agreement
- Recitals
- The start date and duration of the agreement
- The precise description of the lease property (usually depicted by the site plan)
- Conditions for renewal or non-renewal and other covenants
- A specific consideration (a lump sum, or periodic payments, such as ground rent) for granting the use of this object.
- Jurat clauses where appropriate
- Signature and Witness provisions
- Oath of proof

THE DUAL LAND REGISTRATION SYSTEM

Two types of systems operate in Ghana. These are Deed Registration and Title Registration.

Deed Registration

Deed registration involves the recording of instruments/transactions affecting land which provides prima facie evidence of rights and interests in the particular piece of land. In Ghana it operates in nine regions of the country. Through the Ghana Land Administration Project (LAP), a Land Registry has been established in eight regional capitals.

Title Registration

Title registration involves the recording of title to a piece of land. Land title registration made is by reference to the land itself and not the instruments affecting the land. Land title is state guaranteed. Land title registration operates in the Greater Accra Region and Kumasi.

Although the law provides for a systematic approach for deed and title registration, in practice it is chaotic, which is why the use of a competent real estate lawyer is very appropriate in all land transfers in Ghana.

THE PROCEDURE FOR REGISTERING LAND IN GHANA

Below is a summary of the key steps involved in land registration in Ghana.

1. *The Purchaser must conduct a title search and present deeds*
   A search at the Land Registry must be conducted to confirm rightful ownership. A lawyer prepares the transfer document (transfer deed) which is signed by both the vendor and the purchaser and their witnesses. The Title Transfer form is then presented to the Land Registry.

2. *The Purchaser must go for property value assessment and pay stamp duty*
   Stamp duty must thereafter be assessed on the property and paid at the Land Valuation Board. The purchaser starts by presenting the deed to the Land Valuation Board . The property is inspected to ascertain its current open market value. The purchaser then pays Stamp Duty to the Land Valuation Board. The **Stamp Duty Act** of 2005 (Act 689) has reduced the stamp duty from 2% to 0.5%. This Act states that for the conveyance or transfer on the sale of a property, the stamp duty is 0.25% where the property value is less than GH¢ 10,000. For properties valued between GH¢ 10,000 and 50,000, stamp duty is 0.5%, and for properties valued above GH¢ 50,000, stamp duty is 1%.

3. *The Purchaser submits application for Title Certificate at Land Title Registry*
   At this stage the purchaser must submit an application form for Title Certificate and payment of processing fee at Land Title Registry. The documentation must include: (i) Application form (ii) Original and one copy of the deed of assignment, duly completed (iii) Land Certificate (iv) Company's certificate of incorporation

4. *Publication in national weekly newspaper*
   The transaction must be published in the national weekly newspaper in order to issue Land Title Certificate. The prescribed fee for publication must then be paid. Where the Land Certificate is urgently required, the applicant has the option to choose what is known as "special publication" and pay appropriately.

5. *Issuance of Land Title Certificate*
   Where there are no adverse claims after publication a land title certificate is subsequently issued to the purchaser.

BIBLIOGRAPHY

BOOKS

Adjei-Mensah, K. Principles of Business Law. His Grace Publications, Accra (2004)

Bondzi-Simpson, P.E. Company Law in Ghana (2009)

Dowuona-Hammond, C. The Law of Contract in Ghana, Buck Press, Accra (2011)

John, E., Bedingfield, J., Harrison, T. Business Law, 3rd edition, Harrison Law Publishing, Wolters Kluwer, New York, (2000)

Joseph W. G., The Law of Torts, 4th edition, Wolters Kluwer (2010)

Kenneth, W. C. Jentz, G. A, Cross, F.B, Miller, R.L., Business Law, Cengage Learning (2008)

McKendrick, E. Contract Law, 4th edition, Macmillan, London (2000)

Ghartey, J. Doing Business and Investing in Ghana, Legal and Institutional Framework. Janel Publications (2004)

Clarkson, K.W., Miller, R.L., Jentz, G.A., & Cross, F.B., Business Law, Cenage Learning; 12 edition (2010)

Joseph W Glannon. The law of Torts: Examples and Explanations.

Clarkson, K.W., Miller, R.L., Jentz, G.A., & Cross, F.B. Business Law, Cenage Learning; 12 edition (2010)

Upex, R, Davies on Contract, 8th edition. Sweet & Maxwell, London (2002)

Salzedo, S. Brunner, P. Brief case on Contract law, Cavendish Publishers, London, (1999)

ARTICLES

C. Ignacio Suarez Anzorena, Robert Wisner, Jack J. Coe, Jr., Claudia T. Salomon & Kiera S. Gans, International Commercial Dispute Resolution, 40 Int'l Law. 251 (2006).

Fabio Bortolotti, Remedies Available to the Seller and Seller's Right to Require Specific Performance (Articles 61, 62 and 28), 25 J.L. & Com. 335 (2005).

Ronald A. Brand, CISG Article 31: When Substantive Law Rules Affect Jurisdictional Results, 25 J.L. & Com. 181 (2005).

Michael G. Bridge, Issues Arising Under Articles 64, 72 and 73 of the United Nations Convention on Contracts for the International Sale of Goods, 25 J.L. & Com. 405 (2005).

INTERNET RESOURCES

https://obdickson.wordpress.com/

http://www.ilo.org/ifpdial/information-resources/national-labour-law-profiles/WCMS_158898/lang--en/index.htm1/

http://www.nlcghana.org/nlc/privatecontent/document/LABOURACT2003.pdf

http://laws.ghanalegal.com/acts/id/18/contracts-act

https://www.kpmg.com/GH/en/Documents/Doing%20business%20in%20Ghana%20-2012.pdf

http://www.doingbusiness.org/law-library/ghana

http://www.doingbusiness.org/data/exploreeconomies/ghana/enforcing-contracts/

http://www.commerceghana.com/guidance/ghana-judicial-system

http://www.multipartgroup.com/sites/default/files/Information%20on%20doing%20business%20in%20Ghana.pdf

http://ir.knust.edu.gh/bitstream/123456789/528/1/Binder1.pdf

http://www.gipcghana.com/invest-in-ghana/doing-business-in-ghana/laws-regulation.html

www.ingramcontent.com/pod-product-compliance
Lightning Source LLC
Chambersburg PA
CBHW051409200326
41520CB00023B/7164